THE SIMON AND SCHUSTER

POCKET GUIDE TO

# CHAMPAGNE
## AND SPARKLING WINES

BY JANE MACQUITTY

Keys to the symbols used in this book appear on page 4.

Jane MacQuitty's Pocket Guide to Champagne and Sparkling Wines.
Edited and designed by Mitchell Beazley International Limited,
Artists House, 14–15 Manette Street, London W1V 5LB.
Copyright © 1986 Mitchell Beazley Publishers
Text copyright © 1986 Jane MacQuitty
Maps copyright © 1986 Mitchell Beazley Publishers

A Fireside Book,
Published by Simon & Schuster, Inc.
Simon & Schuster Building
1230 Avenue of the Americas
New York, New York 10020

ISBN 0-671-62860-7
Library of Congress Cataloging Information available upon request.

Maps by Sue Sharples
Typeset by Servis Filmsetting Ltd, Manchester, England
Reproduction by Anglia Reproductions Ltd, Witham
Printed and bound in Hong Kong by Mandarin Offset
International Ltd.

| | |
|---|---|
| Editor | Elizabeth Hubbard |
| Designer | Paul Drayson |
| Researcher | Jean Gordon |
| Proofreader | Alison Franks |
| Production | Androulla Pavlou |
| Senior Executive Editor | Chris Foulkes |
| Senior Executive Art Editor | Roger Walton |

# Contents

# —— *How to Use this Book* ——

This book is a country-by-country A–Z guide to champagne and the world's sparkling wines.

The Introduction on pages 5–11 explains how champagne and sparkling wines are made, the grapes they are made from, the different styles of champagne and sparkling wines, and how to buy, store, serve and enjoy them.

Throughout the book, champagne means wine from the Champagne region, sparkling wine means wine from outside the Champagne region.

Each country has an introduction that provides a background to the wines produced including, where necessary, a "labels and the law" section that deciphers the confusing jungle of sparkling wine terminology. This is followed by the producers in that country, listed alphabetically.

As the method by which a sparkling wine is made is an important indication of quality, the method (or methods) used by each producer is shown by a code:

MC *Méthode Champenoise*
CC *Cuve Close*, also known as the Charmat or Tank method
TM Transfer method
CM Continuous, or Russian Continuous Flow method
IM Injection or Carbonated method
MR *Méthode Rurale*
MD *Méthode Dioise*
MG *Méthode Gaillaçoise*

These methods are explained on pages 5–8.

In addition there is a star rating system:

→★ Basic, usually mass produced
★ Acceptable everyday fizz
★★ Recommended; definitely above average
★★★ Highly recommended; excellent quality
★★★★ Finest; rare, prestigious and, alas, expensive
★→★★ Producer whose range includes both ordinary and superior, recommended wine
☆ Indicates the predicted future quality of a wine that has not yet been released

Other symbols are:

76, 82, etc Recommended vintages that have been especially successful for producers appear, where appropriate, between the method and the star rating. Most of these occur in the section on Champagne, where the staying power and supremacy of vintages are well established. A general guide to champagne vintages is on page 15.

*Star buys* Most countries feature several producers with specific "star buys". These represent exceptional quality and value for money.

Abbreviations used in the book are:

g/l grams per litre
ha hectares
km kilometres
m million

All figures are the latest available.

The Glossary on page 160 explains the various terms used in connection with champagne and sparkling wines.

Choosing any wine is a matter of personal taste and style. The views in this book are entirely those of the author.

# — *Introduction* —

Every year we drink some 1,500 million bottles of champagne and sparkling wine. This means that somewhere in the world more than 47 bottles of "fizz" are opened every second.

Europe still produces most of the world's sparkling wines: just 300m bottles are produced outside Europe. Champagne's share, a mere 200m bottles, is not huge either. Nor is the *méthode champenoise* the most popular method of putting bubbles in a bottle – that distinction goes to Monsieur Charmat's swift, economical tank method.

But whether it be Charmat or champagne, sparkling wine continues to be the world's favourite festive drink. And as with every style of wine, there are good, bad and ugly sparkling wines. This book aims to sort one from the other. Never again should you or your guests have to suffer what one early Victorian toast so aptly described as: "Champagne to our real friends and real pain to our sham friends."

## The Grapes

Champagne is made from a blend of white and black grapes, the latter gently pressed to yield only white juice. Pinot Noir and Pinot Meunier are the black grapes used and Chardonnay the white. Champagnes in which the black grapes dominate usually have a deep golden, occasionally pinky glow to them. The Chardonnay-dominated wines are a paler, often green-tinged, straw-yellow colour.

When the *chef de cave* in Champagne comes to put the blend together in the spring after the vintage, he is looking for a balanced collection of full-flavoured (but not overwhelming) base wines with high acidity and low alcohol. Pinot Noir will give him the backbone, strength and depth of flavour he wants, while the Chardonnay imparts elegance, freshness, lightness and finesse. This leaves Pinot Meunier with its aromatic nose and soft, subtle, quick-maturing style to marry the other two and tone down any overtly flavoured edges they may have had.

So far the most successful *méthode champenoise* wines made outside Champagne are those that contain a fair proportion of Chardonnay or Pinot Noir. Outside France the superiority of the Chardonnay and Pinot Noir is slowly being recognized. California as usual appears to be leading the field with Chardonnay widely planted and, to a lesser extent, Pinot Noir. South Africa, Australia and Spain, among others, are increasingly following suit. Once these new plantings come on stream, their sparkling wines will certainly be competition for the Champenois. How great this competition is will be intriguing to observe.

## The Methods

**Carbonated or Injection** The cheapest, quickest and least lovely way of putting bubbles into wine. Still wine is placed in a large closed tank and chilled. $CO_2$, carbon dioxide, is pumped into the wine which is then bottled under pressure. Fizzy lemonade or cola is made in the same way. Carbonated wines have large bubbles that disappear quickly and an off-putting frothy, soda-pop character in the mouth.

**Cuve close, Charmat, Bulk or Tank** Perfected by Eugène Charmat in 1907, based on the theory that if a second bubble-inducing fermentation worked well in a bottle it could also take place in a tank. Still wine is pumped into a giant stainless-steel pressure tank and yeast and sugar are injected, starting the second fermentation. The wine is then left to settle, transferred off its sediment and filtered into a holding tank where it receives a *dosage* prior to bottling. As all these processes take place under pressure, the bubbles given off during the second fermentation remain trapped in the wine. Given the speed and ease of production – it can take just three weeks from start to finish – it is not surprising that this is now one of the most popular methods of producing sparkling wine. The quality, although a noticeable step up from that of carbonated fizz, will never equal that of *méthode champenoise* wines: the bubbles are larger than the pin-head size of champagne and disappear fairly rapidly.

**Transfer** A compromise between *cuve close* and *méthode champenoise*, giving some of the latter's finesse for far less work. The second fermentation takes place in bottle in the normal way and the wines are aged for a short period. There is no expensive riddling and disgorgement. Instead, the wine is transferred under pressure from the bottles into a tank. The sediment sinks to the bottom, the wine is drawn off, given its *dosage* and a final filtration and then bottled, still under pressure. Transfer-method wines are now produced mainly in the USA. Their quality is indeed finer than *cuve close* but still not on a par with *méthode champenoise* wines. Kriter is a famous French transfer-method wine.

**Méthode Rurale** This was the earliest method used to give still wines a sparkle, practised mainly in regions where the wines had a natural tendency to sparkle anyway. Before the wine bottle was introduced in the late 17th century, these naturally sparkling wines would develop a pleasing *pétillance* in cask in the spring after the vintage when the warmer weather would encourage a secondary malolactic fermentation. By leaving the wine in cask in contact with the yeasty sediment, a cloudy, rustic, slightly sparkling wine was produced. Few of these tipples can be found today but one truly *méthode rurale* French sparkler does still exist: Vin de Blanquette. It is not filtered or riddled and the result, like those early wines, is cloudy. It is difficult to obtain outside the Limoux region.

**Méthode Dioise** Clairette de Die, from the Rhône, is the only wine made by this technique, which is a refined version of the *méthode rurale*. It involves long (3–4 months) fermentation and the wine is filtered. The chief advantage of this method is that the fresh, fruity charm of the Muscat grape is preserved and, unlike most *méthode rurale* wines, Clairette de Die Tradition is star-bright and not slightly cloudy.

**Méthode Gaillaçoise** Another variation on the *méthode rurale*, perhaps a little less sophisticated than the *méthode dioise*. *Méthode gaillaçoise* wines come from Gaillac in southwest France and are not often found outside the region. Like all *méthode rurale* wines, they have a "spontaneous second fermentation in bottle" without the aid of sugar and yeast. In practice this second fermentation is a continuation of the first. The wine does not receive a *dosage*.

**Russian Continuous Flow** This ingenious system, where the bubbles stem from a second fermentation in tank, allows the Russians to produce vast quantities of sparkling wine for what must be the minimum possible outlay and manpower. A continuous supply of base wine is fed under pressure through a series of fermentation tanks. At the same time a continuous flow of sugar and yeast solution is fed into one set of tanks and of *dosage* into another. In between are a series of filtering, pasteurizing and stabilization tanks. The whole process takes three weeks from start to finish and, true to its name, a continuous supply of sparkling wine is ready to be bottled from the final tank. Outside the USSR few firms admit to using this process – one that does is Lancers in Portugal.

**Méthode Champenoise** Despite the efforts of modern technology, the costly, time-consuming and labour-intensive *méthode champenoise* is still the best way to make sparkling wine.

The grapes are pressed swiftly and gently, either in traditional vertical wooden presses or in modern automated, horizontal bladder presses.

Each press is loaded with 4,000kg of grapes. Only the first 2,666 litres pressed from these grapes can be sold as champagne. Conveniently, this divides neatly into 13 of the Champagne region's traditional 205-litre oak casks, in which the first fermentation takes place. Today only houses such as Krug use casks. Large stainless-steel fermenters are much more common. The first ten casks (2,050 litres worth) of "free-run juice" literally flows from the press with little or no pressing. This is the *vin de cuvée*, the finest quality juice. The next best quality juice is the *première taille*, or second pressing, and this adds up to 410 litres, or two casks. The final pressing, the *deuxième taille*, consists of just one cask's worth of juice. All three champagne grapes are pressed and fermented separately.

The first fermentation takes place in the cellars of the various champagne houses. This slow, cool fermentation takes 3–4 weeks. Then the wine is racked into a clean cask or tank.

In January after the harvest the *chef de cave* starts to put the various blends of still wines or *cuvées* together. By April the complex and highly skilled task of tasting, analysing and blending is completed on a small scale and the next step is to ensure that the wines in the vast tanks in the cellar are blended in exactly the same proportions. The blended still wine is then bottled with the *liqueur de tirage*, a sugar and wine solution with a little of a selected yeast strain, and the bottle is given a temporary seal – a crown cap in most cases.

Once the wine is sealed in thick, heavy-duty glass bottles, made to withstand pressure, the second fermentation begins and the yeast gradually converts the sugar into alcohol. At the same time $CO_2$ or carbon dioxide bubbles are given off and dissolve in the wine. Once the fermentation has stopped a yeasty sediment falls to the underside of the bottle. It is vital that the wine remains in contact with this sediment during the ageing period for it gives the wine the intriguing complex flavours that are one of the hallmarks of champagne.

Removing the sediment is the next stage. The bottles are placed horizontally in *pupitres* (wooden racks with holes for the bottles). Gradually the bottles are shaken and twisted in the racks by the *remueur* until the bottles are upended and the sediment has collected at the neck and is resting on the cork.

*Remuage* is both time consuming and labour intensive and in the early 1970s automatic *remuage* was introduced. Riddling machines known as *gyropalettes*, square cages containing up to 504 bottles, imitate the movements of the *remueur* by shaking and twisting on a timed programme.

The latest experimental *remuage* techniques are *micro-billes* which could make the *remuage* process defunct. Instead, bottles will be seeded with these porous yeast capsules and, after the second fermentation and ageing process has taken place, the bottles will be upended and the sediment, trapped inside the *micro-billes*, will fall at once on to the cork.

Once the riddling and ageing period is over the champagne is ready for disgorging or *dégorgement*. Most firms use the *dégorgement à la glace* process in which the neck of the upended bottle is dipped into a freezing brine solution. The sediment is frozen into a pellet of ice which shoots out of the bottle when the cork is removed. A little wine escapes at the same time and the bottle is topped up with a blend of wine and sugar mix known as the *dosage*. The amount of sugar used determines whether the wine will be dry or Brut or one of the sweeter styles.

## The Styles

**Non-vintage** Start your appreciation of sparkling wines with the non-vintage wines that are widely available and indeed account for the vast majority of sales. These reflect the typical taste and style of each champagne house and are blended every year to show a consistent "house style". By law all non-vintage champagne must now be aged for a minimum of one year in bottle before it is sold and no champagne is allowed to be bottled in the year of its harvest. The youngest non-vintage champagne available will thus be at least 15 months old. Most non-vintage champagne from the better houses is a blend of two or three recent vintages and has at least three years' bottle-age. The average non-vintage *cuvée* is roughly a blend of two-thirds black grapes to one-third white.

**Vintage** Finer, older and more expensive, these are wines or blends of wines from a single year, and as such they reflect both the character of the house and the year. By law, they cannot be sold until three years after the harvest, but the better producers try to give them at least five years' bottle-age. Not every year in Champagne is declared a vintage year (see page 15 for a guide to champagne vintages).

**Rosé** Pink champagne should not be dismissed as just a lighthearted little drink. It can be superb and can often eclipse its less rosy relations. There are two methods of making rosé champagne. The quickest and least costly is simply to add a touch of the Champagne region's still red wine to the basic white-wine blend. This has the advantage of guaranteeing a consistent colour. A few houses adhere to the traditional method in which black grape skins are left in contact with the juice for a day or two, staining it a pretty pale pink.

**Prestige or Deluxe** Moët & Chandon were the first to produce a deluxe or *cuvée de prestige* in 1921, known as Dom Pérignon. Today almost every house makes a prestige champagne, usually sold in an ornate bottle at a very high price. Whether they are all worth the money is another question. The Champenois point out that they are usually made from the finest wines of the finest years and as such are *la crème de la crème*. After Dom Pérignon, Roederer's Cristal is probably the most famous. Krug, incidentally, claim that all their champagnes are prestige *cuvées*, including Grande Cuvée.

**Crémant** These softly sparkling or "creaming" champagnes have roughly 3.5 atmospheres of pressure behind the cork instead of the usual 5 or 6 for fully sparkling or *mousseux* champagnes. Crémant d'Alsace is slightly more sparkling with about 4. Some people prefer these gently sparkling wines with food.

**Blanc de Blancs** This ultra-fashionable term now crops up on numerous labels – perhaps rather more often than it should. A true Blanc de Blancs champagne (or sparkling wine) is a white wine made exclusively from white grapes. In Champagne this is therefore a 100% Chardonnay wine and, as such, should have a fine, light, fresh and fruity character. Some find Blanc de Blancs champagnes rather too shy and delicate, in which case it is better to keep to the other vintage and non-vintage blends which will have a fair proportion of big, full-bodied black grapes blended in with the white.

Blanc de Noirs A rarity, at least in that the words Blanc de Noirs hardly ever appear on a label. Blancs de Noirs are white wines made exclusively from either or both the black Champagne grapes Pinot Noir and Pinot Meunier. Rich, ripe and full-bodied, they are especially delicious with food. Bollinger's costly Vieilles Vignes Françaises is a Blanc de Noirs.

Single Vineyard A rarity in the Champagne region but rather more common elsewhere. Purists will argue that these lack the harmony and balance of champagnes made from a blend of grapes from different vineyards, but they present a unique opportunity to taste an unblended wine and for that reason alone are worth experiencing. Do not expect them to be cheap. Krug's Clos du Mesnil and Philipponat's Clos des Goisses, both from walled vineyards, are two examples.

Coteaux Champenois The still red or white wines of the Champagne region, not widely available but worth looking for. When the harvest is small, few still wines will be made as most of the crop will be needed to make champagne.

Buyer's Own Brand or BOB These are champagnes that are bottled not, as is usual, under the label of the producer but under that of the seller. It is therefore quite possible to be served a champagne marked with the name of a restaurant, wine merchant or supermarket which will have done nothing more than to select a blend from the producer. (See also How to Read a Champagne Label, page 14.)

Ratafia, Fine and Marc Much admired by locals and knowledgeable champagne lovers, these unusual drinks from the Champagne region take a little getting used to. Ratafia is made from fresh champagne grape juice mixed with brandy or sometimes cognac. The result is rich, strong, sweet and alcoholic. Serve it ice-cold as an apéritif or a *digestif*. Fine and marc are much stronger with about 40% alcohol, about twice the strength of ratafia. Fine, a brandy distilled from the still wine of the region, is the better of the two but difficult to find outside Champagne. Marc, like the marcs produced in other parts of France, is distilled from the skins, pips and stalks left behind after the last pressing. It is a fiery, rustic tipple that not everyone appreciates.

Pétillant These are slightly sparkling wines whose sparkle or *pétillance* is either a natural attribute or has been introduced. Most *pétillant* wines have roughly 2 atmospheres of pressure behind the cork, unlike the fully sparkling or *mousseux* wines that have 5–6. *Pétiller* means to crackle as well as to sparkle, which is why some countries and companies describe their slightly sparkling wines as "crackling" wines. *Perlant* wines have the least sparkle of all at just over 1 atmosphere of pressure.

### Dry or Sweet?
Champagne and other sparkling wines from EEC countries are among the few that specify exactly how dry or sweet they are. The levels set out below apply from September 1986.
Extra Brut (Extra Herb or Very Dry): 0–6 g/l

Brut (Herb or Dry): less than 15 grams per litre
Extra Dry (Extra Trocken): 12–20 g/l
Sec (Trocken, Dry, Secco, Asciutto, Seco): 17–35 g/l
Demi-Sec (Halbtrocken, Abboccato, Medium Dry, Semi-seco,
Meio-seco): 33–50 g/l
Doux (Mild, Sweet, Dolce, Dulce, Doce): more than 50 g/l

It is mandatory for every EEC producer, including champagne producers, to include one of the terms on their labels. The Ultra Brut, Brut Zero and Brut Sauvage non-*dosage* styles of champagne now fit into the new Extra Brut category as will many of the low *dosage* wines produced by houses such as Bollinger and Krug whose styles have always been dry.

The exact amount of residual sugar used in the categories listed above does, however, vary from firm to firm and from country to country. Even in Champagne, one company's Extra Dry could well be drier than another's Brut.

## Buying, Storing, Serving and Enjoying Sparkling Wines

Champagne and sparkling wines are the most sensitive of all wines. Light and heat are arch-enemies: champagne deteriorates alarmingly quickly in hot, bright surroundings – 24 hours is often all it takes to "kill" a bottle. Similarly, bottles left upright rather than horizontal (with the wet cork making an airtight seal) can deteriorate in a matter of days. It is therefore vital that champagne or sparkling wine is not only stored horizontally in a cool, 10°C (50°F), dark place but that it is bought from someone who has kept it in similar conditions.

It is worth storing even non-vintage champagne (as opposed to sparkling wine) for at least six months to a year before drinking it. Given this extra touch of maturity it takes on a richer, fuller, more complex flavour. Vintage champagne should be cellared for 5–10 years, depending on the style of the vintage and your own personal taste. If you like the taste of old, rich, nutty champagne, then by all means keep it for longer. A guide to champagne vintages is on page 15.

All champagne and sparkling wine should be served cool, not frozen. The optimum is around 7.5°C (45°F). This can usually be achieved by placing the bottle inside the refrigerator door for an hour or in a bucket of water and ice for ten minutes or so. Anyone who prefers their bubbly colder can always put the bottle back in the bucket for another five minutes. Much longer and the wine will be robbed of its bouquet and the cold will numb the palate.

Glasses also affect the pleasure of drinking sparkling wine. Avoid the saucer-shaped glasses: they flatten the bubbles and the bouquet, and even filled to the brim give a small measure. Tall, thin, plain, tulip-shaped glasses or champagne *flûtes* are perfect. The bouquet is concentrated and the bubbles should rise in an appealing, vigorous, steady stream to the surface. At all costs avoid swizzle sticks – you have paid for the bubble so why not enjoy them!

Judging the amount of champagne or sparkling wine needed for a wedding or any other event where it is the only wine to be served is not difficult. Most people drink about half a bottle per head at these functions. (A bottle usually contains about six full glasses.) If you like the thought of a big bottle to serve at a party, the following are available but the largest are now very difficult to find: Magnum – 2 bottles; Jeroboam – 4 bottles; Rehoboam – 6 bottles; Methuselah – 8 bottles; Salmanazar – 12 bottles; Balthazar – 16 bottles; Nebuchadnezzar – 20 bottles.

## Wine and Food

As a general rule a dry, light Blanc de Blancs is the wine to choose before a meal, if you are to serve sparkling wines throughout, saving the bigger, richer, more full-bodied wines to drink with the food. In terms of champagne this means a non-vintage Chardonnay-dominated (or indeed exclusively Blanc de Blancs) apéritif followed by a vintage Pinot Noir-dominated, or certainly Pinot Noir-influenced, wine with the meal.

If some palates find these rather too bubbly to go with food, try the softly sparkling *crémant* wines whose gentle bubbles and mousse are roughly half that of the fully sparkling or *mousseux* wines. If even *crémant* disagrees with your digestion, try a still white or red Coteaux Champenois. It may lack the delightful effervescence of champagne but has much of this region's majestic finesse and flavour.

A *doux* or *riche* style is the one to opt for as a dessert wine, but if you dislike sweet wine a slightly sweet Demi-sec is perhaps the ideal choice.

Demi-Sec or even *doux* champagnes, although now (unfairly) rather unfashionable, are worth considering for a wedding reception – not as the bubbly to be served throughout the event because most palates would prefer a non-cloying Brut or dry sparkling wine, but a glass with the wedding cake and for the toasts would be ideal.

## Acknowledgments

This book could never have been written without the help of numerous friends (and family) all over the world. In particular I would like to thank the following for their invaluable help and assistance: David Balls, Pierre Bouard, Christine Campbell, Nicholas Clarke MW, Judy Coleman, Eileen Crane, Brian Croser, Cecilia Daniels, Terry Dunleavy, Ronald Emler, André Enders, Sam Folsom, Sarah Fraser, Richard and Jenny Freeman, Toni Gill, Richard Goodman, Jean Gordon, Philip Hedges, João Henriques, Michael Hill-Smith, Nancy Jarratt, Fritz and Maureen Joubert, Margaret Le Roy, John Lipitch, Catherine Manac'h, Malcom McIntyre, John Page, Jan Read, Max Ringrow, Michaela Rodeno, Errol Slyfield, Dip Ing Traxler, Jean Valentine, John Walter, Jeremy Watson, Simon Watson and Robin Young.

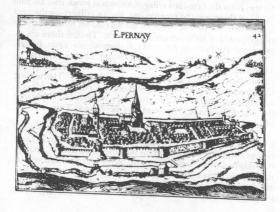

EPERNAY    42

# Champagne

*Le champagne*, the wine, takes its name from La Champagne, the old province of France where it is made. Champagne, 145km (90 miles) northeast of Paris, still produces the Rolls-Royce of sparkling wines. Other *méthode champenoise* wines from both inside and outside France may at times equal and even surpass those produced by some of the lesser-known houses, but so far no sparkling wine produced outside the region has been able to reach the heights achieved by the great names of Champagne. It is doubtful whether they ever will.

The region consists of some 35,000ha (86,000 acres) of which only some 25,000ha (62,000 acres) have been planted. Pinot Meunier and Pinot Noir each account for more than a third of the planted vineyard area, leaving Chardonnay with some 7,000ha (17,000 acres). The proportion of Pinot Meunier is always glossed over by the *Champenois* but it accounts – just – for the largest share of the total and is used in many blends. With great houses such as Krug using about 25% of the Meunier, it is clear that this grape is not a poor relation of the Chardonnay and Pinot Noir but a noble champagne grape in its own right.

There are 250 different *crus* or villages within the Champagne region. Conveniently, these can be divided into four main areas: the compact Montagne de Reims south of Reims and the river Vesle, the meandering Vallée de la Marne from just before Château-Thierry to just after Epernay, the Côte des Blancs that lies to the south of Epernay and ends just beyond Vertus, and the lesser-quality Aube district to the southeast of Vertus. In addition to these four there is the less distinguished Sézanne district that stretches south of Vertrus, and Vitry-le-François east of Sézanne and south of Châlons-sur-Marne. Part of the Vallée de la Marne, known as the Aisne, that lies south of the river and Château-Thierry, also fits into this less distinguished category.

The Chardonnay grape's stronghold within these areas is the Côte des Blancs, whereas the Pinot Noir reigns in the Montagne de Reims, and the Pinot Meunier as well as the Pinot Noir do well in the warmer, sunnier Vallée de la Marne.

Every year just before the harvest the price per kilo of grapes is fixed by a committee consisting of both growers and merchants. Grapes from the first-class villages, known as *grands crus*, are paid 100% of the price; the *premiers crus*, the 41 villages on the next level down, are paid 90–99% all the way down to the outlying villages, rated at 80%, which receive 80%. To date there are 17 *grands crus*: Ambonnay, Avize, Ay, Beaumont-sur-Vesle, Bouzy, Chouilly (for Chardonnay only), Cramant, Louvois, Mailly, Le Mesnil-sur-Oger, Oger, Oiry, Puisieulx, Sillery, Tours-sur-Marne (black grapes only), Verzenay and Verzy. The leading Chardonnay villages are Avize, Chouilly, Cramant, Le Mesnil-sur-Oger and Oger. The rest grow mainly Pinot Noir although the odd Chardonnay vineyard can be found. Two villages, Mareuil-sur-Ay and Tauxières, are now rated at 99%.

With the recent elevation of five villages to the 100%-rated level and others receiving a higher quality rating as well, these ratings are perhaps less important than they used to be. Certainly it is impressive to find a house or blend that exclusively uses 100%-rated grapes. But those who grandly claim that their wines are all rated at an average of 97% or whatever are not necessarily proving anything in terms of quality. It is the delicate art of

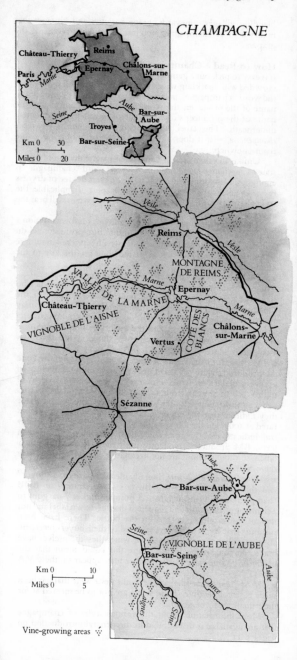

*CHAMPAGNE*

Vine-growing areas ⁖

blending villages, vineyards, grape varieties and vintages that makes a great champagne, not just the quality rating of the grapes.

## How to Read a Champagne Label

It is easy to pick out a genuine French champagne on a shop shelf crowded with sparkling wines. True champagne will simply bear the word "champagne" in large letters on the label plus the brand name of the producer, the words "produce of France" and the name of the producer's town or village in much smaller letters underneath. The label will not bear the words *"méthode champenoise"* — if it does, then your bottle of bubbly has come from elsewhere.

Unlike all other French wines, champagne does not have to state its *appellation contrôlée* status. The one word "champagne" is enough. Champagne bottles also declare their degree of dryness or sweetness, from Extra Brut to Doux, plus, if applicable, the style such as Blanc de Blancs or Rosé. Vintage wines will bear the appropriate date.

The most important and revealing item of information on a champagne label is the CIVC or Comité Interprofessionnel du Vin de Champagne registration code, which is printed in minute lettering. The first two letters of the code are the key to the champagne's origin:

● NM are the most common and stand for *négociant-manipulant*. These indicate wine from a merchant or négociant, someone who is entitled to buy in grapes or wine from elsewhere in the Champagne region to use in his own blends, which may or may not contain wines from his own vineyards. All the big houses produce NM champagnes and the quality should be the most reliable in the region. As with everything in life there are exceptions.

● RM stands for *récoltant-manipulant*. Champagnes with this code are produced mainly by small growers who must use their own grapes to make their wines. However they are allowed to buy in up to 5% of grapes from other sources. The quality varies tremendously. Watch for the words *"grand cru"* on these labels for they indicate that the champagne has been made from grapes rated at 100% on the Champagne village quality scale. *"Premier cru"* indicates that the grapes used have been rated at more than 90%. RM producers frequently omit these words from their labels, so those without are not necessarily of lower quality than the others.

● MA or *"marque d'acheteur"* literally means "mark of the buyer" and that is just what these "Buyer's Own Brand" or BOB champagnes are. Wine merchant X or supermarket Y has gone to a champagne producer and requested that their own label and not that of the producer be put on the bottle. There have been rumours that BOB producers are tired of their buyers receiving all the accolades (or otherwise!) for wines they themselves have made. At some stage in the future this could mean that the producer's name rather than number may appear on these MA labels.

● CM or *"coopérative manipulante"* indicates a wine that has been made by a cooperative. These wines are not to be sneered at for their quality can be good.

More information about the various styles of champagne that are available is to be found in the general introduction on pages 5–11.

## Champagne Vintages

**1985** A last-minute miracle vintage. Spring frosts killed 2,000ha (5,000 acres) of vines, some 8% of the total area, followed by a cold early summer, but a heatwave throughout September and October saved the day and early reports indicate that it is likely to be an exceptionally fine year. The crop, however, is small. 152m bottles.

**1984** An indifferent year. A late flowering and an equally late harvest. The quality is mixed. 199m bottles.

**1983** The second record breaker in a row after the 82. Happily quantity again went hand in hand with quality and most houses view the 83s as very good vintage material. The 82s are thought to just have the edge, but higher acidity may mean that the 83s live longer. 302m bottles.

**1982** An excellent year with abundant quantities of classic vintage wines, although some may show a slight lack of acidity. 295m bottles.

**1981** A good year but a tiny crop which with the small 80 and 78 harvests gave the *Champenois* supply problems. Most 81s went into non-vintage blends. 92m bottles.

**1980** The vintage that most *Champenois* would prefer to forget. Average quality. Smallish crop. 113m bottles.

**1979** A puzzler. The vintage was declared by most houses and many consider this an excellent year whose austere wines just need time to reveal their true glory. Blind tastings in 86 including all the big names proved disappointing with rot a noticeable feature of several wines. Time will tell how good the 79 vintage really is. 228m bottles.

**1978** A small crop but a fairly good year. High acidity is a feature which some houses have attempted to tone down with a high *dosage*. 78m bottles.

**1977** A difficult year. September sunshine helped but overall the quality was mediocre. 186m bottles.

**1976** The year of the sun. Almost overpoweringly rich, ripe, full-bodied wines. The best, which can be superb, are those with sufficient acidity to balance the fruit. 203m bottles.

**1975** A classic year. Magnificent, balanced, harmonious wines full of fruit and flavour. 168m bottles.

**1974** Unripe, disappointing wines. 163m bottles.

**1973** An early vintage with wines that many feel are balanced and appealing, but even the best are now showing their age and should be drunk. 202m bottles.

**1972** Thin, mean wines strictly for blending. 149m bottles.

**1971** A wonderful year with fine, full-flavoured, balanced wines that have grown old gracefully and are still drinking well, but only a small crop. 81m bottles.

**1970** A large vintage of good quality. Many of the round, fruity 70s are still going strong. 210m bottles.

## Older fine vintages

Not everyone enjoys the taste of old champagne with its soft, honeyed, hazelnut-like charms and gentle sparkle. But risky though it may be to hang on to a good vintage for 15 years or more, it is an experience that should be tried at least once. 1969 was an exceptionally good year. Similarly the 66s from leading houses are still rich, elegant wines. Anything much older, or from the lesser producers, means the odds start to work the other way, but try the great 61s or 59s, or even the 55s, 53s or 52s from the top champagne houses.

---

Henri Abelé                MC                73    ★

50 rue de Sillery, 51100 Reims

Now owned by the all-powerful Freixenet sparkling wine group
of Spain, Henri Abelé do not own any vineyards but produce
about 63,000 cases annually. Two-thirds of this appears under the
labels of their buyers. Among wines carrying the Abelé name are
Sourire de Reims plus the non-vintage and vintage Marque
Impériale and a Rosé. Half of the production here is via automatic
*remuage*. Henri Abelé champagne is only available in France and is
of simple, straightforward quality. One of the Abelé ancestors
invented *dégorgement à la glace*.

---

Ayala                      MC                59 70    ★

2 boulevard du Nord, 51160 Ay

One of the great old-fashioned champagne names. Ayala
champagne was apparently much admired by Queen Victoria's
son Edward when he was Prince of Wales. Ayala have a colourful
history: they were founded by Edmond Ayala, the son of a
Colombian diplomat, in 1860. Vicomte de Mareuil, a friend of
Edmond's father, introduced the young man to Champagne
society and he sensibly married one of the Vicomte's nieces –
Gabrielle d'Albretch. Mlle Albrecht's dowry included an important vineyard or two and Edmond promptly founded a champagne house on the strength of this. Today Ayala, despite its
illustrious past, is a somewhat forgotten name, even though some
75,000 cases are produced annually. A little of this comes from the
firm's own 99% Pinot Noir vineyards at Mareuil-sur-Ay. A
typical Ayala blend would be roughly 50% Pinot Noir, 20%
Pinot Meunier and 30% Chardonnay. Ayala champagne is
available in vintage and non-vintage Brut, Brut Rosé, Demi-Sec
and a vintage Blanc de Blancs. The latter is only released in very
good years. About half of their total sales are exported mainly to
the UK, the USA, Germany and Belgium. The quality of Ayala
champagne is simple and straightforward without being very
exciting. The light, biscuity Brut has a curious, almost metallic
nose. The green, disappointing 79 is not recommended.

---

Barancourt                 MC                ★→

Place André Tritant, Bouzy, 51150 Tours-sur-Marne

Three growers, Brice, Martin and Tritant, joined together in the
late 1960s to make and sell champagne under the single label of
Barancourt. Together they own some 50ha of vines and produce
about 46,000 cases annually. Barancourt offer a wide range of
champagnes but their still red Coteaux Champenois wine, Bouzy
Rouge, is their *pièce de résistance*. Apart from a vintage and non-
vintage champagne made from Bouzy grapes, Barancourt also
make Brut Réserve Blanc de Blancs, Rosé and Cramant
champagnes from the three partners' scattered vineyards.

---

Beaumet                    MC                81 85    ★

3 rue Malakoff, 51207 Epernay

Beaumet is a name well known in the USA, the UK, Sweden and
Belgium, which are its main export markets, but not in France.
Since 1977 Jacques Trouillard has been the force behind Beaumet
and in 1980 the firm moved to an old house with splendid cellars
in the Parc Malakoff. The company originally belonged to the
Beaumet family who established the house in 1878. A certain
percentage of Beaumet's own grapes, most of which are from the

Côte des Blancs, go into their *cuvées* but most of the firm's needs
are bought in. The vast majority of their sales are taken up by the
non-vintage Brut made from two-thirds Pinot Noir to one-third
Chardonnay. Other labels are Extra Dry, Demi-Sec, vintage and
non-vintage Blanc de Blancs, plus a vintage-dated Blanc de
Noirs, Rosé and a raw, pear-drop like Brut. Ratafia, marc and fine
are also made here. Beaumet's finest champagne is their Cuvée
Malakoff Blanc de Blancs. The firm have high regard for both the
81 and forthcoming 85 vintage wines. Beaumet is closely
associated with Jeanmaire and Oudinot.

| Besserat de Bellefon | MC | 71 75 | ★→ |

Allée du Vignoble, 51061 Reims

Bought by the Pernod-Ricard group in 1976, Besserat de
Bellefon are a big champagne house specializing in *crémants* which
account for about 40% of their sales. Founded in 1843 in Ay,
Besserat moved in 1970 to rather showy, ultra-modern premises
which cover 14ha (34 acres) at Reims, complete with two large
cellars that can be hired out for conferences and parties. Besserat
de Bellefon's style is light, lean and not very exciting. But their
*crémant* champagnes, both white, and rosé (sold as Crémant des
Moines) are made from a blend of 50 different wines and are well
distributed. Besserat own 10ha (24 acres) of Ay Pinot Noir vines
and buy in another 250ha worth of grapes to produce their
167,000 cases of champagne annually. Apart from *crémant* wines
Besserat make a Pinot Noir-dominant vintage and non-vintage
Brut plus their recently launched non-vintage B de B prestige
*cuvée*. Besserat export a great deal principally to Switzerland and
Belgium as well as to the UK. They are one of the few champagne
houses to make a Crémant Rosé and they suggest it should be
drunk as an apéritif as well as with meats and cheeses. Besserat's
non-vintage Brut is not recommended.

| Billecart-Salmon | MC | 76 | ★→ |

40 rue Carnot, 51160 Mareuil-sur-Ay

Billecart-Salmon, currently directed by Jean Roland-Billecart,
the fifth generation of his family, like to be thought of as one of
France's best-kept secrets. Certainly this small *grande marque*
house founded in 1818 is only just stepping into the limelight.
Their 42,000 cases are at present made almost entirely from
bought-in grapes. The 10% that comes from their own Mareuil-
sur-Ay Pinot Noir vineyards is used exclusively in their flowery,
salmon-pink Rosé wine. Other Billecart wines include a lemony,
flowery non-vintage and vintage Brut, a Demi-Sec and Blanc.
The vintage Brut and Rosé are a Pinot Noir/Chardonnay blend
and the Blanc de Blancs is pure Chardonnay from the three *grands
crus* villages of Cramant, Avize and Mesnil-sur-Oger. The
Billecart-Salmon style is lean, lively and flavoursome without
being particularly special. Their best wine is the 79 Blanc de
Blancs whose complex, lively, chalky character will obviously
mature into an impressive champagne. France is the most
important market, followed by the USA and the UK. The 78
Billecart has an intense green, almost asparagus-like character and
the 79 is an acceptable, light, lean wine.

| Robert Billion | MC | 79 | ★★→★★★ |

Le Mesnil-sur-Oger, 51190 Avize

*Star Buy 79 Blanc de Blancs du Mesnil*

One of the Mesnil-sur-Oger cooperatives, this firm was founded by Robert Billion and grandson of Aimé Salon (the founder of Salon) in 1954. The superb quality of the grapes here combined with the considerable talent of Monsieur Billion have ensured that the wines produced have been wonderful examples of this first-class Chardonnay village. The cooperative sells all of its production in bulk although every year since 1969 a small quantity has been sold under the Robert Billion label. Sadly, since M. Billion's untimely death in 1984 there are now only limited stocks of wines left. Buy up whatever you can find of Robert Billion's fresh, elegant and flowery non-vintage Blanc de Blancs du Mesnil. If you are lucky you might still be able to get hold of a vintage champagne such as the splendid 79 whose golden colour and lovely long, lingering, rich, biscuity taste is a delight.

| Boizel | MC | ★→ |
|---|---|---|
| 14–16 rue de Bernon, 51200 Epernay | | |

Boizel do not have any vineyards of their own and most years produce more than 50,000 cases. In 1985 they made 80,000. The firm has been in family ownership since its foundation in 1834. Boizel Brut non-vintage accounts for the majority of sales here but this wine is also available in Sec and Demi-Sec versions. Blanc de Blancs, Rich, Rosé, Grand Vintage Brut and their *tête de cuvée* Joyau de France complete the range. Their Blanc de Blancs is shortly to be relaunched with a fancy 19th-century label to commemorate their 150th anniversary. Today Christophe and Evelyne Roques-Boizel, the fifth generation, direct the firm. Boizel are keen exporters with more than half their annual sales achieved overseas. The main consumers of Boizel champagne are principally the UK plus Switzerland and the USA to a lesser extent. Krémer is another Boizel brand, a firm that Boizel took over in 1912. Boizel produce a fair number of Buyer's Own Brand champagnes. Boizel Rosé is a frothy, deep red-pink wine and the Brut Réserve is appealingly soft, toasty and fruity.

| Bollinger | MC | 69 70 75 76 | ★→★★★★ |
|---|---|---|---|
| 16 rue Jules Lobet, 51160 Ay | | | |

In 1829, some years before Johann Joseph Krug arrived in Champagne, his countryman Joseph Bollinger from Württemberg in Germany founded Bollinger. In the early days Paul Renaudin was Bollinger's partner. The original nucleus of the firm were the vineyards owned by Joseph Bollinger's father-in-law, the Comte de Villermont. Monsieur le Comte did not wish to sully his name with any trade connections and thus the champagne produced was labelled Renaudin, Bollinger & Co., a name that appeared on bottles of Bollinger until quite recently. Determined Madame Lily Bollinger, who steered her firm through the difficult years of German occupation, was the last Bollinger and today the house is run by her nephew, Christian Bizot. Bollinger are traditionalists and their big, biscuity, almost beefy style of champagne has always reflected this. To achieve this style Bollinger still vinify their vintage champagnes in oak and for all their blends use a noticeable proportion of reserve wines. Unlike other houses Bollinger keep their reserve wines in magnums and at any one time these account for about 10% of their stock. About five years' worth in total. In particular Bollinger's non-vintage champagne Special Cuvée contains a high proportion of reserve wines. Bollinger are also traditionalists when it comes to their vineyards with only the first pressing used. They own 140ha (345 acres) which provide them with roughly

70% of their needs. As the full-bodied Bollinger taste indicates, almost all the vineyards are planted to Pinot Noir, the most important holdings being in Ay, Verzenay, Bouzy, Louvois, Tauxières, Avenay and Bisseuil. Bollinger also own Chardonnay plots in Cuis and Grauves plus a little Pinot Meunier in Champvoisy. The latter is used only in their Special Cuvée.

Perhaps the most traditional wine that Bollinger make is their extraordinarily fine Vieilles Vignes Françaises made from old ungrafted pre-phylloxera vines. The elegant, flowery, perfumed 80 vintage of this classic Blanc de Noirs champagne is young as yet and noticeably different in style from other Bollinger vintages. But it nonetheless has a tremendous depth of flavour and fruit that will mature into a distinguished champagne.

At the other end of the Bollinger price scale is Special Cuvée which accounts for about 70% of their total annual production of 166,000 cases. Clearly there is great demand for this non-vintage wine. Sadly there have been some alarming variations in the quality of Special Cuvée. At its best it is a superb, rich, biscuity, powerful champagne, at its worst a thoroughly disappointing glassful. In recent years Bollinger have suffered from this bottle variability problem more than any other *grande marque* house. Still, there are signs that they have weathered the storm.

The seductive RD 75 (disgorged in November 1985) is a wonderful example of textbook vintage Bollinger: a glorious buttercup-gold colour plus a rich, flowery, biscuity nose backed up by a similarly fine, full-bodied yet balanced palate. The RD stands for "recently disgorged". In other words this champagne was matured on its lees or yeast until in this case November 1985. Bollinger believe strongly that this extra time in contact with the yeast (which varies from 7–10 years) gives the wine additional body and flavour. Certainly anyone who has tasted the 75 or the rich, smoky, hazelnut-like 70 would find it hard to disagree. The musky 73 RD is not as good and neither are the new gold-label 73 RD Année Rare wines that spend even longer on their lees – 10 years or more. Bollinger also sell a vintage-dated Grande Année Rosé (the racy, green 81 is the latest vintage) plus the Grande Année Brut whose 79 vintage is a rich, big, flavourful, meaty wine. But like all the 79s not a *crème de la crème* Bollinger vintage.

Bollinger have recently bought a share in a leading Australian winery, Petaluma, which has just released its first *méthode champenoise* wine. Bollinger have also just joined forces with Whitbread and Antinori to set up a winery in California's Napa Valley. Bollinger also own Langlois-Château in the Loire. More than 70% of their champagne is exported, chiefly to the UK, the USA and Australia. They also make a delicious still red wine, La Côte aux Enfants, whose big, full, ripe, morello cherry-like 82 vintage is well worth tasting.

| Bonnaire | MC | ★ → ★★ |
|---|---|---|

105 rue du Carrouge, Cramant, 51200 Epernay

The Brut non-vintage Champagne de Cramant with its clean, fresh, lively, flowery taste is a good example of the Bonnaire family's expertise.

| F. Bonnet | MC | 64 | ★ → |
|---|---|---|---|

Rue du Mesnil, Oger, 51190 Avize

Not a well-known champagne name, but F. Bonnet, founded by vigneron Ferdinand Bonnet in 1922, are an old family firm. Mlle Nicole Bonnet is the current manager here. The family's 10ha

(24 acres) or so of vines in the top Chardonnay villages of Oger and Avize, plus the slightly less distinguished neighbouring village of Vertus (with a little Pinot Noir) supply almost all their needs. With an annual production of slightly more than 11,000 cases F. Bonnet are a small house but they have a good reputation for their fine, aged, Chardonnay-dominant *cuvées*. Chardonnay-only champagnes include the Blanc de Blancs Reserve Carte Or Brut and the vintage-dated Selection. The one-third Pinot Noir wines include F. Bonnet's Crémant and Carte Blanche. Their most popular wine is the Crémant. 20% of their wines are exported, principally to the UK.

| Bricout & Koch | MC | 69 | ★→ |
|---|---|---|---|
| 7 route de Cramant, 51190 Avize | | | |

Owned by Kupferberg, the giant German sparkling wine concern, Bricout & Koch was founded in 1966 and is one of the newer champagne houses. With an annual production of more than 200,000 cases (aided by automatic *remuage*) B & K is a medium-sized house. The firm uses a blend of all three Champagne grapes to make their Bricout Carte Noire, Carte Or, Rosé and Pol Varême. Production is mostly divided between Carte Noire and Pol Varême. The vintage-dated Cuvée Charles Koch (currently the 81) is Bricout's finest. It is made exclusively from Chardonnay and Pinot Noir. Bricout consider their 69 vintage to be their best offering so far.

| René Brun | MC | | ★→ |
|---|---|---|---|
| 4 place de la Libération, 51160 Ay | | | |

René Brun founded this firm in 1942. Today his descendants run the company and produce some 20,000 cases of champagne annually. Most of this comes from their own vineyards at Ay. The Pinot Noir-dominated vintage and non-vintage Brut are well made and easy to drink.

| Albert le Brun | MC | 64 70 71 | ★★→ |
|---|---|---|---|
| 93 avenue de Paris, 51000 Châlons-sur-Marne | | | |
| *Star buy Blanc de Blancs Brut, Cuvée Réservée Brut* | | | |

Founded by Léon le Brun in 1860 in Avize, this firm moved later to Châlons. Albert le Brun champagnes are definitely worth seeking out for several wines in their range are excellent and the others are often bargain buys – a considerable achievement for this medium-sized family firm that produces almost 30,000 cases annually. The most notable in the le Brun range is the non-vintage Blanc de Blancs Brut, a three-star wine made from Avize Chardonnay including the produce of the family's own 4ha (9 acres) of vines. This wine's fine, smoky bouquet and big, rich, gutsy taste in many ways seems more reminiscent of a Blanc de Noirs and is highly recommended. Le Brun's full-bodied, biscuity, smoky, non-vintage Pinot Noir-dominant Cuvée Réservée Brut is another good buy, as is their big, ripe 76. Albert le Brun also make a Carte Blanche Brut and Demi-Sec plus a Rosé Brut. The house considers its 79 Vieille France Brut in its curious dumpy bottle to be its best wine, but it lacks both balance and charm. Try the others instead! More than half of le Brun's champagnes are exported, principally to Europe and the USA.

| Victor Canard | MC | | ★ |
|---|---|---|---|
| 8 rue Victor Hugo, 51500 Ludes | | | |

Victor Canard must be the newest Champagne house, having

been founded in 1984. It has nothing to do with Canard-Duchêne. Jean-Pierre Canard named the firm after his grandfather who cultivated vines at Ludes in the mid-19th century. Almost all the grapes used come from the family's own Pinot Noir vines at Ludes which is the next-door village to the west of Mailly in the Montagne de Reims. Just 500 cases were made here in 1985 but the family hope this will eventually reach 25,000 cases. Not everyone will be smitten by Monsieur Canard's modern labels. The wines behind them include the Cuvée Or in the non-vintage Jaune, Gris and Rosé styles plus the vintage-dated Vieil Or. Gris is 100% Chardonnay and Jaune predominantly Pinot Noir. The others are a blend of white and black grapes. With so few vintages available at present it is too early to assess the Victor Canard style, but they are already doing well in the UK, Holland and Switzerland.

| Canard-Duchêne | MC | 75 80 | ★★ → |
| --- | --- | --- | --- |
| 1 rue Edmond Canard, 51500 Ludes | | | |
| *Star buy Canard-Duchêne non-vintage Brut* | | | |

Somewhat unfairly this house trails along in Veuve Clicquot's wake, for the two belong to the same group. Canard-Duchêne is however a worthy champagne firm in its own right. Their delicious, elegant, flowery non-vintage Brut is an especially good buy most years despite its lowly provenance and does consistently well in blind tastings even when compared with Veuve Clicquot. Canard-Duchêne, who were founded in 1868, own 17ha (41 acres) at Ludes and Taissy in the Montagne de Reims but these vineyards only supply 4% of their needs. (Production at Canard-Duchêne tops 250,000 cases most years.)

This means that another 400ha (988 acres) worth of Pinot Noir and Pinot Meunier (probably given Canard's low prices from the Aube) plus a smaller amount of Chardonnay are bought in. 200,000 cases of the inexpensive Canard-Duchêne Brut are sold annually but they also make tiny amounts of a Demi-Sec, Rosé, vintage-dated Brut and their prestige Cuvée Charles VII. France consumes most of the wine made but about 10% is exported to the UK and Europe. Visitors must have an appointment to see the modern Canard-Duchêne buildings above ground and the 2km (3 miles) of cellars below.

| de Castellane | MC | | ★ → |
| --- | --- | --- | --- |
| 57 rue de Verdun, 51204 Epernay | | | |

Dominating the mostly traditional Epernay skyline is de Castellane's crazy crenellated tower. This edifice as well as the firm's famous red cross label indicate that de Castellane has an important past. Vicomte Florens de Castellane founded this house giving it his name and choosing its red cross trademark. Production boomed and up until the 1960s much of the 125,000 cases of de Castellane champagne made annually was exported all around the world. Since then de Castellane have gone through a difficult time but are now determined to retrieve their old reputation. De Castellane do not own any vineyards of their own and their current production is 167,000 cases. In 1985 they hoped to export more than 40,000 cases. 80% of their total is taken up by the black grapes-dominated Brut with its red cross label. Other de Castellane champagnes include a vintage and non-vintage Blanc de Blancs, a Brut Rosé plus the top of the line, the vintage-dated pot-bellied Cuvée Commodore bottle. De Castellane have recently introduced a sweet liqueur de la Champagne which the firm feels can be drunk either before or after a meal or as a base for cocktails. De Castellane are the producers of Maxim's champagne with its distinctive label. Its pleasant, soft, easy-to-drink flavour contrasts with an unusual tea-leaf like aspect on the nose. The vanilla-pod scented de Castellane Brut is equally quaffable.

| Charles de Cazanove | MC | 73 | ★ |

1 rue des Cotelles, 51200 Epernay

The Lombard family are the major owners of de Cazanove champagne. The firm do not own any vineyards of their own but buy in grapes during the harvest from various vignerons throughout the major champagne regions. They do however make the wines entirely by themselves. With an annual production of about 12,500 cases de Cazanove is a small firm. Only four different wines are made here: their best-sellers the non-vintage Brut and Demi-Sec, the 81 Brut and the Ruban Azur Blanc de Blancs. The firm launched a Rosé champagne in 1986. De Cazanove's main export markets are the UK, Italy and Hong Kong. Charles Gabriel de Cazanove founded the firm in 1811.

| A. Charbaut & Fils | MC | 71 73 | ★ → |

17 avenue de Champagne, 51205 Epernay

It is difficult to know quite what to make of Charbaut. On the one hand they are a highly-successful champagne firm that has just acquired some magnificent revamped cellars in Epernay's equivalent of the Champs Elysées – the Avenue de Champagne. Clearly their own-label business for wine merchants, supermarkets and the like is thriving. On the other hand the quality of their once stylish blends now appears to have its ups and downs. Perhaps this is the price of success. André Charbaut founded the firm in 1948 at Mareuil-sur-Ay and, although he still comes into the office every day, his two sons René and Guy now run the firm. Charbaut's annual production is more than 140,000 cases and the 56ha (138 acres) of the family's own vines at Mareuil-sur-Ay and the neighbouring village of Bisseuil no longer supply all they need. An additional 120ha (296 acres) worth of grapes are bought in. The Charbaut range consists of a non-vintage Brut, Rosé and Blanc de Blancs plus the vintage-dated Brut and Blanc de Blancs. Charbaut also make a still white, red and rosé Coteaux Champenois plus marc, ratafia and fine. The 79 Cuvée de Reserve has a smoky, fruity palate: good but not great. Similarly the 76 Charbaut Certificate has a soft, vanilla-like and easy to quaff style. At its best the Brut has been a lovely warm, toasty, flavoury champagne with a good mousse, and the Rosé has been an equally delightful fruity, pale pink *fraises de bois* scented wine.

| Chaudron & Fils | MC | 76 | ★ |

Route de Billy, 51380 Vaudemange

The Chaudron family have a long history in both Vaudemange and Verzenay in the Montagne de Reims. The company however did not start to sell its wines on a large scale until 10 years ago. Today they own 15ha (37 acres) of mostly Chardonnay vines on the eastern edge of the Montagne de Reims at Vaudemange and the delightful-sounding Billy le Grand. Their Pinot Noir vines are concentrated in Verzenay, Verzy and Beaumont. Together these supply only a third of Chaudron's needs and the balance needed for their annual 12,500 case production is bought in. Chaudron champagnes are available in Brut, Rosé, Demi-Sec and Sec styles. Most are a blend of 60% Chardonnay and 40% Pinot

Noir and Meunier. France is the major market for Chaudron champagnes which are also exported to the UK, the USA and Germany. Brut Selection is their latest *cuvée* – a blend of the first pressing of the Chaudron family's own 100% quality rated vines, aged for four years. It should be worth trying.

| A. Chauvet | MC | ★ |
| --- | --- | --- |

11 avenue de Champagne, 51150 Tours-sur-Marne

This small family concern owns 10ha (4 acres) or so of its own vineyards which account for almost all of its needs. Production is slightly in excess of 4,000 cases annually divided between a fruity Blanc de Blancs and a non-vintage Pinot Noir-dominant Brut and Rosé.

| A. Desmoulins | MC | ★ |
| --- | --- | --- |

44 avenue Foch, 51201 Epernay

With just 12,500 cases produced annually A. Desmoulins & Cie of Epernay are a small company, in family hands since 1908. Six different champagnes are made and all apart from the Blanc de Blancs are a blend of the three champagne grapes. The Cuvée de Réserve Brut and Cuvée Prestige Brut are the mainstay of the firm followed by Brut Royal, Grand Rosé Brut, a Demi-Sec and the 79 Blanc de Blancs Brut. Germany and Belgium are their two export markets. Visitors are welcome by appointment. Their full-bodied fruity Cuvée Prestige is well thought of.

| Deutz | MC | | 66 75 82 | ★ → ★★ |
| --- | --- | --- | --- | --- |

16 rue Jeanson, 51160 Ay

William Deutz and Pierre Geldermann, who were both born in French Aix-la-Chapelle, now German Aachen, in the early 19th century, founded this firm in 1838. Today the Lallier family, fifth generation descendants of William Deutz, run the company. Dynamic André Lallier clearly believes in international connections for to date the company has sparkling wine interests in four overseas countries (as well as a wine firm in Touraine and another in the Rhône). The Deutz & Geldermann Sektkellerei in Germany with its 208,000 cases output is by far the largest of these offshoots. In 1983 Deutz joined forces with Ste Navarro Correas in Argentina and with DAE SUM in South Korea. Their Pressoir Deutz winery in California is both Deutz owned and run. It will be interesting to see where Deutz go next.

The Deutz style is a traditional one, using hand *remuage*, and about 40% of their grape needs come from their own vineyards. Most of these are situated in prime Pinot Noir country at Ay and Mareuil-sur-Ay, but Deutz has a sizeable holding of Chardonnay at Mesnil-sur-Oger plus a little Pinot Meunier at Moussy and Pierry just south of Epernay. All this is turned into about 67,000 cases of well-made, pleasing, soft, fruity champagne which rarely thrills the tastebuds but does not disappoint them either. Most of it is in attractive, herbaceous, gentle non-vintage Brut. A Demi-Sec, vintage-dated Brut, Rosé and Blanc de Blancs are also available. The painter Georges Mathieu has designed a special bottle for them but the jewel in the Deutz crown is their prestige Cuvée William Deutz. The ripe-fruit, pineapple-like 75 is worth tasting, though it is only produced in limited quantities. Deutz export half their production, mostly to the USA, Germany and Switzerland. Visitors can admire the ornate reception rooms painstakingly restored to an 1860 style by André Lallier. The 82 Deutz is a light, elegant, flowery-fruity wine.

## Duval Leroy   MC   73   ★→★★

rue du Mont Chenil, 51130 Vertus

*Star buy Fleur de Champagne*

Jules Duval merged his firm with that of Edouard Leroy in 1859. Duval Leroy are today one of those go-getting négociant houses who sell an impressive 325,000 cases of champagne every year. Even more impressive perhaps is that the Duval-Leroy Brut (generally under an own-label guise) regularly comes top in blind non-vintage champagne tastings that include all the famous *grandes marques*. To attain both quantity and quality in champagne is a tremendous achievement, one which Duval manage, although their quality does slip from time to time. Under their own label the firm offers a Carte Blanche Brut and Demi-Sec, a Fleur de Champagne Brut and Demi-Sec plus vintage, rosé and Cuvée des Roys Brut. These champagnes account for half of the firm's sales and the remainder are sold as Buyer's Own Brand Brut and Demi-Sec wines. Given such a vast output it is understandable that Duval's own 100ha (247 acres) of vines in the Côte des Blancs, plus others at Loisy, Sézanne and Bligny, account for only a fifth of their needs, with the rest bought in. At a recent tasting their Brut was excellent: elegant, rich, big, biscuity and fruity. The firm however consider that their fresh, flowery Fleur de Champagne Brut is the best ambassador for the house. Duval Leroy make a still Coteaux Champenois red and white wine. By far the biggest export market for Duval is the UK followed by Germany, the Low Countries, Ireland and the USA.

## Roland Fliniaux   MC   ★★→

1 rue Léon Bourgeois, 51160 Ay

*Star buy Fliniaux Rosé*

Roland Fliniaux and his wife head this family firm that was founded in 1938 but which inherits winemaking traditions in the region going back to 1905. The Fliniaux style is one that is wholeheartedly and uncompromisingly that of Ay. Although the family own just 3ha (7 acres) of their own Ay vines (giving them a third of their needs) the other two-thirds also come from this important Grand Cru champagne village. Newcomers to the Fliniaux range will probably find the overwhelmingly ripe musk-melon scent and taste almost too much to cope with. Certainly the enormously powerful Carte Noire Brut has this character in abundance, wrapped up with other ripe fruit flavours including pineapple and banana. Fliniaux also make Carte Bleue, Rouge and vintage-dated Noire in addition to their Cuvée Prestige Tradition. The real star however is their splendid Rosé. This full-flavoured Ay Rosé is one of the few exclusively Rosé de Noirs available in Champagne. Its pretty salmon-pink colour and attractive *fraises de bois* bouquet are backed up by a wonderfully rich and gutsy, fruity flavour. Definitely the pink'un to choose if you are fed up with pale insipid rosé champagne. The old champagne traditions are still much in evidence here and disgorging is still *à la volée*, that is to say done by hand without the use of ice. Fliniaux are a very small family firm producing just over 6,000 cases annually so you will have to hunt to find them. The wines are exported to the UK, Germany and Switzerland.

## H. Germain & Fils,   MC   ★

36 rue de Reims, 51500 Rilly-la-Montagne

83,000 cases are made in most years of Germain champagne and its baby brother Binet. Binet is the brand that goes to small, specialist outlets whereas Germain is sold in supermarkets and the like. America drinks large quantities of Germain. A vintage and non-vintage Brut and a Rosé are produced.

| Paul Gobillard | MC | 76 | ★ |
| --- | --- | --- | --- |

Château de Pierry, Pierry, 51200 Epernay

Madame Paul Gobillard and her son Jean-Paul Gobillard run this firm that dates back to 1858 in Pierry but has only been a company since 1972. A small plot of Pierry's Pinot Meunier comprises this family's own vineyard holding but in addition they buy in some 30ha (74 acres) worth of mostly Pinot Meunier and Chardonnay plus a little Pinot Noir. 12,500 cases are made annually of the firm's fruity Pinot Meunier-dominated non-vintage Carte Blanche and Brut Réserve plus four other Gobillard wines. These are a Rosé, Blanc de Blancs, Cuvée Régence and vintage sparklers. The latter are Chardonnay-dominated wines. Cuvée Régence is a 50/50 blend of Chardonnay and the two black Pinot grapes. Most Gobillard champagne is sold in France but a little is exported to Switzerland. The grand 18th century Château de Pierry is available for receptions and other gatherings. Paul Gobillard will receive visitors provided a prior appointment is made. Ratafia and marc are also made here.

| Gosset | MC | 76 79 | ★→ |
| --- | --- | --- | --- |

69 rue Jules Blondeau, 51160 Ay

Somewhat unfairly perhaps, Gosset is one of those champagne houses that tend to get overlooked. Yet the traditions and history of this Ay firm, dating back to 1584, make it the oldest winemaker, as opposed to champagne maker, in the region. Today Gosset is run by the 13th and 14th generation descendants of the founder Pierre Gosset. About 20% of the Gosset family's grapes come from their own Montagne de Reims Pinot Noir vineyards. In addition they buy in grapes from 30 different Côte des Blancs villages. All this adds up to some 40ha (99 acres) of vines which together with an annual production of just 25,000 cases makes Gosset one of the smaller houses. The average blend is two-thirds Pinot Noir to one-third Chardonnay and the house believes in giving its champagnes a lengthy sojourn in the cellar before releasing them. At any one time they have more than five years stock in their cellars. Gosset have no wish to expand, preferring to remain a small, family-run quality-conscious house. With four centuries under their belt the Gossets released a special Cuvée Quatrième Centenaire in 1984. The range now includes the non-vintage Brut Réserve, the recently launched Grande Réserve, a Rosé and the vintage-dated Grand Millésime Brut and Rosé. The full-flavoured Gosset style will not be admired by everyone. But the pungent, truffley, Pinot Noir-dominant Grande Réserve, the equally odoriferous, frothy, almost cheesy 73 Grande Millésime and the sweet, cherry-like Rosé represent an unusual range. The UK, the USA and Germany are the major export markets for Gosset. Visitors are welcome during office hours by prior appointment. The 79 Grande Millésime with its fresh, green, lively, flavoury palate is recommended.

| Alfred Gratien | MC | 76 | ★★→ |
| --- | --- | --- | --- |

30 rue Maurice Cerveaux, 51201 Epernay

*Star buy 76 Alfred Gratien*

The Seydoux family own this champagne house in addition to

their Gratien & Meyer Saumur operation. The full title of the company is actually Gratien, Meyer, Seydoux. It opened its Epernay branch in 1864. For a small house producing just 12,500 cases annually Alfred Gratien has a big reputation, which is entirely justified if their delicious, big, green herbaceous 76 is anything to go by. Alfred Gratien buy in all the Chardonnay, Pinot Noir and Pinot Meunier needed to create the current 79 vintage Brut, the Rosé Brut and the Cuvée de Réserve Brut. The English much enjoy the mature, nutty, slightly oxidized style that is the hallmark of all their champagnes, with the exception of the fruity grapey Rosé. The UK is a big export market followed by the USA, Germany, Denmark and Sweden. Visitors are welcome at Alfred Gratien during working hours by appointment.

| Emile Hamm & Fils | MC | 75 ★ |
| --- | --- | --- |

16 rue Nicolas Philipponnat, 51160 Ay

Hardly the most celebrated name in Champagne, yet Emile Hamm produce a respectable 16,000 cases annually. With slightly more than 3ha (7 acres) of vines at Ay this firm buys in the vast majority of its grapes from elsewhere. The Hamm family have been running the firm since 1943 and today make five different *cuvées* plus still white Coteaux Champenois wine. 15 complementary villages supply the backbone of their blends, which are turned into Grand Vin, Sélection, Réserve 1er Cru, Rosé Brut as well as a vintage-dated Brut. The Hamms have high hopes for their 85 vintage. Most of their champagne is drunk in France but a little is exported, mainly to the Common Market countries and Switzerland. Hamm will receive visitors during office hours preferably by appointment.

| Charles Heidsieck | MC | ★→ |
| --- | --- | --- |

3 place des Droits de l'Homme, 51055 Reims

Charles-Camille Heidsieck, or Champagne Charlie as his American clients nick-named him, founded this firm in 1851. Like the other Heidsiecks of Reims Charles-Camille was a relative of Florens-Louis and broke away from the main firm to set up on his own. It must have been hard for the 29 year-old Charles-Camille to compete with the two other already well-established champagne Heidsiecks but success in the USA saved the day. Since then five generations of Heidsiecks have run the house. From 1976 Henriot briefly held a majority shareholding but in late 1985 Rémy Martin, who also own Krug, bought Charles Heidsieck. It is unlikely that this will mean dramatic changes for there are still numerous Heidsieck family shareholders.

Charles Heidsieck do not own any vineyards but buy in what they need to create almost 300,000 cases annually. Most of this is the Brut non-vintage but there is an Extra Dry, Sec and Demi-Sec, all made roughly from the same quick-maturing blend: 15% Chardonnay and 85% Pinot Noir and Meunier. The longer-lasting vintage range includes a Brut, Rosé and Blanc de Blancs made usually from three-quarters Pinot Noir to one-quarter Chardonnay. The Charles Heidsieck style is light and soft, which the firm hopes has wide appeal, for, unusually for any *grande marque* house, more than 60% is exported. The standard of their non-vintage Brut has been very disappointing during the last few years, perhaps due to the uncertainty of ownership. However their new prestige champagne, the 79 Cuvée Champagne Charlie made from a blend of 55% Pinot Noir and 45% Chardonnay, is a step in the right direction with its delicate, peach-like fruit. A marc and a Coteaux Champenois, the Cuvée des Augustins, are also available. Visitors may admire the giant new, modern, stainless steel fermenters, but only by appointment.

| Heidsieck & Co Monopole | MC | ★→ |
| --- | --- | --- |
| 83 rue Coquebert, 51054 Reims | | |

Sorting one Heidsieck from another is a confusing business – but then everyone in Champagne is related to or associated with everyone else in some way. German-born Florenz-Ludwig Heidsieck set up his champagne firm in 1785 and became Florens-Louis. He had no children of his own so his German nephews came to Reims to help him run the business. The descendants of the first nephew Louis Walbaum-Heidsieck are connected with this firm. Other nephews eventually broke away to set up on their own, hence Piper-Heidsieck and Charles Heidsieck. Heidsieck & Co did not officially acquire the Monopole tag until 1923. The firm actually introduced their famous Dry Monopole brand in 1860 and customers were already referring to the company as Heidsieck Monopole (to distinguish it no doubt from the other Heidsiecks) not long after that. Heidsieck, like Mumm and Perrier-Jouët, is now part of Seagram's mighty champagne empire. More than 150,000 cases are made in most years.

Heidsieck's own 85ha (210 acres) of vineyards supply roughly a third of their needs. The most famous of these is at Verzenay, dominated by a huge old windmill that Monopole bought in 1923 and which has served as both observation point and entertainment venue. The Heidsieck range now includes a red-top Sec and a green-top Demi-Sec plus a rosé and vintage wine. The Heidsieck Dry Monopole non-vintage Brut is currently a dull and disappointing glassful with some curious nuances of flavour. The amazingly strong, over-ripe, exotic fruit smell and taste of Heidsieck's 76 Diamant Bleu prestige *cuvée* has its loyal followers, though. This wine is 50/50 Pinot Noir and Chardonnay, whereas Heidsieck's other range tends to be Pinot Noir-dominated. The straight 79 Heidsieck Dry Monopole vintage has some of Diamant Bleu's full-blown character.

| Henriot | MC | 66 73 | ★→★★ |
| --- | --- | --- | --- |
| Boîte Postale 457, 51066 Reims | | | |

Keeping up with the champagne trade is almost a full-time occupation. Suffice it to say that Henriot, who were once connected with Charles Heidsieck, are now linked with Veuve Clicquot. Quite what changes this will bring, if any, is difficult to judge. The Henriot family first became involved in Champagne in 1808. Today they are one of the very few champagne houses who are almost self-sufficient in grapes. With 103ha (248 acres) providing 80% of their needs, and the remaining grapes coming from Henriot's workers' own vineyards, this house is fortunate indeed. Henriot's own vineyards are spread throughout the three main regions but almost two-thirds are planted to Chardonnay, primarily in the Côte des Blancs. Together they yield some 100,000 cases annually, most of which consists of the unusual beefy, fruity non-vintage Brut. A Blanc de Blancs, Rosé and vintage-dated Henriot Brut complete the standard range. Henriot however have two prestige *cuvées*: the vintage-dated Chardonnay-dominated Cuvée Baccarat and the fearfully expensive Réserve Baron Philippe de Rothschild. (Both of these are aged for about five years.) Henriot feature prominently in three-star restaurants and hotels in France and on the direct-mail order market in France. Export markets include Germany, Switzerland, Belgium, Italy and the USA. In general the Henriot style is usually light and fairly invigorating. However the 79 Baron Philippe de Rothschild Réserve with its elegant, flowery-toasty taste is a wonderful champagne.

| Ivernel | MC | | 71 | ★→ |
|---|---|---|---|---|

4 rue Jules Lobet, 51100 Ay

Ivernels have been in Ay since 1500, and although this firm only dates from 1963, an earlier Ivernel champagne house was founded in 1889. Bernard Ivernel learnt the champagne business from his father Henri (a *chef de cave* at both Roederer and Krug) and revived the family firm in the early 1960s. With only 2ha (5 acres) of their own Ay Pinot Noir and Meunier vines, the Ivernels buy in grapes from a further 25ha (62 acres). Almost 16,000 cases of Ivernel Brut, Rosé, Cuvée du Roi François 1er, Blanc de Blancs and a vintage champagne are made here annually. Red and white still Coteaux Champenois are also produced in very small quantities. Cuvée Vincent Ivernel is their latest champagne. The UK, Switzerland, Belgium and Holland are the chief export markets. Ivernel champagnes are highly regarded in France.

| Jacquart | MC | | ★→ |
|---|---|---|---|

5 rue Gosset, 51066 Reims

The CRVC cooperative which produces this brand is one of the few in the region to sell champagne direct to the public. Most cooperatives prefer to stick to the own-label business. CRVC are obviously determined that their Jacquart brand should be a rip-roaring success.

Since its introduction in 1981 its flying horse trademark has been aggressively marketed in France and is now being introduced elsewhere. The cooperative's members own 1,000ha (2,470 acres) between them and produce some 667,000 cases of champagne annually. Roughly 167,000 cases are sold as Jacquart, the rest as Buyers' Own Brands. Jacquart champagne is available in both a non-vintage Brut Tradition and the classier Brut Selection. In addition there is a non-vintage Rosé and a vintage champagne made from 60% Pinot Noir to 40% Chardonnay. Jacquart hope to launch a prestige *cuvée* soon. Jacquart's Brut Tradition is a fresh, green fruity champagne.

| Jacquesson | MC | 75 76 | ★→★★ |
|---|---|---|---|

68 rue du Colonel Fabien, Dizy, 51318 Epernay

Jacquesson champagne is heavily billed as "originally supplied to Napoléon the Great". Bonaparte even went so far as to present the house with a gold medal in 1810 "for the beauty and richness of their cellars". Latter-day Wellington admirers should not be put off by this historical trifle. Jacquesson champagnes are worth getting to know, especially their Cuvée de Prestige: big, bold and delightfully rich, and the full-bodied 76 Signature Brut which was fermented in oak. Founded in 1798, this firm today owns 22ha (54 acres) of vines of an average 97% quality rating. Most of these Chardonnay and Pinot Noir vineyards are to the north and south of Epernay. Jacquesson also own Pinot Meunier vineyards at Lagery and buy in some 10ha (25 acres) worth of Meunier from outside. 60% of Jacquesson's needs come from their own vineyards; and their annual production is almost 30,000 cases. Apart from the 50/50 Chardonnay and Pinot Noir Signature, Jacquesson produce a Blanc de Blancs plus a Pinot Meunier-dominated non-vintage Perfection Brut and Rosé Brut. The vintage-dated Perfection Brut and Millésime Ancien are made from a blend of all three grapes. Jacquesson feel that the hallmark of their champagnes is suppleness: in other words they are soft, attractive and easy to drink. It would be hard to disagree. Jacquesson is exported to the USA, the UK and Germany.

| Jeanmaire | MC | | 81 | ★ |

12 rue Godart-Roger, 51207 Epernay

Owned by Oudinot and sharing the same address, Jeanmaire is now also run by the Trouillard family. Exactly the same policies rule here as they do at Oudinot, and Jeanmaire share the Oudinot facilities. Eight different champagnes are made here. These include a vintage and non-vintage Brut, an Extra-Dry, Demi-Sec, Rosé, Blanc de Blancs, Blanc de Noirs and a deluxe *cuvée* sold as Cuvée Elysée. Jeanmaire also make a ratafia, marc and fine. Jeanmaire champagnes are Pinot Noir-dominated. The Low Countries, the UK and Germany are the chief export markets. Jeanmaire is also associated with Beaumet.

| Krug | MC | | 69 73 75 76 | ★★★ → ★★★★ |

5 rue Coquebert, 51051 Reims

*Star buy Grande Cuvée*

Krug is quite simply the king of champagne. Private Cuvée devotees may have had some worrying moments when this robust and much-prized Krug was replaced by the lighter Grande Cuvée. It did take time to get used to the new Krug, with its noticeably higher proportion of Chardonnay. But now the non-vintage Grande Cuvée blend with its rich, seductive, biscuity smell, fruity, full-bodied taste and long firm finish is so mouthwateringly delicious that all doubts have long gone. Grand Cuvée accounts for 80% of their sales.

Johann Joseph Krug from Mainz in Germany founded the firm in 1843, after working for Jacquesson for nine years. Today the fifth generation of Krugs – Henri and Rémy – are in charge and as always it is they who put the blends together. The Krugs are perfectionists. Often as many as 50 different wines from 25 villages and 10 separate vintages go into their Grande Cuvée blend, which is roughly 45% Pinot Noir, 23% Pinot Meunier and 32% Chardonnay. Similarly their latest 79 vintage (36% Chardonnay, 36% Pinot Noir, 28% Meunier) is a blend of 29 different *crus* or villages. Krug Rosé, launched in 1983, (52% Pinot Noir, 24% Pinot Meunier, 24% Chardonnay) is a less burdensome blend of 11 different *crus* from four vintages. There is however no set recipe – each spring the various blends are painstakingly put together and the proportions therefore differ slightly from year to year.

About 20% of Krug's grapes come from their own 16ha (39 acres) of vines at Ay and Le Mesnil-sur-Oger. Other important sources of supply include Mareuil-sur-Ay and Ambonnay for Pinot Noir, Oger and Avize for Chardonnay and Leuvrigny for Meunier. Krug consider the Meunier grape to be an important part of any fine champagne. They insist on fermenting all their wines in traditional 205-litre wooden casks, firmly believing that much of the distinctive Krug style stems directly from this process. Krug also use only the first pressings for their wines. The wines are aged for an exceptionally long time before sale and the house holds an unparalleled six years' stock in their handsome old cellars. All this adds up to just 41,000 cases per annum, all deemed by the Krugs to be prestige *cuvées*.

The Krug style is extraordinarily fine, characterized by a deep golden colour, an intense, biscuity, almost hazelnut-like nose, a rich, harmonious, complex palate and a long, firm lingering finish. It is as majestic and magnificent as any champagne drinker could crave. But vintage Krug in particular embodies all these characteristics and more. Its powerful charms need time to be seen at their best, but hold on to any Krug vintage for ten years or more and you will be rewarded with all these flavours. Certainly anyone who has been lucky enough to taste the sensational 69, with its incredibly strong, rich, mouthfilling, biscuity-buttery finesse and flavour; or the rich, flavoury 53, or the smoky, almost Yquem-like 28 will have tasted Krug at its greatest. Minor Krug disappointments have included the lemony Rosé plus the young green 79 Clos du Mesnil from the Krug's own walled vineyard of Chardonnay vines. Italy, the UK and the USA are its major export markets. Sales are almost always "on allocation" i.e. rationed. Rémy Martin took an interest in Krug in 1970 and became the major shareholder in 1977.

| Lang Biemont | MC | 76 | ★ |

Les Ormissets, Oiry, 51200 Epernay

With production of more than 41,000 cases a year, Lang Biemont are obviously not an unknown firm. The name of this century-old house is rarely seen abroad however, although the firm do export to the UK, Holland and North Africa. Lang Biemont use grapes from the Côte des Blancs and Sézanne as well as the less illustrious Aube and Aisne areas. The range includes a Cuvée Réservée, Rosé, Carte d'Or plus the vintage top wine, Cuvée III. Most of the light, lively Lang Biemont champagnes are 60% Chardonnay, 30% Pinot Noir and 10% Pinot Meunier. Cuvée III, a Chardonnay-dominant blend, is protected from ultra-violet rays by a plastic wrapper.

| Lanson | MC | 71 76 | ★→ |

12 boulevard Lundy, 51056 Reims

People either love or loathe Lanson's young, light, lively-lemon style typified by the immensely successful Black Label Brut. This powerful concern, with annual sales adding up to half a million cases, is now along with Pommery part of the even more powerful French BSN group. François Delamotte founded the house in 1760. Despite Lanson's prolific output a quarter of their needs still come from their own 203ha (501 acres) of vines scattered throughout the three champagne regions and processed at six press houses. Most of these appear to be planted with Pinot Noir. Like all of the big champagne houses Lanson are somewhat secretive about the exact blends of their brands. But Black Label introduced in 1937 and which accounts for about 80% of Lanson's sales is thought to be a blend of 40% Chardonnay to 60% Pinot Noir and Meunier. Other Lanson labels include a Sec, Demi-Sec and Rosé plus a vintage Brut and a Chardonnay-dominant 225th Anniversary Special Cuvée from the 1980 vintage. Lanson's prestige *cuvée* is their new Noble Cuvée de Lanson whose beefy, musty character is not a good advertisement for the company. This firm also make a still red and white Coteaux Champenois plus a ratafia and marc. Lanson are thought to be the Number Two on the French market and also sell well in the UK, the Low Countries, Germany, Australia and the USA. (An associated company, Massé, is now also part of the BSN group.) The frothy, full-flavoured, almost beefy 79 is not recommended. But the flowery, elegant, toasty 76 is balanced and well-made. If only all Lanson vintages had this class.

| Larmandier Père & Fils | MC | ★→ |
|---|---|---|

43 rue du 28 aout, 51130 Vertus

Jules Larmandier founded this house in 1930. His grandson Dominique Larmandier now runs the firm. Although Larmandier no longer exclusively uses its own vines to create the 100,000 bottles or so it produces every year, it does have access to 9ha (22 acres) of family vineyards at Cramant plus additional vineyards elsewhere. Larmandier's non-vintage Cramant accounts for roughly 25% of their total production and is a speciality of the house. With its fresh, green, racy style and lively finish it makes an excellent apéritif champagne.

| Laurent-Perrier | MC | 70 75 79 | ★→★★★★ |
|---|---|---|---|

Domaine de Tours-sur-Marne, 51150 Tours-sur-Marne

*Star buy Cuvée Grande Siècle*

Modern, well-equipped Laurent-Perrier lies some distance to the east of Epernay at Tours-sur-Marne. Like many champagne houses Laurent-Perrier's name is that of a husband and wife: Eugène Laurent founded the firm in 1812 and when he died in 1887 his widow Mathilde Perrier took over, adding her name to his. The firm passed to the Nonancourt family in 1936 and they own it today. Currently Laurent-Perrier bring in 850ha (2,099 acres) worth of grapes each harvest of which they own about 10%. This adds up to roughly 625,000 cases which makes Laurent-Perrier one of the biggest and most powerful champagne houses. Laurent-Perrier's range is one of the most imaginative and varied in the region. It is mostly Chardonnay-dominated ranging roughly from 57% down to 50% for the Brut. There is a style, it seems, to suit every customer. It includes a well-made, bone-dry non-*dosage* Ultra Brut which, with its raw, flowery, astringent style, is not dissimilar perhaps to this firm's "Sugarless 1893 Grand Vin"? LP are one of the very few houses who are still making a traditional rosé whose coral pink colour and faint strawberry flavour stem from the Pinot Noir skins delicately staining the juice. Other non-vintage wines include the unexciting but again well-made fruity, appley Brut plus an Extra Dry, Demi-Sec and a Crémant (the latter only for the French market). This house's non-vintage *pièce de résistance* is the wondrous prestige Grand Siècle, a four-star wine whose classic, intense, toasty, flowery taste makes it one of the most majestic champagnes available, on a level with, if not superior to, Moët's Dom Pérignon and Roederer's Cristal. LP make just two vintage champagnes: a Brut (try the vigorous, fruity 79) and the intriguing Millésime Rare. The latter wine is old champagne from fine vintages primarily reserved for the Grand Siècle blend but any left over is bottled and sold as Millésime Rare. The 73 vintage had a deep gold colour, heady, herbaceous nose and soft, buttery taste. Laurent's Coteaux Champenois wines are a speciality and worth trying, especially the fresh, fruity Blanc de Blancs Chardonnay on which the firm in many ways made its reputation.

| Leclerc Briant | MC | ★ |
|---|---|---|

Cumières, 51200 Epernay

Still a family firm, Leclerc Briant was founded in 1872. This

Epernay-based house owns substantial vineyards of its own and produces some 24,000 cases annually. Leclerc Briant's labels include a Cuvée de Réserve Brut plus a Demi-Sec and Rosé. The quality of these champagnes does vary but their Cuvée Special Club is well thought of.

| R & L Legras | MC | 73 | ★ → ★★ |
|---|---|---|---|

10 rue des Partelaines, Chouilly, 51200 Epernay

Not a well-known name, but Legras Blanc de Blancs is apparently the house fizz for several French Michelin-approved establishments. Their superior prestige Cuvée St Vincent is well worth experiencing, especially the 73 vintage. R & L Legras' Brut Integral was the first non-*dosage* champagne.

| Abel Lepitre | MC | | ★ |
|---|---|---|---|

4 avenue de General Giraud, 51055 Reims

Abel Lepitre is the best known of Les Grands Champagnes de Reims' offerings. The other two brands in this stable are George Goulet and Saint-Marceaux. About 84,000 cases of all three champagnes are produced annually, of which Abel Lepitre accounts for about half with the balance split equally between the other two. Outside France the most important consumers of these champagnes are the UK, the USA and Switzerland. Abel Lepitre was once a celebrated champagne in Europe. It is available in both a Brut and a Crémant Blanc de Blancs version. The 79 Crémant with its powerful, herbaceous, almost green cabbage-like taste will not appeal to everyone. The St Marceaux Extra Quality Brut has a similarly off-putting grassy bouquet backed up by an aggressive lemony-smoky taste.

| Mailly-Champagne | MC | | ★ → |
|---|---|---|---|

51500 Rilly-la-Montagne

This group of Mailly producers founded in the 1920s is one of the most celebrated cooperatives in Champagne. Today Mailly make some 41,000 cases from about 70ha (173 acres) of vines. Surprisingly for a cooperative, most of the wine is sold under its own label. The Mailly range is generally based on a blend of three-quarters Pinot Noir to one-quarter Chardonnay. It offers among others a Brut, Demi-Sec, Rosé, vintage Brut and a deluxe *cuvée*, the Cuvée des Echansons. Mailly champagnes are sound if unexciting examples of the cooperative art. The Cuvée des Echansons is the best.

| Champagne Marie Stuart | MC | | ★ |
|---|---|---|---|

8 place de la République, 51100 Reims

Although they have an imposing building on the corner of the Place de la République Marie Stuart are perhaps a little less impressive than they might appear. This house is run by the Comptoir Vinicole de Champagne who in turn are owned by the Société Anonyme de Magenta or S.A.M.E. Founded in 1867 Marie Stuart now make more than 100,000 cases of champagne a year, all of which is made from bought-in grapes or wine. The Marie Stuart Brut which bears this ill-fated Queen's likeness, as do all the labels, accounts for most of the sales. Small amounts of a Demi-Sec, Blanc de Blancs, Rosé, vintage Brut and a Cuvée de la Reine are also produced. The style of Marie Stuart champagne is light and not particularly memorable. France consumes most of this bubbly but a little is also sent abroad, mostly to Germany, Belgium, the UK and the USA.

## Marne & Champagne    MC    ★→
22 rue Maurice Cerveaux, 51205 Epernay

Even the most determined champagne sleuths are unlikely to find
this name on many champagne labels. Marne & Champagne are
the second largest stockholders in Champagne and most of their
energies are devoted to being a "bank" for other houses. Thus if
one of the big concerns runs out of a certain style of wine Marne &
Champagne can step in to fill the gap. Apart from their sizeable
stockholding activities this house, owned by the hardworking
but now elderly Gaston Burtin, specializes in Buyer's Own Brand
champagnes. Many supermarkets and wine merchants in the UK
and elsewhere sell Marne & Champagne bubbly under their own
labels. Despite the large size of this firm the quality of its Buyer's
Own Brand wines has often been excellent. Many of their non-
vintage efforts have been well-made, lively, green, yeasty
champagnes. However this house has been known to turn out
coarse and raspingly green wines too. Recently the firm has been
taking more interest in the wines it markets itself under the
Giesler, Alfred Rothschild and Eugène Cliquot labels.

## Médot    MC    ★
19 route de Dormans, Pargny les Reims

This tiny champagne house producing slightly more than 6,000
cases annually owns just 4ha (10 acres) on the Montagne de
Reims. These supply only 15% of their needs and the rest is
bought in. Despite the small quantities made of the four Médot
champagnes (Cuvée Classique, Cuvée Réserve Direction, vintage Brut and Blanc de Blancs) the firm still exports to Europe and
the USA. Médot are proud of their limited edition Clos des
Chaulins champagne. It is one of the few in the region to come
from a walled vineyard.

## Mercier    MC    70 75    ★→
75 avenue de Champagne, 51200 Epernay

Eugène Mercier thought big: when he founded his champagne
house in 1858 he rejected the traditional convoluted rabbit-
warren champagne cellars and chose long straight galleries
instead. The end result was 47 wide galleries covering some 18km
(10 miles). Today visitors to Mercier are driven round in a small
train to admire these galleries plus a collection of wine presses and,
of course, to be shown the various stages in the making of
champagne. First-time visitors to Champagne will find Mercier
an enjoyable house to visit. Mercier became associated with Moët
& Chandon in 1970 and a year later both houses became part of
the giant Moët-Hennessy group. Inevitably Mercier's role is now
one that fits in with the group's plans rather than following any
independent path. Thus while Moët is the export champagne,
Mercier is principally designed for the French market: of the
330,000 cases total production some 283,000 cases are consumed
by the enthusiastic French. Mercier have 196ha (484 acres) of
their own vines but 80% of their needs have to be bought in. Like
many large champagne concerns Mercier are reluctant to reveal
their blends, but it is highly likely that Mercier is a Pinot Meunier-
dominant wine. Its low price certainly indicates this as do its own
outlying holdings, three-quarters of which are planted to
Meunier. Mercier champagnes therefore will never be in the first
league. At their best they enjoy a golden colour and a rich, full-
bodied taste that makes them good with food. At their worst they

can be dull and somewhat metallic is style. Mercier non-vintage Brut is no doubt the big seller here but there is a non-vintage Demi-Sec and Extra Rich – the latter intended for the UK market. Vintage wines include a Brut and Brut Réserve in both white and rosé styles. The 80 Mercier Brut is a full-flavoured, lemony champagne. The UK is an important export market.

| Moët & Chandon | MC | 70 73 75 78 | ★→★★★★ |
|---|---|---|---|
| 20 avenue de Champagne, 51200 Epernay | | | |
| *Star buy 78 and 81 vintage Moët & Chandon* | | | |

To be as enormous as Moët is and to produce the quality they do must be a minor miracle. Their total yearly production is now almost 2m cases which makes Moët the biggest selling champagne in France and the world. A very large chunk of this must be taken up by their non-vintage Brut Impérial (sold as Première Cuvée in England). But Dom Pérignon, Moët's deluxe *cuvée* first sold in 1936, must now account for some sizeable sales given the extraordinary demand for this liquid status symbol. The USA in particular just cannot get enough of DP as they call it or DPR as its pink sister is known. Other Moët wines include a white and rosé vintage-dated Brut Imperial plus an Extra Dry (only for the US market) and a Crémant Demi-Sec which is rarely seen. Moët also make a fine Coteaux Champenois Blanc de Blancs named after their beautiful Château Saran near Epernay. Ratafia, marc and a red Coteaux Champenois Bouzy complete the range. Moët's size and premier position amongst the champagne houses did not happen by chance. There have been Moëts in Champagne since the early 15th century but the earliest reference to Claude Moët of Epernay as a champagne maker is dated 1743. Madame de Pompadour was a devoted customer apparently but it was Claude's son Jean-Rémy who made Moët the most famous and fashionable champagne of the time, not just in France but worldwide. The house still occupies this position today. In 1832 Claude's son-in-law, the Comte Chandon de Briailles, linked his name to that of Moët. This house has owned vineyards since the beginning and these now total 461ha (1,139 acres) scattered throughout the region. These represent just 20% of their needs. Moët's taste today is a very distinctive one. About five years ago there were some alarming ups and downs in both quality and style. But even the non-vintage Brut has now settled down to a rich golden colour backed up by a warm, fruity taste with a firm backbone of flavour that has a little of the metallic aspect that Mercier has. Not a great glass of champagne but an agreeable and drinkable one nonetheless. Vintage Moët has also much improved over the years – the 78s in particular were excellent. The white is a big, ripe, bouncy wine with a lot of fruit and a dramatic bouquet reminiscent of passion fruit. The Rosé is a pretty rose-pink colour and has a taste like crushed strawberries. The 81 vintage Brut is a delicious, balanced, full-flavoured wine. Dom Pérignon is of course the firm's flagship, made from a blend of about 60% Pinot Noir to 40% Chardonnay from Moët's best vineyards and from an average of 40-year-old vines. Its dark green 18th century-style bottle has been much imitated but so far not the taste. The 76 vintage was a big, rich, fruity wine with a steady stream of bubbles and a multi-layered soft, biscuity and honeyed taste. The 71 DPR or Rosé with its pinky-orange colour and slight taste was less impressive. This champagne is named after the blind Benedictine monk who is credited as being the first to finalize the champagne process. The USA, the UK, Italy and

Germany are the major Moët export markets. This house is one of the most technologically advanced in Champagne and has outposts in California (Domaine Chandon), Brazil (Provifin), Argentina (Proviar), Germany and Austria (Chandon Handels-gesellschaft). Moët & Chandon welcome visitors and have a small Dom Pérignon museum.

| Montaudon | MC | 76 | ★ |
| --- | --- | --- | --- |

6 rue Ponsardin, 51100 Reims

It would be hard to miss the big red M emblazoned on all but one Montaudon champagne bottle. Yet even though Montaudon is exported to the USA, UK, Australia, Belgium, Switzerland and Germany it is rare to see a bottle on sale. Perhaps the French keep most of the annual 41,000 cases of Montaudon that is made for themselves? This medium-sized, lesser-known, champagne firm founded in 1891 is still owned by the Montaudon family. The most interesting wine in the range is the Montaudon Rosé and still red Coteaux Rouge made from the family's own vines and one of those rare Rosé des Riceys Pinot Noir wines which should definitely be worth trying. In addition Montaudon have to buy in another 50ha (124 acres) worth (split equally between the three champagne grapes). Most of Montaudon's production is still riddled by hand and in addition to the Rosé the range includes a Brut, Demi-Sec, a vintage-dated champagne plus a Blanc de Blancs. The black grapes-dominated non-vintage Brut accounts for the vast majority of sales. This wine's strong, herbaceous taste will not appeal to everyone.

| G. H. Mumm | MC | 79 82 | ★→★★ |
| --- | --- | --- | --- |

29 rue du Champ de Mars, 51053 Reims

With the distinctive bright-red sash on both foil and label it is easy to note that the next door table is drinking Mumm in either its vintage or non-vintage Brut guises. A salespoint that probably did not escape Seagram, the giant wine and spirits group, when they bought Mumm in 1972. Equally eye-catching is Mumm's Demi-Sec bubbly with its emerald green sash. Mumm's vintage Rosé in its appropriately pale pink livery looks positively introverted by comparison. All three are made predominantly from black grapes. The quality of these standard Mumm champagnes is sometimes less impressive than their looks. Launched in 1876 Mumm Cordon Rouge is a very big seller. At a recent tasting Mumm's non-vintage Cordon Rouge was an agreeable, fresh, young, green, yeasty champagne albeit with a short finish. Extra Dry and the Double Cordon Sec are other standard wines. One step up from this is Mumm's Crémant de Cramant. This champagne used to provide a wonderful, fresh, flowery, appley mouthful but in recent years as its postage-stamp-sized label has got bigger its flavour seems to have diminished. It is still however a great rarity for it is made entirely from Chardonnay grapes grown in the village of Cramant in the heart of the Côte des Blancs and as such should not be missed. Mumm's finest champagne is the prestige *cuvée* René Lalou whose 79 vintage was a lovely, delicate, fragrant, flowery wine. Definitely a three-star champagne. Mumm's straight 79 vintage with its raw, aggressive taste is not recommended. Mumm sounds a German name which it is, for the original Herr Mumm came from Rudesheim and founded his champagne firm in Reims in 1827. It remained a family business until 1914. After the First World War the firm was taken over by French management with

René Lalou as one of its first directors and eventually Chairman. Today Mumm own 218ha (538 acres) of vines of which their Pinot Noir holding at Bouzy and their Chardonnay holding at Cramant are the most important. Domaine Mumm is their new California enterprise. The USA is the main export market.

| Oudinot | MC | 81 | ★→ |
|---|---|---|---|

12 rue Godart-Roger, 51207 Epernay

Jules Edouard Oudinot founded this firm in 1889 but Michel Trouillard, one of the well-known Trouillard champagne family, took it over in 1981. Michel Trouillard moved the Oudinot business soon afterwards to Epernay. Oudinot own vines in some important champagne villages. These vines represent half of their grape requirements and they buy in the rest. The Trouillards obviously try to cater for all tastes for their range offers eight different wines. The non-vintage Brut accounts for the majority of sales. Apart from this champagne, Oudinot make an Extra Dry, Demi-Sec, non-vintage Blanc de Blancs, a vintage-dated Blanc de Noirs plus a Brut and Rosé and finally the Cuvée Particulière BB Millés. Ratafia, marc and fine are also available. The Oudinot style is fruity and Pinot Noir-dominated. The Blanc de Noirs is their newest idea. Oudinot are heavily involved in the export market, and the USA, the Low Countries, Switzerland and Italy are their most important markets. Oudinot also control the firm of Jeanmaire and are closely associated with Beaumet with whom they share the same address. Production of this group that owns 62ha (153 acres) of vines is thought to be about 41,000 cases per annum.

| Bruno Paillard | MC | 73 | ★→ |
|---|---|---|---|

Rue Jacques Maritain, 51100 Reims

Bruno Paillard obviously admires Baron Philippe de Rothschild for his vintage champagne labels are illustrated by paintings from different artists as are the Rothschild wine labels. Each painting endeavours to reflect the style of the year. 79 is therefore a young lively village celebration and 76 is a sunny scene of bounteous prosperity. Young M. Paillard comes from an old champagne family of both vignerons and brokers. And although he is still involved in broking, the champagne house that he founded in 1981 now takes up rather more of his time. As yet only 20,000 cases of Champagne Bruno Paillard are produced annually. More than 80% of that is exported to countries such as the USA, the UK, Belgium and Switzerland. But the energetic Monsieur Paillard is keen to expand his small champagne house and to become a recognized champagne name. This achievement could be some way off as yet for the crisp, streamlined Paillard champagnes are still rather too young and lean for most tastes. The firm does not own any vineyards of its own. Bruno Paillard is however a firm believer in the low or non-*dosage* approach for he makes no Sec or Demi-Sec wines. He can also produce a "Dosage 0" or Brut Zero style if customers wish. Other Paillard champagnes include the Pinot Noir-dominated Rosé, a Crémant Blanc de Blancs, vintage Brut plus the non-vintage Brut predominantly made from Pinot Meunier and Pinot Noir with a little Chardonnay. The vintage *cuvées* vary from year to year: 76 and 79 were Chardonnay-dominated whereas 81 was predominantly Pinot Noir. The Paillard vintage labels carry disgorge dates. M. Paillard considers his Crémant Blanc de Blancs to be one of his most successful champagnes.

## Pannier                    MC                                    ★
23 rue Roger-Catillon, Château Thierry

Pannier, based in the Aisne, to the west of the region, produces
166,000 cases a year. Most of this is sold in France and about a third
of it is Buyer's Own Brands. Pannier are keen however to
promote their own label. So we can expect to see Pannier on sale
increasingly in markets such as the UK, the USA and Germany.
Currently Pannier's most important champagnes are Pol du
Breuil, sold in France, and de Brienne, sold in Germany. Pannier
champagnes have a noticeable proportion of Pinot Meunier in
their blends. Pannier Brut is a fresh, pear-drop-like champagne.

## Joseph Perrier              MC                         73    ★→
69 avenue de Paris, 51005 Châlons-sur-Marne

Joseph Perrier, the son of a négociant at Châlons, founded this firm
in 1825. But the Perrier family ran out of heirs and in 1888 Paul
Pithois took the house over. Today the Pithois both own and run
Joseph Perrier. Of all the *grandes marques* houses Joseph Perrier,
situated in outlying Châlons, has one of the lowest profiles
probably because only 54,000 cases or so are made here annually.
The firm owns about 20ha (49 acres) of vines situated at Cumières
Damery, Hautvilliers and Verneuil in the Vallée de la Marne.
Most of these supply Joseph Perrier with Pinot Noir grapes but
Verneuil supplies the Pinot Meunier. In addition a further 20ha
(49 acres) of grapes are bought in, principally from the Montagne
de Reims and the Côte des Blancs, to give this house the blending
tools it needs. The non-vintage Cuvée Royale Brut which
accounts for three-quarters of Joseph Perrier's sales is made from
equal portions of the Chardonnay/Pinot Noir/Pinot Meunier
grapes. Vintage wines contain a higher proportion of
Chardonnay, usually 50%. The Joseph Perrier selection consists
of a Demi-Sec, Blanc de Blancs, Rosé, and vintage Brut besides
their non-vintage Brut. The 79 both tasted and smelt of cheese
straws. Their rarest and most expensive wine is the non-vintage
prestige blend, the Cuvée du Cent Cinquentennaire introduced
in 1975 to commemorate the 150th anniversary of the house. The
current blend probably contains wines from the 75, 76 and 73
vintages. Unlike most prestige *cuvées* it contains a high proportion of Pinot Noir (about 50%) with the remainder being
Chardonnay. Non-vintage Joseph Perrier Brut has a somewhat
chameleon character, one minute full-bodied and chocolatey, the
next equally firm but toasty and almost woody in style. The Cent
Cinquentennaire is worthwhile with its *tisane*-like mint and lime
blossom bouquet and taste. The UK, Belgium, Australia,
Germany and the USA are Joseph Perrier's chief export markets.

## Perrier-Jouët               MC               69 71 73    ★→★★
24–28 avenue de Champagne, 51200 Epernay

PJ, as the wine world refers to this house, has always had one of
the most glamorous and fashionable reputations amongst the
champagne firms. Probably since the days of the pre-First World
War Belle Epoque era, when everyone from actress Sarah
Bernhardt who apparently bathed in it to Queen Victoria who no
doubt merely drank it was a Perrier-Jouët devotee. Pierre-
Nicolas-Marie Perrier founded PJ in 1811 and to distinguish it
from other Perrier champagne concerns added his wife's maiden
name Jouët to the firm's title. Perrier-Jouët's main 40ha
(100 acres) of vineyards surround Cramant and Avize in the Côte

des Blancs and the house feels that it is these grapes above all that
give their champagne its clean-cut light, flavoury style. Another
40ha (100 acres) of PJ vines are situated at Dizy and Ay in the
Vallée de la Marne and at Verzenay and Mailly in the Montagne
de Reims. Vinay and Orbais are two other vineyard holdings.
The firm is now, like Heidsieck Monopole and Mumm, part of
Seagram's champagne interests and produces about 227,000 cases
annually. PJ's most famous champagne and the one that sums up
this firm's style is the pretty Emile Gallé *art nouveau* Belle Epoque
bottle where a garland of enamel anemones are fired directly onto
the surface of the glass. The predominantly Chardonnay 78 Belle
Epoque with its rich golden colour, persistent bubbles and full,
warm, flowery smell and taste, albeit let down by a slightly
aggressive finish, is a good example of PJ's art. Similarly the non-
vintage Brut is usually a golden and agreeable rich, biscuity wine.
Other champagnes in PJ's range include a pink, faintly fruity
version of Belle Epoque which is not recommended plus their
ultra-prestige blend the Blason de France together with a vintage
PJ Rosé and Brut. The rich, golden, biscuity 79 is recommended.
About half of Perrier-Jouët's production is exported with the
UK, Italy and the USA being the chief markets. The USA is a
major consumer of Belle Epoque. Perrier-Jouët were the first
house to sell a dry champagne in the UK in 1848.

| Philipponnat | MC | ★ |

13 rue du Pont, Mareuil-sur-Ay, 51160 Ay

This small family firm with almost 12ha (30 acres) of vineyards is
now owned by Gosset. Its most celebrated champagne is the
robust vintage-dated Clos des Goisses made from the family's
own vines. In most years Philipponnat produce about 40,000
cases of which roughly half is exported. Philipponnat non-
vintage Brut is an agreeable, fruity, if unexciting champagne.
Their non-vintage Rosé with its pale salmon-pink colour is of a
similar standard. It has a fresh, green, almost fig-like taste.

| Jules Pierlot | MC | ★ |

15 rue Henri Martin, 51207 Epernay

France consumes 70% of Jules Pierlot's 10,000 case production
which is why this house is little known elsewhere. Founded in
1889, Jules Pierlot do not own any vines and simply buy in
whatever base wines they need. Their Carte Rouge Brut and
Demi-Sec and Casque d'Or Brut and Demi-Sec are a mix of both
Pinot Noir and Meunier. The Cuvée Speciale and Blanc de
Blancs Bruts are both exclusively Chardonnay. A Rosé Brut plus
the Cuvée des Archers complete the range. Jules Pierlot wines are
generally light, young and easy to drink. Apart from France, the
UK, Switzerland, the Low countries and Belgium each import a
small amount of Jules Pierlot champagnes.

| Piper-Heidsieck | MC | 69 76 | ★ → ★★ |

8 rue Piper, 51100 Reims

Everyone it seems from 17 Royal or Imperial courts to Marilyn
Monroe has had a preference for Piper-Heidsieck. Christian
Heidsieck, another nephew of the original Heidsieck, started
trading on his own in 1834 but unfortunately died within the
year. His widow married Monsieur Piper in 1837, hence Piper-
Heidsieck. Today the Marquis d'Aulan and his family are the
major shareholders, an association that dates back to 1850. Piper
do not own any vines and buy in grapes from some 500ha

(1,235 acres) to make about 416,000 cases annually. This house was the first in Champagne to use *gyropalettes* for *remuage* and by 1982 Piper's total production was riddled in this way. Piper's style is light, mostly without any special character or depth, and geared to consumers' tastes. The non-vintage Demi-Sec and Brut are dominated by black grapes, with Pinot Noir and Meunier making up 70% of the blend. The vintage range has higher proportions of Chardonnay. It is probably best to avoid the dull, anonymous non-vintage Brut here and go straight to the vintage wines. The pear-drop-like 79 had a good, frothy, foamy mousse. The splendid non-*dosage* Brut Sauvage, only recently vintage-dated, is one of the finest bone-dry bubblies available. Its handsome 18th-century style bottle contains a refreshing, flavoursome, zippy champagne, 50/50 Pinot Noir and Chardonnay, that is worth its premium price. It is an apéritif champagne. Piper's most magnificent *cuvée*, the Chardonnay-dominated 76 Champagne Rare, is also worth seeking out with its fine frothy bubbles and light, elegant, chalky-flowery taste. Rare lives up to its name however for, like the Brut Sauvage, only 12,000 cases are made annually. The price reflects this. Piper own half of Piper Sonoma in California, they are also responsible for Vivency Crémant de Loire and through their associates Champagne Technologie advise clients in Mexico, Argentina and India. Piper exports chiefly to the USA, the UK, Italy and Belgium. Their vast cellars are open to the public and visitors are driven around in small trucks.

| Ployez-Jacquemart | MC | ★ |
|---|---|---|

8 rue Astoin, 51500 Ludes

Four generations of growers have been involved in this firm. But even so their 2ha (5 acres) of vines provide only 15% of their needs. Slightly more than 8,000 cases are made here annually of Extra Quality, Grande Réserve Sélection and Rosé plus a vintage-dated champagne and a Cuvée de Prestige – the L. d'Harbonville. All bar the last two are a 50/50 blend of Pinot Noir and Meunier. The UK, Low Countries, Germany and Switzerland are Ployez-Jacquemart's chief export markets.

| Pol Roger | MC | 71 73 75 | ★ → ★★★ |
|---|---|---|---|

1 rue Henri Lelarge, 51206 Epernay

*Star buy 1979 Pol Roger*

"The world's most drinkable address" is how Sir Winston Churchill described his favourite champagne's Avenue de Champagne residence. When Sir Winston died in 1965 Pol Roger returned the compliment by printing a black border of mourning on their labels. This was followed in 1984 with a new prestige champagne – Cuvée Sir Winston Churchill. Pol Roger's style is a fine yet flowery traditional one and every Pol Roger champagne is especially noted for its small persistent bubbles and rich creamy mousse. Founded in 1849 by Monsieur Pol Roger, today the firm is still family owned and run by Christian Pol Roger and his cousin Christian de Billy. Pol Roger own some 70ha (173 acres) of vines surrounding Epernay in both the Côte des Blancs and Vallée de la Marne which give them some 40% of their needs. The remainder required to produce their annual 108,000 cases are mostly Chardonnay and Pinot Meunier and are bought in. Pol Roger has always cultivated the English market and in the UK both their pleasant non-vintage yeasty Extra Dry White Foil and Pinot Noir-dominant clean, fruity, creamy Extra Dry 1979 bear the words "Reserved for Great Britain". Pol Roger also make a fine Rosé, the 79 vintage of which had a deep pink colour and pleasant, flowery, cherry-like flavour. Definitely one of the finest Rosés, made from 60% Pinot Noir to 30% Chardonnay. Pol's other brands include a vintage-dated Blanc de Chardonnay, which is not often seen, made from fine Côte des Blancs fruit plus the Réserve Spéciale PR, also vintage-dated – a premium Pol Roger *cuvée*, made from 50/50 Chardonnay and Pinot Noir. Pol Roger's finest champagne however is the Cuvée Sir Winston Churchill, a prestige *cuvée*, whose 75 vintage is a full flavoury wine with the scent of lilies and, once again, those famous creamy Pol Roger pinhead bubbles. About 55% of Pol Roger is exported, chiefly to the UK, the USA, Germany and Australia. Pol Roger's cellars may be visited by the public during office hours by appointment.

| Pommery | MC | 79 | ★→★★ |
| --- | --- | --- | --- |
| 5 place du Gal Gouraud, 51053 Reims | | | |

Pommery & Greno to use their full title are now, like Lanson, part of the giant BSN group. Although the firm was founded in 1836 it was Mme Louise Pommery, one of the famous champagne widows, who really put this champagne house on the map. Her most enterprising move was to buy a large plot of land near Reims containing 120 Roman chalk pits. On the land above she built some bizarre baronial buildings, styled apparently after famous English country houses and surrounded by lawns. Below she connected the pits with an 18km (11 miles) labyrinth of passages and galleries. Not content with this Madame Pommery bought land opposite where her daughter, who married the Comte de Polignac, built a grand property – the Château de Crayères. Nearby a more recent sports-loving Polignac gave up 32ha (80 acres) of parkland to be turned into a vast sporting centre for the people of Reims, known as Parc Pommery. Today Château de Crayères is a three-star hotel and restaurant offering the finest food and accommodation in Champagne. Parc Pommery thrives and the cavernous cellars with their ornate carved bas-reliefs are some of the most spectacular in Champagne. Pommery's 300ha (741 acres) now account for 45% of their needs and their annual production adds up to some 475,000 cases. Unfortunately all this does not detract from the fact that most glasses of Pommery are not all they should be. Non-vintage Pommery Brut has improved slightly over the years and now has a welcoming yeasty nose but its fresh light taste still has an aggressive finish. The other Demi-Sec, Sec, Rosé and vintage Brut Pommery wines can also disappoint. The 80 Pommery was for instance an unusual lime-juice like champagne. However things are looking up at Pommery for their new 79 Louise Pommery champagne made from Avize and Cramant Chardonnay and Ay Pinot Noir is everything a *grande prestige cuvée* should be: rich, complex and delicious. Madame Pommery herself would have heartily approved. Pommery's cellars are open to the public, even at weekends.

| Rapeneau | MC | | ★ |
| --- | --- | --- | --- |
| 69 avenue de Champagne, Epernay | | | |

Rapeneau are big sellers in France where all except 10% of their production is sold. In most years Rapeneau make 125,000 cases. The USA is their most successful export market. Martel is a Rapeneau brand name.

| Louis Roederer | MC | 75 81 82 | ★★ → ★★★★ |

21 boulevard Lundy, 51053 Reims

Roederer is truly one of *the* champagne greats. It says much for the sheer breed and distinction of the Roederer style that their great prestige champagne, Cristal, was still utterly delicious even in poor years such as 75 and 77. If Roederer's competitors complain that every vintage since 66 (with the exception of 68, 72, 78 and 80) has appeared on a Cristal label, their customers certainly do not. The firm was founded in 1776 but Louis Roederer did not become involved until more than half a century later. Young energetic Monsieur Roederer soon boosted sales to more than 200,000 cases with Russia a keen Roederer consumer. When Tsar Alexander III asked the makers of the Russian imperial court's favourite champagne to produce a superior bottle to the plebeian green variety Roederer obliged with the chic Cristal bottle, made in crystal-clear glass. Today Roederer own 180ha (445 acres) of vines of which 75ha (185 acres) are in the Côte des Blancs and the remainder in the black grape strongholds of the Montagne de Reims and Vallée de la Marne. These supply 80% of Roederer's requirements, a unique situation for any leading champagne house and one which explains why Roederer's champagnes are so remarkably consistent. The remaining 20% is Pinot Noir and is bought in. Production is limited to 208,000 cases, on the small side for such a leading name, and yet another Roederer quality factor. Roederer's method of working is traditional and old fashioned with noticeable use of reserve wines that have been both kept in wood and left to age in bottle on their yeasts plus old wines used again in the final *dosage*. The end result is a rich, honeyed, biscuity, full-bodied wine whose two-thirds Pinot Noir to one-third Chardonnay blend is all too apparent. Roederer's Extra Quality non-vintage blend is generally a delicious, rich, yeasty wine that with age takes on some fine, biscuity overtones. A new superior, non-vintage style with four years ageing called Brut Premier has just been launched. Other non-vintage champagne here includes the palest of pink Rosé's, Demi-Sec, Carte Blanche and Extra Dry. The vintage range consists of a Brut and Blanc de Blancs which are finer still. But the glorious Cristal (also made in a Rosé version), such as the 77 with its steady mousse, warm, toasty smell and intense biscuity, honeyed taste, is everything a great champagne should be. Perfection. Roederer have an operation in California and another in Tasmania, Australia. 60% of their champagnes are exported, chiefly to the USA, Germany, Italy, Switzerland and the UK.

| Théophile Roederer | MC | | ★ → |

20 rue Andrieux, 51058 Reims

Théophile Roederer are entirely owned and run by Louis Roederer. Although the finest grapes and wines are kept for big brother Louis, Théophile's range, which includes a vintage and non-vintage Brut plus a Demi-Sec, is admirable.

| Ruinart | MC | 76 75 | ★★ → ★★★ |

4 rue des Crayères, 51053 Reims

*Star buy 76 Dom Ruinart Blanc de Blancs*

Ruinart is the oldest champagne house, founded in 1729. Gosset, who date back to 1584, are the oldest still winemakers in the region but it was Nicolas Ruinart it seems who first sold champagne. Nicolas's uncle was Dom Thierry Ruinart, a

Benedictine monk and friend of Dom Pérignon, and it seems likely that he knew the secret of champagne and handed it down to his nephew. Successive generations of Ruinarts increased the family fortunes and by 1832 Ruinart champagne was well regarded worldwide especially in Russia and the USA. In 1963 Ruinart became part of the large Moët-Hennessy group and thereby associated with Moët and Chandon.

Today 15ha (37 acres) of Ruinart's own Chardonnay vines at Sillery supply only 20% of their needs. The total production here adds up to a modest 100,000 cases annually. Ruinart is usually overshadowed by its giant associates, Moët and Mercier. This is unfair because the light, flowery-citrussy Ruinart style can and does stand on its own two feet. It has also been known to surpass that of its two big brothers. Ruinart champagnes also represent extraordinarily good value for money, especially Dom Ruinart, their prestige *cuvée*, which is half the price of Dom Pérignon. The 76 vintage of the Dom Ruinart Blanc de Blancs was a lovely, racy, flowery champagne with intriguing citrussy undertones. An elegant four-star champagne. The 79 with its dull fruit and frothy palate is not recommended. The Rosé version of Dom Ruinart, a predominantly Chardonnay wine, is rather faint-hearted by comparison. In addition Ruinart has a vintage "R" de Ruinart, a predominantly Pinot Noir wine, plus the non-vintage "R" de Ruinart made from a blend of all three champagne grapes. The USA, Germany and Switzerland are the main export markets.

| Sacotte | MC | 76 78 | ★ |

13 rue de la Verrerie, Magenta, 51190 Epernay

This house celebrates its centenary in 1987 and is still a family firm. They own no vineyards but buy in grapes each vintage from different vignerons. 25,000 cases are made annually of vintage and non-vintage Brut, Rosé Brut and a vintage-dated Blanc de Blancs. A special Cuvée du Centenaire from the 82 vintage is available.

| Sacy | MC | 76 | ★ |

6 rue de Verzenay, 51380 Verzy

This family firm was founded fifteen years ago. André Sacy runs the company but Louis de Sacy's name appears on most of the labels. They own 30ha (74 acres) of vines that, apart from a plot in Avize, are mostly in outlying areas. These supply them with 90% of their needs. Sacy is a medium-sized house producing about 25,000 cases annually. A Brut, Demi-Sec and vintage Rosé comprise the Sacy range. All three have a high proportion of Pinot Noir in the blend. Sacy is exported to the UK, Germany and Switzerland.

| Salon | MC | 64 71 79 | ★★★ |

Le Mesnil-sur-Oger, 51190 Avize

So closely entwined with the top Chardonnay village of Le Mesnil-sur-Oger is this distinguished champagne house that everyone refers to it as Salon Le Mesnil. It would be difficult to have a more prestigious or rarefied approach to the creation of champagne than Salon. Only the first pressing of Mesnil Chardonnay is used by Salon and, more exclusive still, only from the finest vintage years. Since 1928 only 22 vintages of the one style of Salon have been made. And, what is more, only 12,500 cases maximum were made of any one of these. Given the scarcity and impeccable credentials of Salon its high price is justified.

Champagne Salon was founded in 1921 by Eugene-Aimé Salon whose family lived near Champagne. M. Salon bought his own vineyard at Mesnil and made the first Blanc de Blancs champagne. Demand increased and Salon bought in the finest Chardonnay grapes from other Mesnil-sur-Oger growers, just as they do today. Salon currently own 1ha (2 acres) at Mesnil and buy in 15ha (37 acres)-worth in addition. The most traditional champagne techniques are still employed here, including ageing the base wine in small wooden casks using hand *remuage* and disgorging also by hand. From the 1950s until 1984 talented champagne maker Robert Billion created the Salon *cuvées* to the same exacting standards set by M. Salon. Salon has since 1976 been controlled by Besserat de Bellefon, who in turn are owned by the Pernod-Ricard group. Since M. Robert Billion's death in 1984 there is some doubt over future *cuvées*. Salon *aficionados* should therefore buy up whatever they can of the rich, full and flowery 73, the glorious, intense, almost meaty 71 and the still youthful, zippy and fresh 69. 1979 is the latest Salon vintage. It has a fine, elegant, biscuity-toasty flavour. Australia, the UK and Denmark are Salon's chief export markets.

| **S.A.M.E.** | MC | ★→ |
| --- | --- | --- |

1 rue des Cotelles, 51200 Epernay

Société Anonyme de Magenta-Epernay to use S.A.M.E.'s unabbreviated title goes back some sixty years. The Lombard family own and manage S.A.M.E. and this organization's entire output is exclusively geared towards Buyer's Own Brands. The firm does have some labels of its own such as Marguerite Christel and Marcel Rouet. S.A.M.E. try to be as quality conscious as they can, given their substantial annual production (about 167,000 cases annually) and produce wines with a minimum of three years' cellar age. Magenta is another S.A.M.E. brand. Magenta's Carte Blanche Brut has a rich buttery palate and solid fruit let down by a slightly metallic finish.

| **A. Secondé-Prevoteau** | MC | ★→★★ |
| --- | --- | --- |

2 rue du Château, Ambonnay

*Star buy Princesses de France Brut*

André Secondé-Prevoteau's grandfather founded this firm but the family were involved in making champagne long before then. Monsieur Secondé-Prevoteau owns 12ha (30 acres) of top Ambonnay vines, predominantly Pinot Noir but with some Chardonnay too. The Secondé-Prevoteau style is a big, gutsy, full-bodied one that goes well with food. The non-vintage Princesses de France Brut with its three-quarters Pinot Noir and one-quarter Chardonnay blend is a good introduction to this house. Its positive bouquet, flowery and perfumed, is backed up by a real mouthful of well-vinified Pinot Noir flavour, albeit a touch short and aggressive on the finish. Heftier still is the Fleuron de France Blanc de Noirs, again a non-vintage wine whose big, beefy, biscuity taste definitely needs food to accompany it – and even then some palates may still find it too positive. Secondé also make a big, firm, fruity, still Ambonnay Rouge Coteaux Champenois that has all sorts of attractive raspberry and beetroot-like flavours on the palate.

| **Jacques Selosse** | MC | ★→★★ |
| --- | --- | --- |

61 rue Ernest Vallé, 51190 Avize

This small, traditional, family-run house owns vineyards at Avize and Cramant. Only the first-class fruit from their own vines is used here. This factor and the ultra-traditional Selosse techniques such as fermentation in small oak casks and hand riddling and disgorging makes these champagnes so worthwhile. Jacques Selosse also age their wines for longer than normal before releasing them onto the market. Three years for the non-vintage champagne and four years or more for the vintage wines is usual. The non-vintage Blanc de Blancs is indeed a two-star-plus wine, with its elegant, green, herbaceous nose and zippy, stream-lined palate. A great achievement from a small grower who produces only 2,500 cases annually. Anselme Selosse, Jacques' son, is now in charge here and he also makes a vintage-dated Blanc de Blancs, a non-vintage Vieille Réserve and a vintage-dated Cuvée Club Special whose 79 vintage with its strong musty perfumed smell and taste is not recommended.

| Taittinger | MC | 76 78 81 | ★→★★★★ |
| --- | --- | --- | --- |
| 9 place Saint Nicaise, 51061 Reims | | | |

Taittinger have the name, the wines and the reputation of one of the grandest of *grandes marques* firms. Yet Pierre Taittinger did not found his celebrated champagne house until 1930. As a young French officer he had been stationed during the First World War at the impressive Château Marquetterie just south of Epernay. After the War he bought both the château and its vineyards and started to make champagne. In addition he bought two cellars, one under the 13th century St Nicaise Abbey and the other also in Reims. Taittinger now own 240ha (593 acres) of vines, 30% Chardonnay, 50% Pinot Noir and 20% Pinot Meunier. These give Taittinger about 40% of their needs. Total production here is about 341,000 cases. The taste of Taittinger at its finest is an elegant, delicate, heavily Chardonnay-influenced style with a unique flowery perfume all of its own. This does not always manifest itself with the non-vintage Brut, but is present in abundance with Taittinger's prestige *cuvée*, the glorious 100% Chardonnay Comtes de Champagne. Taittinger do not like to give too much away when it comes to the composition of their blends. But it seems likely that the unusual, perfumed non-vintage Brut Reserve that accounts for the lion's share of sales contains a significant portion of Chardonnay, perhaps as much as 50%. Demi-Sec is the other non-vintage wine here. The rest of the range includes a vintage Brut – the 80 was perfumed, flavoury and easy to drink – besides the Comtes de Champagne, whose 76 vintage was a wonderful, stylish, flowery champagne. The Comtes is also available as a Rosé. Taittinger's latest idea is the deluxe expensive Taittinger Collection, whose bottles are protected from harmful heat and light by a protective plastic coating. The Hungarian painter Victor Vasarely designed the first gold-encased 78 vintage bottle and Arman, the French painter, created the 81. The Pinot Noir-dominant 78 had a delicious, rich, warm, flowery character. Taittinger now own the champagne house Irroy plus Monmousseau and Bouvet-Ladubay in the Loire. Their cellars are open to the public.

| J. de Telmont | MC | | ★→ |
| --- | --- | --- | --- |
| 1 avenue de Champagne, 51200 Epernay | | | |

These inexpensive champagnes are definitely worth tracking down. Founded in 1920 and owned by the l'Hôpital family, only small amounts of J. de Telmont are produced every year. The non-vintage Grande Réserve Brut is made partly from Pinot

Noir grapes grown in their own 24ha (59 acres) vineyards at Damery in the Marne valley. This blend consists of 45% Pinot Noir, 45% Pinot Meunier and 10% Chardonnay. Its ripe elderflower bouquet and flowery-biscuit black grapes character is recommended. The l'Hôpitals also make a Crémant Blanc de Blancs which, with its fresh, soft, sweet taste and higher price, is less impressive.

| **Union Auboise** | MC | ★→ |
|---|---|---|

Domaine de Villeneuve, BP 17, 10110 Bar-sur-Seine

Union Auboise des Producteurs de Vin de Champagne is just what it sounds like – a group of Aube cooperatives. 11 producers make some 97,000 cases between them. Abel Jeannin and Léonze d'Albe are their two main labels. This pair are currently available only in non-vintage versions but vintage and rosé styles are about to be launched. Union Auboise currently export to Germany and the Low Countries plus a little to the USA and the UK. Production is likely to increase dramatically here.

| **Union Champagne** | MC | ★→ |
|---|---|---|

7 rue Pasteur, 51190 Avize

This vast, modern cooperative with its 10 smaller branches looks after 1,000 growers in total. It is an enormous concern, responsible for more than 400,000 cases annually. Like many champagne cooperatives, it produces own-label wines, but it also has several brand names of its own, including St-Gall. 80% of its production is returned to its numerous growers to be sold under their own labels. Union have a well-made, fresh, crisp, clean vintage Blanc de Blancs, whose Chardonnay elegance shows. Their St-Gall non-vintage Brut Rosé, with its curious pink colour complete with blue overtones, has a fresh, fruity bouquet but an aggressive palate. Their vintage-dated 1980 St-Gall was a cheesy, over-ripe champagne.

| **Vranken-Lafitte** (C. Lafitte) | MC | ★ |
|---|---|---|

Le Pavé, 51130 Vertus

Clever marketeer and technician Paul-François Vranken set up his champagne business in 1976. At first the firm simply sold Buyer's Own Brand champagnes to outlets such as supermarkets, but Monsieur Vranken was soon also selling his own Veuve Monnier. Sales went well both in France and abroad and in 1983 a new bubbly was launched called Charles Lafitte. Not a shameless lift of the famous Bordeaux name as it happens, for there is a real Charles Lafitte sitting on the company's board. The Vranken-Lafitte group has a modern automated winemaking plant at Vertus in the Côte des Blancs, plus a recently-acquired château nearby called des Castaignes. They use about 40% to 50% of Chardonnay in their blends plus sizeable amounts of Pinot Meunier, buying in *première* and *deuxième taille* wines. Charles Lafitte labels include vintage and non-vintage Brut, Demi-Sec, Rosé and Brut Prestige. The latter is roughly 70% Chardonnay. La Cuvée du Dessert in both Special and Rosé styles, specifically designed to accompany desserts, has recently been launched. Veuve Monnier champagnes are available in Grande Cuvée, Brut, Demi-Sec and Rosé plus a vintage-dated Special. Annual production of the group is now thought to top 108,000 cases with Veuve Monnier accounting for about half of that and a sizeable amount of own-label wines for others. Quality is average rather than special.

## De Venoge                    MC                    ★ →
30 avenue de Champagne, 51204 Epernay

De Venoge have palatial premises on the Avenue de Champagne. Their wines are rather more prosaic. De Venoge are, however, inventive marketeers, from their vintage-dated Champagne des Princes sold in a reuseable glass decanter through to their champagne-cork-man-of-a-logo complete with top hat and monocle. Founded in 1837 this firm has no vineyards of its own but buys in whatever it needs every year to create 100,000 cases of champagne. In addition to Champagne des Princes, De Venoge sell a Crémant Brut, pleasant, fruity-peppery Cordon Bleu, and Crémant Brut Rosé besides their vintage-dated Brut, Blanc de Blancs and Rosé. The firm are especially proud of their recently-launched Crémant Rosé. De Venoge are heavily involved in the own-label business and are associated with Trouillard, another Epernay champagne house.

## Veuve Clicquot              MC          75 80    ★ → ★★
12 rue du Temple, 51054 Reims

Nicole-Barbe Ponsardin, who married François Clicquot in 1799, was the greatest of all the champagne widows. Tragically widowed in 1805 she took over the firm founded in 1772 (although her father-in-law wished to sell it) and renamed it Veuve Clicquot-Ponsardin.

This name still graces every bottle of "the widow" to this day. By the time she died 61 years later at the age of 89 she had founded a bank, invented a vital new stage in the *méthode champenoise* process and had made her champagne world famous. Other *coups* executed by this remarkable woman included the launch of this firm's famous yellow label (in practice more of a vivid orange) and the eventual exportation of three-quarters of their production. Russia was an important market. Today Clicquot champagnes reflect the traditions of the past with their fruity, full-bodied, almost peppery style. Clicquot now own some 265ha (654 acres) which supply almost a third of their needs. Another 600ha (1,482 acres) (two-thirds Pinot Noir to one-third Chardonnay) are bought in. All this adds up to 593,000 cases. Clicquot are reluctant to reveal their exact blends but it is clear that they are dominated by black grapes, perhaps by as much as two-thirds. The big, bouncy flavours of the Pinot Noir grape are an integral part of all Clicquot styles. Non-vintage Yellow Label Clicquot Brut has had its ups and downs, as have other famous *grandes marques* Bruts. Sales of this champagne top 458,000 cases in most years. At its best it is a rich, full, fruity wine. The gold label vintage Brut is better and the 79 was blessed with a big, rich, biscuity taste. The 80 was full, flowery and yeasty. Clicquot make a little vintage Rosé and the orangey-pink metallic 78 is not recommended. Also in their range are a non-vintage Sec, Demi-Sec and Rich. Clicquot's finest champagne is La Grande Dame whose generously curved bottle must surely be reminiscent of the great lady herself? The 79's warm, full-bodied peppery style has a pleasing aroma of walnuts. It is a two-thirds Pinot Noir, one-third Chardonnay blend.

# Other Champagne producers:

Collery, Ay; Doyen, Reims; Ellner & Fils, Epernay; Gardet & Co., Rilly-la-Montagne; Granier, Sézanne; Louis Kremer, Epernay; Charles A. Prieur, Vertus; Trouillard, Epernay.

# The Loire

The sparkling wines of the Loire are the chief challenger to those of Champagne in terms of quantity – indeed some would say in quality too. The vineyards along this attractive, winding river produce substantial amounts of sparklers, most of which come from its central regions of Anjou, Saumur and Touraine. Roughly 2m cases are produced annually with about 1m cases coming from Saumur.

Loire sparkling wines are light, fruity and generally very easy to drink. Not perhaps the kind one wants to linger over and savour, but the majority do make useful apéritif and party wines. Unfortunately some large Saumur firms today seem keener on quantity than quality. Thankfully there are others such as Ackerman-Laurance where both walk hand in hand.

One of the most agreeable aspects of Loire sparkling wine is its low price. You may not get the distinction or grandeur of champagne, but you will get a pleasant, fresh, *méthode champenoise* alternative for less than half the price. This has not escaped the *Champenois*. Several champagne firms have Loire interests.

The grapes behind sparkling Saumur are principally the Chenin Blanc, or Pineau de la Loire as locals call it, plus a wide range of other white (including Chardonnay) and black Loire grapes. Almost three-quarters of Saumur is Brut, the rest is Demi-Sec; and there are both white and pink versions..

To the west of Saumur is the Anjou district whose slightly sweet white and rosé wines play second fiddle to those of Saumur. Most lack the acidity and life necessary for a fine sparkling wine. To the east of Saumur is Touraine whose white, red and rosé sparklers may not be in the same class as Saumur but nonetheless have a place in the sparkling wine spectrum. Inexpensive *méthode champenoise* Touraine *mousseux* such as the popular Blanc Foussy may not be the best sparkling wine in the world but it is appreciated by cost-conscious customers.

In the heart of Touraine on the north bank of the Loire, lies Vouvray, where the finest Loire sparkling wines are produced. Sparkling Vouvray is made in two different styles: the fully-sparkling or *mousseux* variety and the slightly-sparkling *pétillant* style. The *pétillant* kind is much more difficult to make than *mousseux* and its gentle bubbles should stem from a slight second fermentation in bottle. Marc Brédif is one of the few remaining firms who specialize in genuine *pétillant* Vouvray.

On the opposite side of the Loire from Vouvray is Montlouis and its *pétillant* and *mousseux* wines (just like its still wines) are similar to, if not as good as, those of Vouvray. Sparkling Montlouis is however much lighter and less intensely fruity.

The last category of Loire sparkling wine is Crémant de Loire, introduced in 1975. This can come from anywhere in the region but in terms of quality it should be finer than the others. (In practice most sparkling Vouvray is actually rather better.) Crémant de Loire should have a lower yield and longer ageing than other Loire sparklers and only the first cuts of its gentler pressing should be used. About 167,000 cases of Crémant de Loire are produced annually.

| Ackerman-Laurance | MC | ★★ |
| --- | --- | --- |

Rue L. Palustre, St-Hilaire-St-Florent, 49416 Saumur

In 1811 Monsieur Ackerman married Mademoiselle Laurance

and thus the important Saumur house of Ackerman-Laurance was founded. Today Ackerman produce some 292,000 cases annually. Not all of this is taken up by Ackerman's own 1811, Brut Royal and Crémant de Loire wines as this firm produces "own label" sparkling wines for numerous outlets. Founder Jean Ackerman learnt the *méthode champenoise* process in Champagne and for 37 years his 7km (4 miles) of Loire hillside cellars, once a stone quarry, were the only ones in Saumur to house wines made by this method. Ackerman-Laurance now use bought-in Chenin Blanc, Chardonnay, Cabernet Franc and Groslot grapes from 400ha (988 acres). With such vast production it is surprising that Ackerman still perform *remuage* by hand although other equipment here is ultra-modern. The range consists of the big-selling 1811 Saumur and Brut Royal, plus their Crémant range consisting of Cuvée Princes de Loire and Cuvée Privée Grand Crémant. For Ackerman's rosé sparklers such as the Cuvée Privée Grand Crémant the Cabernet is the major grape. The quality of Ackerman's sparkling wine is reliably consistent. The 1811 is fresh with a flowery-fruity character. The Cuvée Princess de Loire Crémant is excellent: clean, fragrant and chalky.

| Aimé Boucher | MC | ★→ |
|---|---|---|

Huisseau-sur-Cosson, 41350 Vineul

This large négociant firm selects wine from all over the Loire and has numerous cellars scattered throughout the region. An intense, ripe, fruity sparkling Vouvray and Crémant de Loire are two of its specialities. Quality is good for a firm of its size.

| Blanc Foussy | MC | ★ |
|---|---|---|

95 quai de la Loire, Rochecorbon

Blanc Foussy in its dumpy bottle is the biggest Touraine sparkler of them all. Annual production is about 210,000 cases of Blanc Foussy's Vin Vif de Touraine, in white Brut and Demi-Sec and a pink Brut version. The makers are Société des Vins de France, who use Chenin Blanc grapes partly from their own vineyards but mostly bought in from numerous growers all over the Touraine region. While the quality of Blanc Foussy is fairly consistent the sweet, yeasty taste is not very exciting. However their new upmarket sparkler, the Cuvée de Comte de Touraine, has a proportion of Chardonnay in its mix and should be worth trying. Société des Vins de France also produce Château Moncontour sparkling Vouvray in a wide range of styles, much of which is exported to the USA. The 83 Crémant Extra Brut is an agreeable ripe, cheesy wine. Veuve Oudinot is another sparkler produced by the same firm. Try the Château Moncontour Crémant Extra Brut Blanc de Blancs.

| Bouvet-Ladubay | MC | ★→ |
|---|---|---|

Rue Ackerman, St-Hilaire-St-Florent

It is ironic that one of Saumur's finest *méthode champenoise* houses should be situated in a street named after one of its leading competitors. Bouvet-Ladubay, owned by Champagne house Taittinger since 1974, show no signs of concern however. After Ackerman-Laurance Bouvet is the oldest Saumur house, founded in 1851 by Etienne Bouvet. Like Jean Ackerman, Monsieur Bouvet married a local girl, Mademoiselle Ladubay, which was a canny move as she was the firm's accountant. Financial problems forced the firm to sell out to the Monmousseau family in 1933 and since then three generations of Monmousseaus have guided

Bouvet-Ladubay. Today 8km (5 miles) of limestone cellars behind Bouvet's handsome turretted courtyard produce 125,000 cases of sparkling wine via automatic *remuage*. Bouvet is a keen export house with roughly one-third of their total production kept for the French market, the rest going principally to the USA and the UK. Bouvet try to buy in only grapes or juice rather than base wine and this policy ensures that quality is kept up. Numerous different wines are made, including basic non-appellation red and white sparklers. The white Saumurs use Chenin Blanc, the rosés a mix of Cabernet Franc and Groslot. The sparkling Saumur range consists of Brut, Blanc de Blancs and Extra Demi-Sec. Better still is the Excellence range in a fresh, fruity Rosé and a Crémant style followed by a Crémant Or Rosé. Finest of all however are the vintage-dated Crémant Or Blanc de Blancs and the warm, peppery Crémant Brut Saphir sparklers. Both the Brut, aged for 18 months, and the Saphir, only made in selected vintages and aged for two years, are worth trying, the Brut having a reasonable, earthy flavour.

## Marc Brédif                                MC                        ★→★★
87 quai de la Loire Rochecorbon, 37210 Vouvray

Marc Brédif's cavernous limestone cellars are among the most spectacular in Vouvray and culminate in a vast circular *cave* where tastings usually take place. The very old Brédif vintages may now all have been sold but the sparkling Vouvrays made here are still impressive. Marc Brédif has long been associated with Vouvray Pétillant, a slightly sparkling wine that gains its mild bubbles from the *méthode champenoise* but is tricky to make. Apart from the chalky, musty Pétillant sparklers (Sec and Demi-Sec), Marc Brédif produces fully-sparkling or *mousseux* wines in Brut, Sec and Demi-Sec versions. Brédif Pétillant is kept for about five years before it is sold. Drink any of these sparkling or *mousseux* wines and you will find that the quality is good. Marc Brédif has recently been taken over by Patrick de Ladoucette.

## Caves de la Bouvraie                       MC/CC                      ★
49123 Ingrandes-sur-Loire

Unravelling the various affiliated sparkling wine firms in the Loire could take a lifetime as everyone appears to be related in some way to everyone else. Suffice it to say that the Caves de la Bouvraie were founded by Henry Grandin in 1885 and are now owned by the Berger group – an important French wine and spirit organization. Berger produce vast quantities of *cuve close* sparklers that sell well within France. Caves de la Bouvraie buy in base wines made from the Chenin Blanc, Folle Blanche and Ugni Blanc grapes and turn them into 166,000 cases of sparkling wine in most years. Non-vintage Brut versions of the Noblet Crémant de Loire and the non-appellation Grandin French sparkling wine account for most of their sales. The vast majority of Bouvraie's wines are sold in the USA with only a little reserved for the European market.

## Cave Coopérative de Haut-Poitou            MC     ★→
Neuville de Poitou

This southern Loire VDQS outpost is increasingly admired by both the trade and public alike for its constantly-improving range of inexpensive and well-made wines. Founded in 1948, this cooperative now has some 1,200 members with 911ha (2,250 acres) between them. Producing wines of good quality on such a large scale is no mean feat and the cooperative hopes to acquire AC status in the near future. Two different sparkling wines are produced here, the excellent, clean, fruity Diane de Poitiers Brut Rosé from the Cabernet Franc grape, and the somewhat oily Chardonnay-based Diane de Poitiers Blanc de Blancs Brut.

## Caves de la Loire                         MC                  ★→
Boîte Postale, 49380 Thouarcé

This cooperative exports its sparkling wines to the UK and elsewhere. Most is sold under the Crémant de Loire Comte de Treillière label in both a pleasant, yeasty Brut and a fresh, fruity, pretty-hued Rosé Brut style. The straight Brut recently won a gold label at Mâcon.

## Cave Coopérative des Vignerons de Saumur    MC    ★→
St-Cyr en Bourg, 49260 Montreuil-Bellay

This highly efficiently run cooperative has an excellent and thoroughly deserved reputation for both its still and sparkling wines. With 250 members owning some 396ha (978 acres) between them, production of sparkling wine exceeds 87,000 cases in most years, all of which is made from their own grapes. Gyropalettes speed along production in the 4km (2 miles) of the cooperative's old limestone quarry cellars. The cooperative controls the malolactic fermentation of their base wines destined for sparkling wine and this they feel makes lighter and more supple sparklers. The cooperative rates its Crémant de Loire, in both the Blanc Brut and Rosé Brut styles, as its finest wine. The latter comes in both Sec and Demi-Sec versions. In addition, a straight Saumur Brut (vintage-dated) and Demi-Sec are made, plus their "curiosity" – the Cuvée de la Chevalerie, a red Demi-Sec *mousseux*.

## Le Cellier du Beaujardin                 MC                  ★
19 rue Nationale, 37150 Civray de Touraine

Jointly owned by the Caves Coopératives of Civray de Touraine and Bléré-Athée, this *cellier* makes several different sparkling wines. Case sales usually exceed 16,000 per annum. Non-vintage Touraine *méthode champenoise* wines in a straight and Demi-Sec version are on offer as well as a not-dissimilar Chenin Blanc-based Brut and Demi-Sec Pirettes brand. Le Cellier's 42ha (104 acres) of Chenin Blanc vines are mainly in the Touraine communes of Civray, Bléré and Athée. Automatic *remuage* aids production.

## Le Clos Baudoin                          MC            ★★→★★★
Vallée de Nouy, 37210 Vouvray

"Estate-bottled by Prince Poniatowski" proudly proclaims the Aigle d'Or sparkling Vouvray label. Prince Poniatowski became the sole proprietor of Le Clos Baudoin in 1971 but the estate had been in his family's hands for 70 years. The Prince has 22ha (54 acres) of Chenin Blanc vines and like most sparkling Vouvray producers he states that it is the harvest that determines the propo·tion of still to sparkling wine produced every year. However during the last 12 years or so he calculates that about two-thirds of the total production has been turned into *méthode champenoise* wine, commenting that very ripe years such as 1976 and 1985 are unsuitable sparkling wine vintages. Apart from the Aigle d'Or sparkling Vouvray, Prince Poniatowski also makes a Touraine Rosé from 2ha (5 acres) of Cabernet Franc grapes. Old-fashioned traditions continue here: the *méthode champenoise* wines are disgorged by hand. Aigle d'Or is delicious: fragrant, flowery and elegant. The somewhat jammy rosé is less successful.

| Daheuiller | MC | ★ |
|---|---|---|

28 rue du Ruau, 49400 Varrains

This small producer makes just 1,250 cases annually of sparkling Saumur, labelled Perle des Varinelles. The Daheuiller family use their own Chenin Blanc grapes to form the base of this *cuvée*, adding a little of their own Chardonnay. All of their tiny production is riddled by hand. No exports.

| Dutertre Père & Fils | MC | ★ |
|---|---|---|

20 rue d'Enfer, Place du Tertre, Limeray

This small Touraine house at the extreme east of the region makes just over 4,000 cases of sparkling wine annually. The quality here is of the simple *mousseux* standard and Dutertre's wines are sold under Rosé Crémant (Brut and Demi-Sec) and Blanc Crémant (Brut or Demi-Sec) labels. Chenin Blanc grapes from the family's 8ha (20 acres) of vineyards plus Gamay and Pinot Noir are the varieties used. The Rosé is 50/50 Gamay and Pinot. 5% of their production is exported.

| A. Foreau | MC | ★ |
|---|---|---|

Clos Naudin, 37210 Vouvray

One of the most respected names in Vouvray. The Foreau family's policy of giving their wines lengthy ageing prior to selling has been known to result in bottles of varying degrees of quality. The Foreaus own about 12ha (30 acres) in total and produce tiny quantities every year. A recent bottle of their Brut sparkling Vouvray was a mature, beefy wine.

| Gratien & Meyer | MC | ★→ |
|---|---|---|

Château de Beaulieu, Route de Montsoreau, 49401 Saumur

Gratien, Meyer, Seydoux is the official title of this firm now owned by the Seydoux family who also own the champagne house of Alfred Gratien. With an annual production of about 167,000 cases, Gratien buy in their grapes from 200 growers. One of the larger Saumur houses, they are well known abroad due to their good distribution system, plus the fact that almost 50% of their wine is exported. Founded in 1864 by Alfred Gratien, the firm now owns 20ha (49 acres) of vineyards which are planted to Chenin Blanc and Cabernet Franc. Automatic *remuage* and the old human hand-powered version are both used here. Half a dozen different sparkling wines are made, of which the most popular must be the Gratien & Meyer Brut (a sweet, toasty Demi-Sec and an over-ripe fruity Rosé are also in this range). Also made are the dangerous-sounding Cuvée Flamme Crémant Brut, an Anjou Rosé, a dry red non-appellation Mousseux, and a Crémant de Loire.

| Huet | MC | ★★→ |
|---|---|---|

Domaine du Haut-Lieu, 37210 Vouvray

Monsieur Gaston Huet's sparkling wine production must be one of the most frustratingly variable in the world: in 1984 almost 9,000 cases, the next year nothing. But it is the harvest and only the harvest that dictates the eventual style of the Huet Vouvrays. Sparkling wine lovers will just have to hope that another green year like 1979 comes along when almost no still Huet Vouvray was made at all. Of the 32ha (79 acres) estate, divided into three plots known as Clos du Bourg, Le Mont and Haut-Lieu, all is planted to Chenin Blanc except for 2ha (5 acres) of Gamay. This is used for the Touraine Mousseux Rosé in both Brut and Demi-Sec styles. Huet is widely acknowledged as being the finest estate in Vouvray as anyone who tastes their non-vintage Brut, Sec or Demi-Sec will agree. 10% is exported. The Brut Vouvray Pétillant is a rich, biscuity, toasty wine.

## Langlois-Château                              MC                        ★→
Rue L. Palustre, St-Hilaire-St-Florent

Slightly more than a century old, Langlois-Château is another of these Loire husband-and-wife enterprises. In this case M. Edouard Langlois married Jeanne Château. The family still own about 15% of this firm but the rest now belongs to the champagne house of Bollinger. Langlois make still and sparkling wines and only grapes from 4ha (10 acres) of their Chenin Blanc and Chardonnay vineyards are utilized for sparkling wine. As this only supplies 10% of their needs Langlois buy in Chenin Blanc grapes from another 35ha (86 acres). Just 25,000 cases per annum of sparkling wine are made here – a fairly limited total given the mighty Bollinger connection. But Langlois-Château do make numerous own-label sparkling wines for others and hoping to expand soon. It is possible that they will expand their automatic *remuage* system, which currently deals with just a third of their total production. Six different Langlois wines are made and the quality is reasonable. Top of the line is the vintage-dated Saumur Blanc de Blancs followed by the Crémant de Loire in an ordinary as well as a Blanc de Blancs version. Less distinguished sparklers include the intense green, cassis-like non-vintage Brut Demi-Sec, the strange, blackcurranty Dry Rosé and a red Carte Rubis Demi-Sec Mousseux wine from outside the region.

## J. M. Monmousseau                             MC                          ★
41400 Montrichard

More than 8,000 cases of Touraine sparkling wine are made here every year by the Monmousseaus, most of which is sold under the Brut de Mosny, Cuvée JM 93 and JM Rosé labels. 61ha (150 acres) of the firm's own vineyards at Azay-le-Rideau, Montlouis and St-Georges-sur-Cher supply 25% of their sparkling wine needs. The champagne firm Taittinger now own Monmousseau.

## De Neuville                                   MC                          ★
31 rue Ackerman, St-Hilaire-St-Florent

De Neuville founded in 1856 and with an annual production figure of some 67,000 cases is not well known outside France, perhaps because only 20% of de Neuville's sparklers are exported. This firm buys in grapes from about 100ha (247 acres) of Chenin Blanc/Cabernet Franc and, pleasingly, Chardonnay vineyards. Four sparkling wines are made here: the fresh, minty de Neuville Extra Quality Blanc and Rosé plus the superior Crémant de Loire Grand Crémant Cuvée Prodige.

## Rémy-Pannier                                  MC                          ★
Rue L. Palustre, St-Hilaire-St-Florent

One of the largest sparkling Saumur firms, Rémy-Pannier think big whatever they do. This means that in addition to a wide range of still Loire wines they also make vast quantities of sparkling Saumur wines as well as other sparklers. The Rémy family also own most of Ackerman-Laurance.

### Claude Verdier                    MC                    ★
Boulevard Jean Moulin, 49400 Saumur

This little-known Saumur house produces 25,000 cases annually of sparkling Saumur plus a little Crémant de Loire. Founded in 1962, this family firm utilizes, as do most Saumur companies, the Chenin Blanc, Cabernet Franc and Groslot grapes. Claude Verdier labels include Carte d'Or A.J. Lecluse Blanc de Blancs, A.J. Lecluse Saumur Brut, Claude Verdier Saumur and Nicholas Verdier Crémant de Loire. The latter is the best wine.

### Veuve Amiot                    MC                    ★
19–21 rue Jean Ackerman, St-Hilaire-St-Florent

Named after the widow Elisa Amiot who founded this firm in 1884, Veuve Amiot are now part of the internationally-minded Martini & Rossi group. Like many Saumur houses, Veuve Amiot buy in all they need to produce 250,000 cases annually of reasonable-quality non-vintage sparkling wine. Gyropalettes are partly used here and encouragingly the Chardonnay grape is beginning to appear in several of the firm's blends. Of the wide range of sparkling wines they produce, Veuve Amiot consider the earthy, perfumed Cuvée Haute Tradition to be their finest followed by the Cuvée Réservée. The firm also makes Saumur Brut, Dry and Demi-Sec plus a Crémant de Loire Brut. Cheaper sparklers from the wider Anjou district include a Crémant Rosé, a Pétillant Blanc and Rosé and a Rouge Mousseux whose base wines come from outside the region.

### Les Vignerons de la Noëlle                    CC/MC                    ★
Boîte Postale 102, 44150 Ancenis

This group of vineyard owners with some 30ha (74 acres) of Chenin Blanc and Chardonnay between them was set up in 1955. Situated in the eastern Loire, most of their annual production of 16,000 cases consists of a low-priced *cuve close* Vin Mousseux made from Folle Blanche among other varieties. The *méthode champenoise* Prince de la Noëlle (from Folle Blanche and Chenin Blanc grapes) and the superior Crémant de Loire (Chenin Blanc-and Chardonnay-based) are also made.

### Les Vins Touchais                    MC/CC                    ★→
25 avenue du Maréchal Leclerc, Doué la Fontaine

The Touchais family are probably better known for their sweet dessert wines than they are for their sparkling range. But in suitable years a proportion of the fruit from their 150ha (370 acres) of vineyards (divided into four different estates) is turned into sparkling wine. Four different sparklers are made: a sparkling Saumur known confusingly as Perles d'Anjou (Brut and Demi-Sec) and a Vouvray Brut, plus two non-appellation wines, the Cuvée Royale (Brut and Demi-Sec) and a *cuve close* wine, the Duc des Nuits. Quality is ordinary.

## Other Loire
## sparkling wine firms:

Albert Besombes, "Moc Baril", Saumur; R.E. Dugast, "Domaine des Moulins", Monnières; Berger Frères, Montlouis; André Freslier, Vouvray; René Gouron, Chinon; Daniel Jarry, Vouvray.

# Alsace

Alsace has been making sparkling wines for more than a century. However, little was done to encourage production until 1976, when the Appellation Contrôlée Crémant d'Alsace was launched. Today almost all sparkling wine produced is *méthode champenoise* Crémant d'Alsace. This is slightly less sparkling than champagne or any other fully *mousseux* wine but at 4 atmospheres of pressure is slightly more sparkling than either Crémant de Loire or Crémant de Bourgogne.

Dopff "Au Moulin" claim to have made the first sparkling Alsace wine at about the beginning of this century. Before the First World War much of this wine, supposedly made from base wine or grapes from the Champagne region, was sold by Alsace merchants as "champagne". Thankfully, the Treaty of Versailles in 1919 put a stop to this practice. Unfortunately, those producers who were making a genuine Alsace sparkling wine also suffered and the industry did not fully recover until 1976.

Since then Crémant d'Alsace producers have rapidly made up for lost time. Where there was once only one producer there are now about 330. Similarly, annual production is now about 4m bottles in an average year. Prior to 1979 it was less than 1m. It is not just the large cooperatives and grower-négociants who are making it: dozens of small independent growers are now also producing Crémant. With only a tiny proportion of Crémant exported it is clear that the demand is coming from within France. Crémant d'Alsace is clearly in vogue.

Crémant d'Alsace is mostly made from the light, fruity Pinot Blanc grape. But the Riesling and the more full-bodied Pinot Noir, Pinot Gris and Auxerrois grapes can also be used. (Crémant d'Alsace rosé is a 100% Pinot Noir wine.) The classy Chardonnay grape is now also grown in the Alsace region, specifically for the production of Crémant d'Alsace. This should mean a gradual increase in the quality of Crémant as new plantings come on stream. In the meantime if you want to drink the finest Crémant d'Alsace it is worth paying extra for the premium sparklers, as most of these should contain a percentage of Chardonnay.

With such a range of grape varieties and flavours the Crémant d'Alsace character is a chameleon one, changing according to the producer. One cooperative's Riesling-based sparkler could be intensely green and herbaceous whereas a small grower's Crémant, made exclusively from Pinot Blanc, could be a soft, mildly fruity wine. Having found a wine you like there is no guarantee that the next vintage will be of the same style. Crémant d'Alsace producers, given below-average Alsace harvests, are often forced to make do with the grapes or base wine that no one else wants. If Crémant production is to continue at such a phenomenal rate it is clear that long-term contracts between Crémant producers and growers will have to be made.

Currently most Crémant d'Alsace sparklers are of average to good quality. It is rare to find an unacceptable or substandard bottle. However it will be some years yet before the sparkling wine producers of Alsace can challenge the *Champenois*.

| Blanck | MC | ★★ |
| --- | --- | --- |

32 Grande Rue, Kientzheim

Bernard and Marcel Blanck run Maison Blanck together with their brother-in-law Jacques Barthelme. Their Crémant d'Alsace in either the non-*dosage* Brut Sauvage or Extra Brut versions comes exclusively from their own 2ha (5 acres) of vineyards at Kientzheim. The traditionalist Blancks are interested in quality, not quantity, and this quest for the best shows in their wines of which just 1,000 cases are made annually. The Extra Brut accounts for the majority of this and like the Brut Sauvage it is an unusual blend of two-thirds Pinot Blanc to one-third Riesling and Tokay. The Blancks first made sparkling wine in 1982 and so far consider their 1983 vintage to be the finest they have made.

### Emile Boeckel    MC    ★→★★
2 rue de la Montagne, Mittelbergheim

"Over a hundred years of experience" boasts M. Boeckel's sales literature but the firm has, like many Alsace wine producers, only been making Crémant since 1980. Boeckel are the most important firm at Mittelbergheim but even so their Crémant production barely tops 1,500 cases annually. Boeckel's 5ha (12 acres) of Crémant vineyards are partly planted to Chardonnay in addition to Auxerrois and Pinot Blanc. The small amount of Crémant d'Alsace Brut Zero, made entirely from Chardonnay, is definitely worth seeking out. Boeckel also produce a Crémant d'Alsace Brut made from the other grape varieties. 25% of their Crémant is exported to Belgium and the rest is sold in France.

### Cattin    MC    ★→
18 rue R. Fremeaux, Voegtlinshoffen

The Cattin family have been associated with the unpronounceable village of Voegtlinshoffen for generations. Today Joseph Cattin produces a respectable amount of Crémant d'Alsace – just over 4,000 cases – from 6ha (15 acres) of Voegtlinshoffen vines. Cattin believe in the traditional methods, including hand *remuage* but with controlled fermentation nevertheless. Their one sparkler, the Crémant d'Alsace Brut (made mostly from Pinot Blanc but with a little Pinot Gris and Riesling), is good rather than great.

### Cave Vinicole de Beblenheim    MC    ★
14 rue de Hoen, 68980 Beblenheim

One of the biggest producers of Crémant d'Alsace, Beblenheim has an impressive 220 or so members who own in the region of 220ha (545 acres). The quality of the cooperative's wines however is only average. Caves de Hoen is one brand name.

### Cave Vinicole d'Eguisheim    MC    ★→
6 Grande Rue, 68420 Eguisheim

The functional, tidy and well-equipped Eguisheim cooperative is one of the most important in France and certainly the largest in Alsace. Founded in 1902, it now boasts 750 members with 950ha (2,346 acres) between them. In any one year an impressive 170–250ha (420–617 acres) are given over to Crémant d'Alsace production which often exceeds 200,000 cases. It is therefore surprising to learn that part of their sparkling wine is still riddled by hand. This cooperative is one of the very few Alsace firms to offer a range of sparklers and there are five different Wolfbergers to choose from. The Pinot Blanc-based Crémant Brut is the biggest seller, but other Alsace firms would be very happy to sell as much of the intense green and herbaceous Crémant Riesling as this cooperative does. The Pinot Noir-based Crémant Rosé and the Crémant Prestige made from Riesling and Pinot grapes also sell well. In fact the only specialist, limited Crémant line that Eguisheim produce is their vintage-dated Wolfberger Millésime in its gaudy, enamelled bottle made from Pinot Noir and Pinot Blanc with a touch of Riesling. Eguisheim are quick to point out the similarities between their Crémant d'Alsace and champagne but even tasting blind it would be difficult to confuse the two. Wolfberger sparklers are of reasonable quality and during the next five years the cooperative hopes to step up annual production to some 250,000 cases. Wolfberger Crémant is sold in France but a little is exported elsewhere in Europe.

## Cave Vinicole de Hunawihr    MC    ★
Hunawihr

Hunawihr was first mentioned in a papal bull of Pope Calixte II in 1123. This explains why the Hunawihr cooperative founded in 1954 has chosen Cuvée Calixte II as its sparkling brand name. The cooperative has 145 members who own 15ha (37 acres) between them for the production of Crémant d'Alsace. More than 16,000 cases of a non-vintage sparkler are made here annually using mostly Pinot Blanc and Auxerrois with a dash of Riesling. Given the relatively large production by Alsace standards it is not surprising that gyropalettes are in use. Quality is reasonable.

## Cave Vinicole de Pfaffenheim    MC    ★
Pfaffenheim, 68250 Rouffach

This cooperative's full title is Cave Vinicole de Pfaffenheim, Gueberschwihr & Environs. Founded in 1955, it has 200ha (494 acres) and is self-sufficient in Pinot Blanc and Pinot Gris grapes, of which a small proportion is turned into 4,000 cases of sparkling wine annually. Hartenberger is the sparkling brand name and the best wine, the Brut, is made exclusively from Pinot Blanc. A Pinot Gris Hartenberger is also available as is a rosé. Riddling is by way of automatic gyropalettes and the quality is average.

## Cave Coopérative de Ribeauvillé    MC    ★→★★
2 route de Colmar, 68150 Ribeauvillé

This important cooperative is a rare bird in the wine world for it manages to produce both quantity and respectable quality. It is also the oldest cooperative in France – it was founded in 1895. Today it has 90 members who between them own 176ha (435 acres) although only 12ha (30 acres) are used for their Crémant d'Alsace. This sparkling wine is sold under the brand name of Giersberger and in only a Brut style. Unlike other Crémant d'Alsace producers Ribeauvillé make their wine entirely from Pinot Blanc. Riddling is partly by hand and partly by the automatic method. Consequently the annual production of 5,000 cases of the fresh, flowery Giersberger may well soon increase.

## Cave Vinicole de Traenheim    MC    ★→
67310 Traenheim

This little-known cooperative in the most northern part of Alsace controls 400ha (988 acres) of which 10ha (25 acres) of Pinot Blanc are used for their Crémant d'Alsace. More than 6,000 cases of the Saint Eloi sparkler are made annually. The quality here is above that of most cooperatives.

## Caves Vinicoles de Westhalten    MC    ★→
Route de Soultzmatt, 68111 Westhalten

170 growers belong to this cooperative, with 251ha (620 acres) in

Westhalten and various neighbouring villages. Like other Alsace cooperatives, they are among the largest producers of Crémant d'Alsace, which they make from Pinot Blanc. Annual production of their strangely-titled Producteur Brut Blanc de Blancs is now about 13,000 cases. It is soft and buttery, but nothing particularly special.

| Dopff & Irion | MC | ★ |
| --- | --- | --- |

"Château de Riquewihr", 68340 Riquewihr

Riquewihr is the most enchanting village in Alsace. The half-timbered houses, cobbled streets and riot of colourful flowers look like something out of an opera set. Guy Dopff and Jean-Louis Irion joined forces after the War but both families had previously made wine at Riquewihr for three centuries. Dopff & Irion make wine on a vast scale and are the largest Alsace firm by far. As is customary in Riquewihr, much of Dopff & Irion's wine is matured, bottled and made in the village; behind that window box and ancient doorway lies not a house but a modern cellar complete with stainless steel tanks and the latest wine equipment. Dopff & Irion buy in many of their grapes and are keen exporters. Their Crémant d'Alsace is a green sparkler, slightly redolent of rubber, but acceptable nonetheless.

| Dopff "Au Moulin" | MC | ★ |
| --- | --- | --- |

68340 Riquewihr

With wine traditions that date back to 1574, Dopff "Au Moulin" are one of the most important Crémant d'Alsace firms today. Julien Dopff visited the Paris exhibition in 1900 and was so impressed with the *méthode champenoise* he saw demonstrated there that he was determined to make a sparkling Alsace using the same process. After two years' study at Epernay in the Champagne district, Julien Dopff launched the first ever Alsace sparkler at the turn of the century. Originally known simply as Dopff, this firm added "Au Moulin" in order to avoid confusion with Dopff & Irion. Dopff "Au Moulin" now own some 20ha (49 acres) of mostly Pinot Blanc vines, but with some Pinot Noir too, close to Colmar and Turckheim. In order to meet their annual production levels of some 38,000 cases the firm has to buy in grapes from another 50ha (123 acres) planted to Pinot Blanc, Pinot Noir and Auxerrois. With such a healthy production figure (by Alsace's standards) Dopff "Au Moulin" use gyropalettes for the *remuage* of two-thirds of their wine, with the remainder still being done by hand. The Dopff family (with Pierre and Pierre-Etienne now at the top) still run this firm and have since 1982 shared their equipment in a joint arrangement with both Dopff & Irion and Laugel. Dopff make seven different sparkling wines, two of which are sold simply as Dopff Dry Méthode Champenoise and Dopff Blanc Brut Méthode Champenoise without the appellation designation. These are therefore blends made from wines from outside the region, and are not in the true Alsace style. A better choice would be the beefy and somewhat aggressive Pinot Blanc- and Auxerrois-based Cuvée Julien Brut, or the similarly-based alarming-sounding non-*dosage* Dopff Wild Brut. Other Dopff sparklers include the Blanc de Noirs and Au Moulin Rouge Rosé, both from Pinot Noir. The finest wines the firm makes, though, are the vintage-dated Cuvée Bartholdi, a wine specially bottled to commemorate the 100th anniversary of the Statute of Liberty, and the magnum bottle of Dopff Réserve Personnelle. About 30% of Dopff's Crémant is exported.

## Geschickt          MC                               ★
1 place de la Sinne, Ammerschwihr

The firm of Jérome Geschickt & Fils is 50 years old and has been handed down from father to son since the beginning. 1,250 cases are made here annually from Geschickt's own 2ha (5 acres) of vines around Ammerschwihr. Only one Crémant d'Alsace is produced, the vintage-dated Brut made from equal parts of Auxerrois, Pinot Blanc and Riesling. Hand riddling and the limited production conspire to keep most of the Geschickt sparkling wine sales within Alsace and France but a little is exported to Germany.

## W. Gisselbrecht          MC                          ★→
3A route du Vin, 67650 Dambach-la-Ville

For a firm as important as Willy Gisselbrecht it seems slightly incongruous that they should be situated at No. 3A. However, Dambach's largest firm, founded in 1936, is a pleasant, modern establishment. The Gisselbrecht family have a tradition of buying in grapes in addition to those from their own 15ha (37 acres) of vines. 30% of Gisselbrecht's own Pinot Blanc and Pinot Noir grapes go into their Crémant d'Alsace blends and they buy in the remainder from other Pinot Blanc producers. Most of Gisselbrecht's 6,000 cases annual production is taken up by their Pinot Blanc-based Crémant d'Alsace Brut, the Cuvée Prestige. W. Gisselbrecht's Pinot Noir-based Crémant Rosé d'Alsace accounts for about 800 cases of the total. *Remuage* here is performed partly by hand and partly by automatic means. Apart from the French market, Germany, the UK and Benelux buy Gisselbrecht sparklers.

## Heim          MC                                    ★→
68111 Westhalten

Important exporters Heim have a good reputation for both their still and sparkling wines. Most of their Crémant d'Alsace is made from grapes from a group of small growers who have some 90ha (222 acres) between them. Heim insist on the very best quality from their growers (unlike some concerns) and this is obviously reflected in the wine. Heim's Crémant d'Alsace is called Imperial Brut.

## Laugel          MC                                  ★
102 rue de Gaulle, 67520 Marlenheim

This prosperous well-equipped family firm is run by Léon, Gérard, Jean-Michel and Philippe Laugel. Michel Laugel founded the firm in 1889 but there have been Laugels at Marlenheim since 1650. Exports are of prime importance here with about 40% of Laugel's Crémant exported to Germany, Canada and the USA among other countries. Laugel first made sparkling wine in 1982 – a non-vintage Pinot Blanc-based Blanc de Blancs. Today this wine still accounts for the lion's share of their production – some 11,000 cases out of a total of some 12,000. In addition Laugel make a Pinot Noir-based Blanc de Noirs and Rosé wine plus a vintage-dated Grand Millésime of which the 81 is the latest vintage. Laugel share the same *méthode champenoise* equipment (including automatic *remuage*) as Dopff & Irion and Dopff "Au Moulin". Laugel's latest idea is the Perles de Framboise apéritif – a blend of Crémant d'Alsace, raspberry liqueur and a dash of raspberry *eau de vie*.

## Mayerling               MC                    ★→★★
Turckheim Coopérative, 16 rue des Tuileries, 68230 Turckheim

The impressive modern Turckheim cooperative is the producer
behind the Mayerling label. 260 members own 30ha (74 acres)
between them. Mayerling is made entirely from the cooperative's
own grapes. 10,000 cases of just one sparkling wine are produced
annually – the non-vintage Mayerling Blanc de Blancs Brut,
made from equal proportions of Pinot Blanc and Auxerrois.
Automatic *remuage* helps speed up production here but as yet the
cooperative does not export its sparkling wine. Mayerling is
definitely worth seeking out: with its elegant, flowery nose and
racy, green palate it is one of the best Crémant sparklers that
Alsace produces.

## Muhlberger             MC                              ★
1 rue de Strasbourg, Wolxheim

François Muhlberger and his son Robert, like many of the
Crémant d'Alsace producers, are heirs to ancient traditions. The
first Muhlberger vigneron documented at Wolxheim was in
1777. However it was more than two centuries before the family
made their first sparkling wine in 1982. Production has been
growing steadily since then and now they produce in the region
of 1,000 cases per annum of Crémant – a Blanc de Blancs Brut
made from Auxerrois. *Remuage* is by hand and most of this wine is
drunk by the French, although the Danes and Germans buy a
little too.

## Muré                   MC                              ★
Route du Vin, 68250 Rouffach

Reine-Thérèse and her brother René Muré run this attractive
place where the Murés have been growing vines since 1630. Old
traditions are still much in evidence here and many wines are both
fermented and aged in cask. Just over 4,000 cases of three different
Crémant wines are made here annually. Most of this is the
Reserve Muré Brut made from a blend of Pinot Blanc, Auxerrois
and Tokay but a fair amount of Crémant d'Alsace de Riesling is
also made in both a Brut and a non-*dosage* Brut "O" style. The
Murés' own grapes provide only 40% of their sparkling wine
needs – they buy in the rest. The sparkling wines produced here
are of average quality.

## Runner                 MC                              ★
1 rue de la Liberté, Pfaffenheim

Almost 4ha (10 acres) of the commercially-minded Monsieur
Runner's vines are set aside for Crémant d'Alsace. This family
firm bases its sparkling wines principally on Pinot Blanc and
Auxerrois grapes topped up with a little Tokay and Pinot Gris.
The Runners use both hand riddling and gyropalettes and their
Crémant is made in either Brut or Sec styles according to
demand. Germany is the only export market.

## Schaller               MC                          ★→
1 rue du Château, 68630 Mittelwihr

The firm of Schaller was founded in 1609 and Edward Schaller
and his son Patrick (who studied in Champagne) have been
making Crémant d'Alsace for more than a decade. With 2.5ha (6
acres) of vines (with an additional 1ha [2.5 acres] of Chardonnay
grapes bought in) Schaller are currently producing 1,500 cases

annually. Extra Brut is the only Schaller sparkler and this is still riddled by hand. The Schallers feel that their Extra Dry Blend has universal appeal. This wine is mostly Pinot Blanc which, they say, gives structure to the wine, plus Riesling which gives the typical fruity Alsace taste, backed up with a little Pinot Gris which gives the wine body.

| Louis Sipp | MC | ★ |
| --- | --- | --- |

Ribeauvillé

Louis Sipp are one of the principal exporters of Crémant d'Alsace. A husband and wife team run this firm and besides their own 30ha (74 acres) of vines they also buy in grapes from numerous small growers. Do not expect the Sipp Crémant d'Alsace to be spectacular. It isn't.

| Pierre Sparr | MC | ★→ |
| --- | --- | --- |

2 rue de la 1ère Armée, 68240 Sigolsheim

Sigolsheim, as Pierre Sparr's address suggests, was entirely destroyed during the Second World War. But this firm, founded in 1892 and with winemaking traditions going back to 1680, is now housed in a handsome new building and is one of the leading exporters of Alsace wine. René and his brother Charles direct operations here and their sons, who are the eighth generation, also work in the firm. 5ha (12 acres) of their own Pinot Blanc and Auxerrois vines produce the base wine for their Crémant and the Sparrs also buy in 4ha (10 acres) of Pinot Blanc. Some 6,000 cases of their only sparkling wine, the Blanc de Blancs Brut, are made in most years. The Sparrs, like most of the big Alsace houses, use automatic *remuage*. Their Crémant d'Alsace is always blended from a minimum of two different vintages to ensure continuity. The quality is good.

| Wunsch & Mann | MC | ★ |
| --- | --- | --- |

2 rue des Clefs, 68000 Wettolsheim

Just southwest of Colmar is Wettolsheim and the firm of Wunsch & Mann, founded in 1948. Originally the firm was run by both the Wunsch and Mann families but today only the Manns are left. With 8ha (20 acres) of their own Crémant d'Alsace Pinot Blanc and Auxerrois vines the Manns now make some 7,500 cases of sparkling wine annually. They make only a Brut here via automatic *remuage*. In addition to the Pinot Blanc and Auxerrois the Manns use a little Chardonnay to lighten their somewhat full-bodied, hearty style.

# Other Crémant d'Alsace producers:

Lucien Albrecht, Orschwihr; Fréderic Berger & Fils, Riquewihr; Jean-Paul Ecklé, Katzenthal; Hering Fils, Barr; René Klein, St-Hippolyte; Marc Kreidenweiss, Andlau; Landmann Ostholt, Soultzmatt; Charles Muller & Fils, Traenheim; André Wackenthaler, Ammerschwihr; Bernard Weber, Molsheim; Louis Wintzer, Soultz.

# ─── *The Rest of France* ───

Making sense of a row of French *vins mousseux* bottles takes both keen eyesight and determination. Any wine that simply carries the words *vin mousseux* without any regional or village designation will have been made from base wines that could come from anywhere in France. So don't be swayed by a famous producer's or company's name on a label if the words *vin mousseux* or French sparkling wine – and nothing else – accompany it. What you will be buying is not Monsieur X from the Loire's celebrated Loire sparkling wine, but his less distinguished *vin mousseux* made perhaps from the Charentes district's Ugni Blanc grape. Frustratingly these *vins mousseux* can be made either by the *méthode champenoise* or the *cuve close* processes, and the method will not always be printed on the label. Most of the wines are made by the *cuve close* system. Despite the often humble base wines used, the quality, as demonstrated by the Caves de Wissembourg's G. F. Cavalier brand, can be excellent.

The next step up in the French sparkling wine hierarchy are the *vins mousseux de qualité*. These wines have to meet stricter regulations than ordinary *vins mousseux*, including longer ageing. They will have *Vin Mousseux Qualité* or the letters VMQ on the label. There are few wines in this category. Most will have been made by the *méthode champenoise*.

Another step up brings in those *appellation contrôlée* wines that come from a specific region or village. Most of these are made by the *méthode champenoise* and some are made by the *méthode dioise* or *méthode rurale* (see p.6). The transfer method is very occasionally used. Annoyingly, the specific method does not always appear on the label. But the words *appellation contrôlée* plus the region or village name will appear.

The finest French sparklers of all, outside Champagne, are the softly sparkling Crémant wines. So far only three regions are producing Crémant: Alsace (see p.54), Loire (see p.47) and Burgundy (Crémant de Bourgogne). Other regions may follow. Initially it seems contradictory that a regional appellation such as these should produce better wine than one confined to a specific area or village. But the Crémant rules stipulate a lower yield per hectare, finer grapes, a longer ageing period and a gentler pressing with only the first cuts used. The quality shows.

Starting in northern France and working clockwise around the country, the first sparkling wine region after Champagne is Alsace (see p.54). Next is Burgundy with its Crémant de Bourgogne wines, introduced in 1975, of which about 3m bottles are produced annually from Pinot Noir, Pinot Blanc, Chardonnay and Aligoté. Quality can be excellent, especially if the producers (many of whom are cooperatives) use high proportions of either Chardonnay or Pinot Noir in their blends. Burgundy also produces white, pink and red *vins mousseux*. These wines tend to rely heavily on the less worthy grape varieties such as Aligoté, Gamay and Sacy.

Farther south and east of Burgundy lie the mountainous Jura and Savoie districts. The sparkling wines from these regions, made from numerous different local grapes, are generally only available in the area of origin. This is no doubt partly due to the unquenchable thirsts of a never-ending horde of skiers. The various appellations include Arbois, L'Etoile and Seyssel besides the generic Vin de Savoie and Côtes du Jura. There is one VDQS wine, Vin du Bugey. The best known of these sparklers (and also the best quality) are the white, red and rosé Arbois wines plus the white Seyssel *mousseux*. A *pétillant* Vin de Savoie is also made.

The Rhône region produces two sparkling wines: tiny amounts of the full-flavoured St-Péray from opposite Valence, and Clairette de Die which comes from a large area southeast of Valence around the town of Die. About 5m bottles of Clairette de Die are made every year in two totally different styles. The finest is the slightly sweet, grapey, flowery Clairette de Die Tradition made by the *méthode dioise* (*see* p.6) predominantly from Muscat. Clairette de Die wines without the Tradition tag are likely to have been made mostly from Clairette via the *méthode champenoise*. The Mediterranean coast vineyards produce the odd sparkling wine, the most important by far being Blanquette de Limoux from Roussillon. The town of Limoux lies just south of Carcassonne. The region is a large one, producing some 7m bottles of sparkling wine annually. The grape varieties used are the robust local Mauzac, plus Chenin Blanc and the recently-allowed Chardonnay. The quality of Blanquette de Limoux appears to have taken a slight dip in recent years but nonetheless it is still a fresh, yeasty and fruity sparkling wine.

Southwest France provides the base wine for many sparklers, but most of these are bought by outside firms and receive their bubbles elsewhere. A few sparkling wines are made locally such as the Armagnac area's Vin Sauvage. One notable exception is Gaillac. The still wines of Gaillac have a tendency to sparkle naturally, due to a combination of soil, grape and climate. The Mauzac grape is the chief one here but other varieties are found including the charmingly-named Loin de l'Oeil or "far from view". The best Gaillac sparklers are made by a variation of the *méthode rurale* known as the *méthode gaillaçoise* (*see* p.6).

Farther north is the Bordeaux region, home, like Burgundy, to numerous sparkling wine firms. Most of these houses produce non-appellation sparklers, but about 2m bottles are made annually of Bordeaux *mousseux* in white and pink versions.

---

### Georges & Roger Antech     MC     ★
Domaine de Flassian, 11300 Limoux

This little-known Blanquette de Limoux is owned by the Antech brothers and is one of the smaller Blanquette producers, making about 25,000 cases annually. Antech's own Mauzac, Chenin Blanc and Chardonnay grapes supply 40% of their needs, the balance being bought in. Their superior Maistre Blanquetier with its tiny slip of a label and its dumpy flagon bottle has a good reputation. The white-and-black label wines are also well thought of. Cuvée Saint Laurent and the green label Prestige Antech are two other brands. Considerable recent investment in both vini- and viticulture augurs well for the future.

---

### Producteurs de Blanquette de Limoux     MC/MR     ★→
11300 Limoux

No one will ever know whether it was the Benedictine monks of St-Hilaire who were truly the first to produce a sparkling wine in 1531, or whether it was Dom Pérignon almost two centuries later. This cooperative however claims to produce "the oldest Brut in the world" and it would be difficult to prove them wrong. The cooperative, with 650 members, dominates the appellation, producing three bottles in every four. Blanquette's quality is due to the region's chalky soil plus the trio of grape varieties: Mauzac, Chenin Blanc and Chardonnay. The distinctive white downy underside of the Mauzac leaf gives Blanquette its name, and also much of its flavour, with the Chenin Blanc contributing fruit and the recently-allowed Chardonnay adding elegance and finesse. The cooperative is one of the biggest producers of sparkling wine in France and in 1985 their automatic gyropalettes were thought to have produced roughly half a million cases. The range comprises a prestige vintage *cuvée* plus non-vintage Brut and Demi-Sec styles. Producteur Aimery, Alderic Brut is this cooperative's French brand name. In export markets, the name Fleur de Lys is used for the vintage Blanquette. At a recent tasting the Brut was a fresh, yeasty mouthful and the 1979 was a lively, fresh appley wine. The cooperative also produce tiny amounts of a cloudy *méthode rurale* Vin de Blanquette sparkler, most of which is consumed locally.

## Bouchard Aîné   CC/MC   ★

36 rue Ste-Marguerite, 21203 Beaune

Bouchard Aîné, as a serious Burgundy house, really should know better. But they sell Cold Duck, the ubiquitous pink *cuve close* fizz, with their name proudly on the label beneath a yellow baby duck floating in a saucer-shaped sparkling wine glass! Other *vins mousseux* include the Cuvée Bouchard Aîné Blanc de Blancs in both Brut and Demi-Sec versions. The only *méthode champenoise* wine they sell is Blason de Bourgogne, a Crémant de Bourgogne. All Bouchard's sparkling wines are made for them by other firms.

## Louis Bouillot   MC   ★→

42 rue des Blés, 21700 Nuits-St-Georges

Maison Louis Bouillot turn out about 34,000 cases of sparkling wine every year, most of which is made from bought-in grapes or wine. Bouillot make vintage and non-vintage Bourgogne Blanc and Rouge from a mix of Chardonnay/Pinot Noir and Aligoté, plus a small amount of Crémant de Bourgogne. Other Bouillot sparklers made from non-burgundy base wines include Carte Noire and Monopole Blanc de Blancs. The Pinot Noir- and Chardonnay-based Crémant wines are worth trying.

## Café de Paris   CC   ★

Cubzac-les-Ponts, 33240 Saint-André-de-Cubzac

Café de Paris, made by the Caves at Cubzac, is a lot less exciting than it sounds. However it is a vintage-dated Blanc de Blancs wine which is at least a quality step up from its competitors. Like most of the cheap *cuve close* French sparklers it is made from various different base wines. The 1982 vintage is just acceptable: a slightly coarse, burnt-toffee nosed wine.

## G. F. Cavalier   CC   ★★→

67160 Wissembourg

*Star buy G. F. Cavalier Brut*

A recent name change from Chevalier to Cavalier was forced on this firm by E. Chevalier of the Loire. No matter, for the Caves de Wissembourg's *cuve close* wines are still of the same high quality selling at the same low price. What seems remarkable about this highly efficiently-run place north of Strasbourg is that the *cuve close* wines (unlike their numerous competitors) are cheap, fresh, lively and deliciously drinkable. This German-owned firm only makes *cuve close* wines, virtually all from French wine that is bought in by the train-load from all over France. The majority probably comes from the Charentes region. G. F. Cavalier is available in Muscat rosé, sweet red and Muscat-based Muscat Blanc versions as well as the more desirable Brut and Blanc de Blancs styles of which a Demi-Sec is also produced. Two prestige *cuvées* are sold under the Feist Belmont Blanc de Blancs and Pierre Larousse labels, G. F. Cavalier also produce own-label sparklers for big supermarket groups and the like.

### Caves de Bailly                           MC                     ★
89530 Saint-Bris-le-Vineux

This modern cooperative, founded in 1972, lies just south of Auxerre close to the Chablis district, and has a reputation for its Crémant de Bourgogne. It has impressive cellars (carved out of limestone) and equipment which includes giant stainless steel fermentors that just scrape in under the cave's ceiling. 80 growers supply the grapes, and a winemaking staff of 20 turn the local Auxerrois grape into vintage-dated white and rosé Crémant de Bourgogne. These wines are made in a variety of different styles. The pale, almost blue-pink, 82 Rosé Brut has an intense grassy herbaceous style. Comte de Bailly with its jagged label is their newest sparkling wine. Meurgis is another brand name. Bailly also make a *vin mousseux* from grapes grown outside the region.

### Caves des Coteaux de Gaillac            TM/MR              ★→
Labastide de Lévis, 81150 Marsac-sur-Tarn

Gaillac in southwest France has long had a reputation for its naturally-sparkling wines. The slightly sparkling wines made by the *méthode rurale*, known sometimes locally as the *méthode gaillaçoise*, are perhaps better than the fully-sparkling *mousseux* made by the *méthode champenoise* or transfer method. This cooperative, founded in 1951, uses mostly the transfer method to create its Gaillac Brut and Demi-Sec, but they use the *méthode rurale* too. The cooperative's members have 70ha (173 acres) of Mauzac grapes plus some of the local Loin de l'oeil. Total annual production is 25,000 cases of lively, fruity sparkling wine. These traditional Gaillac wines are something of a curiosity within the sparkling wine world but worth experiencing.

### Cave Coopérative de Die                  MC/MD               ★→
Avenue de la Clairette, 26150 Die

Before this cooperative was founded in 1950 the Drôme region produced very little of the delightful fresh Muscat Clairette de Die. Almost 40 years later this cooperative now produces half a million cases annually. The slightly sweet Tradition is made by the rural *méthode dioise* whose fermentation preserves all the fresh lively fragrance of the Muscat grape. An excellent wine, flowery and grapey. The cooperative also makes a green-apple-like Clairette de Die Brut from Clairette grapes using a second *méthode champenoise* fermentation in bottle. Voconces Brut, which is made from a blend of different grape varieties, is also made by the *méthode champenoise*. This large and impressively-equipped cooperative has 500 members with 1,000ha (2,470 acres) between them scattered across the region's 32 communes.

### Caves les Vignerons de St-Péray          MC        ★→
07130 St-Péray

This tiny appellation, on the opposite bank from Valence in the heart of the Rhône, produces more sparkling wine than still wine. The quantities however are still minute. But with their growing reputation, low-alcohol content, full-bodied flavour and rarity value they are worth trying. St-Péray is made mostly from the Marsanne grape plus a little of other local Rhône grapes, the Rousanne and Roussette. St-Péray Brut is a biscuity, slightly coarse wine.

## Cave de Viré                MC                ★★→
71260 Viré

*Star buy 1983 Crémant de Bourgogne Brut*

The Viré cooperative that lies just south of Mâcon in the heart of Burgundy's Mâconnais makes only one sparkling wine. This Crémant de Bourgogne is made exclusively from the cooperative members' own Chardonnay – they have 40ha (99 acres). The quality therefore, given the grapes, should be well above the usual cooperative level. 25,000 cases are made every year and production is helped along by semi-automatic *remuage*. Viré are greatly interested in the export market especially to the USA, Germany and the UK. Their 1983 Crémant de Bourgogne Brut is a lovely firm, fresh, pineappley wine with a good, creamy mousse and a clean, biscuity finish.

## Chaverou                CC                →★
10 rue Galilée, 33200 Bordeaux

Chaverou is one of several Bordeaux-based sparkling wine firms who buy in base wine from all over the southwest to turn into low-price *cuve close* sparklers. Chaverou has a multiplicity of labels including Café de France, Henri Bontant, Galilée and M. & P. Chaverou. The quality is what you might expect: coarse, dull and not very nice.

## Hubert Clavelin                MC                ★→
Le Vernois, Voiteur

For once with a French regional sparkling wine it is immediately apparent from Clavelin's label where it comes from: it is simply labelled by its appellation name – Côtes du Jura. Four generations of Clavelins have run this traditional place and today the firm produces about 12,500 cases of *méthode champenoise* wine a year. They own 24ha (59 acres) of vineyards, mostly Chardonnay, which provide two-thirds of their needs. More grapes, again mostly Chardonnay, are bought in. Most of the wine is drunk in France, but a little is exported to Germany and the USA. If you manage to find any, try it.

## Compagnie Française des Grands Vins                CC/MC                ★
Zone Industrielle, Tournan-en-Brie

This large wine group, founded in 1909 and now situated just east of Paris, has outposts in both Burgundy and Saumur. It is now owned by Martini & Rossi. Its production is enormous – around 2.5m cases a year. Most of this sea of wine comes from the Ugni Blanc grape from Charentes, plus Chenin Blanc from the Loire and a little Chardonnay and Cabernet from elsewhere. Most of the sparkling wine is made by the *cuve close* method but the gyropalettes *méthode champenoise* output is substantial too. The cheapest wine in their range is André Gallois, followed by the marginally classier Blanc de Blancs version, Grand Impérial and Opéra Sec. One up from there is the Muscat-based plus Pol Acker. *Méthode champenoise* wines include Monopoles Alfred Rothschild and Cadre Noir – an earthy, musky, slightly atypical Saumur Brut from the Loire. The group also produces a Crémant de Bourgogne sold as Imperiale Bourgogne, and a sparkling Vouvray sold as Vouvray Club. Martin Laurent is their champagne brand. Compagnie Française des Grands Vins export a third of their production and a quarter of all the *mousseux* (excluding champagne) that France makes.

## Les Coteaux de Gardie Coopérative    MC    ★
Gardie, 11250 St-Hilaire

This Blanquette de Limoux cooperative has 65 members and produces 40,000 cases annually of sparkling wine sold mostly under the Blanche de Gardie label. The non-vintage Brut and Sec sparklers are based on the local Mauzac grapes while the vintage-dated Brut now has a large proportion of Chardonnay and a touch of Chenin Blanc in its blend. The cooperative's members own 200ha (494 acres), so it is entirely self-supportive in grapes. The wine is exported to Belgium and Germany. Edouard de Clauzel is another brand name.

## André Delorme    MC    ★→
rue de la République, Rully, 71150 Chagny

More than 41,000 cases of sparkling wine are made here annually making the Caves Delorme-Meulien a medium-sized firm. As is usual with most Crémant de Bourgogne producers, Jean-François Delorme uses a blend of different grapes. The Blanc de Noirs and Rosé are mainly Pinot Noir with a little Gamay. The Blanc de Blancs is mostly Aligoté with a dash of Chardonnay. Apart from these Crémants de Bourgogne, André Delorme make *méthode champenoise* Bourgogne Rouge and Blanc Brut, both made from grapes or wine from outside the region. The firm considers their Crémant de Bourgogne Blanc de Noirs to be their best wine and they are very interested in the export market to countries such as the UK, Belgium, the USA and Germany.

## Kriter    TM    ★
5 rue du Collège, 21201 Beaune

Kriter is to Burgundy what Veuve de Vernay is to Bordeaux: a modestly-priced bulk-method sparkler that the world drinks in vast quantities. It is sold in 96 different countries, doing especially well in the USA and Germany, and is the biggest-selling sparkling wine in France. Anyone travelling on the autoroute through Burgundy cannot fail to notice Kriter's giant production plant, complete with fields of blackcurrant bushes whose fruit is turned into Kriter cassis. Unlike Veuve du Vernay, Kriter is made by the transfer method – a superior process to the *cuve close*. Kriter's grapes are thought to include Burgundy's straightforward, fruity Aligoté variety, although they must also use grapes from outside the region. Kriter is available in Brut, Brut de Brut, Demi-Sec and Rosé styles, some of which are vintaged, some not. Two deluxe Kriter wines also made by the transfer method include the vintage Impérial and the sweet Délicatesse. More than 1m cases of Kriter are sold every year. The company is part of the Patriarche Père & Fils group.

## Producteurs de Lugny-St-Gengoux-de-Scissé    MC    ★→
71260 Lugny

This cooperative at Lugny in the heart of the Mâcon area is, along with its southerly next door neighbour at Viré, the chief source of Crémant de Bourgogne. Opinions are divided as to which cooperative produces the best Crémant: it varies from vintage to vintage. This Pinot Noir and Chardonnay blend is a big, yeasty almost chocolatey wine.

## Henri Mugnier    MC    ★→
1 rue du Perthuis, 71850 Charnay-les-Mâcon

Henri and Pierre Mugnier make more than 18,000 cases of *méthode champenoise* Blanc de Blancs *mousseux* and Crémant de Bourgogne. The bought-in base wines are Chardonnay, and this plus the traditional methods used in the 17th-century Mugnier cellar indicate that quality should be better than most. Export markets include the USA and Italy.

## Piat Réserve    CC    ★
71570 La Chapelle-de-Guinchay

There is little to say about Piat Réserve except perhaps to point out that this fizz shares the same pot-bellied bottle as its relative in the Piat d'Or range of still wines. This *vin mousseux* is made from a blend of base wines that are drawn from all over France and acquire bubbles via the *cuve close* method. When tasted recently it was not unpleasant; sweet, though somewhat musty.

## Picamelot    MC    ★
Rully, 71150 Chagny

Established as recently as 1970 but with a history going back to the 1920s, Picamelot has had a complicated series of owners. Their annual production of 25,000 cases is made entirely from bought-in base wine: Picamelot merely add bubbles via the *méthode champenoise*. Crémant and other Bourgogne sparkling wines sadly account for a small percentage of the total. The majority is a straightforward Vin Mousseux Blanc made apparently from the non-Burgundian Pinot de Tourenne grape. Bourgogne wines are made principally from Aligoté plus Pinot Blanc with the Crémant from Chardonnay and Aligoté. All wines are non-vintage. Quality is no more than basic.

## William Pitters    CC    →★
Rue de Banlin, 33310 Lormont

A hefty 583,000 cases of sparkling wine are made here annually. Club Prestige (Brut and Demi-Sec) made from the southwest's ubiquitous Ugni Blanc grape, accounts for the lion's share of this. But other companies would no doubt be very happy with yearly sales of 84,000 cases a piece of both De Vaubrun (Brut and Demi-Sec) and Muscat Rosé de Reinevald. De Vaubrun has some Loire Chenin Blanc added to the Ugni Blanc. All William Pitters sparklers are non-vintage, *cuve close* wines and no stock is kept of any of them – thus they have no bottle-age. Do not therefore expect too much from this firm..

## Simonnet-Febvre & Fils    MC    ★→
5 avenue d'Oberwesel, 89800 Chablis

It is odd to discover that a firm so well-known for its Chablis also produces a decent quantity (some 12,500 cases) of sparkling wine. The Simonnet family still own this firm, founded in 1840, and they use the *méthode champenoise* to produce all their sparkling wines. Non-appellation Blanc de Blancs (plus a little rosé) accounts for most of their output but there is a Bourgogne Mousseux Blanc and Rosé too. The best of the bunch is undoubtedly their attractive Crémant de Bourgogne Blanc and Rosé, both of which do well in the USA and the UK.

### La Tête Noire                    MC                    ★→
32 avenue de Verdun, 13340 Rognac

Not the ideal name for a sparkling wine firm perhaps. Grapes
from 200ha (494 acres) of the firm's own Aix-en-Provence
Chardonnay, Ugni Blanc and Mourvèdre are utilized here, plus
the produce of 30ha (74 acres) of Chardonnay bought in from
outside. Production given these quantities of grapes is under-
standably large – some 125,000 cases a year. Automatic *remuage*
helps to oil the wheels. Virant Blanc de Blancs is the big seller but
Rosé d'une Nuit does reasonably well too. La Cuvée de
l'Archeréque, their latest release, is a deluxe sparkling wine made
from 60% Chardonnay and is definitely worth tasting.

### Jean Teysseire                    MC                    ★→
Avenue du 11 novembre, 07130 St-Péray

Jean Teysseire's father was a vine grower in 1899 and the old
traditions are certainly being continued with the next generation.
Monsieur Teysseint only owns 2ha (5 acres) of Roussette and
Marsanne vines himself but his *méthode champenoise* St-Péray Brut
still has its own label.

### Varichon & Clerc                    MC                    ★→★★
Les Séchallets, 01420 Seyssel

Seyssel is another of those odd French regional sparkling
specialities that few outsiders have ever heard of and even fewer
tasted. It comes from mountainous skiing country on the road
between Lyon and Geneva in the Savoie. Tiny amounts are
usually made but this négociant house cleverly has an arrangement with the local producers' *syndicat* to buy their harvest every
year. This way Varichon & Clerc manage to produce a handsome
50,000 cases of their *méthode champenoise* wine annually. Sparkling
Seyssel has a character all of its own due to the blend of local
Savoie grapes – the Roussette (or Altesse) and the Molette. In
addition Varichon & Clerc use Jacquère, Clairette and Chenin
Blanc grapes. Seyssel is still made by the *méthode champenoise* and
hand-riddled. Varichon & Clerc also sell *vins mousseux* from
outside the region without the appellation Seyssel tag at the
bottom of the label. Their Carte Blanche with its elegant, fresh,
flowery style is excellent. Wines with the Seyssel distinction
include Royal Seyssel, Seyssel Brut and Diner's Blanc de Blancs.
A Pétillant de Savoie is also available but not recommended.
Vintage-dated Royal Seyssel is considered to be their best wine.
The firm exports heavily to the USA, Italy and the UK.

### Veuve Ambal                    MC                    ★→
Boîte Postale 1, Rully, 71150 Chagny

Simplicity is everything, it seems, at Veuve Ambal. Unlike other
sparkling wine firms the Veuve Ambal label is attached to only
three different qualities of sparkling wine of which 66,000 cases
are sold. The lowest grade is the *méthode champenoise mousseux* that
comes from outside the region (Brut, Demi-Sec, Rosé Brut and
Demi-Sec). The middle Bourgogne Mousseux range consists of a
Blanc, Rosé and Rouge (all available in Brut, Sec and Demi-Sec).
The top category of the Crémant de Bourgogne range, made
mostly from the Pinot Noir grape plus Chardonnay and a touch
of Aligoté, is the one that will interest most palates. Today
Madame Ambal's grandson runs this firm and his wines are
exported to Belgium, Italy and elsewhere.

### Veuve du Vernay                    CC                         →★
Cie Girondine des Vins Mousseux, 33700 Bordeaux

The name of this sparkling wine sounds as if it could be champagne. Only it isn't. Veuve du Vernay is a simple *cuve close* wine with very successful sales figures; The base wines come from Bordeaux, Loire and Charentes with the latter's Ugni Blanc supplying the lion's share. Veuve is available in Brut, Demi-Sec and Rosé. The sweet pink version is made from the Muscat Alexandria grape grown at Carcassonne near the Mediterranean coast. The Brut has a frothy mousse plus an exotic, almost bananary nose and taste. In France this company sells a sweet, white sparkler called Muscabar plus a sweet Rosé called Rosabel. Paul Bur is an associated champagne house. Veuve du Vernay is exported all over the world.

### Vin Sauvage                       MC                         ★→
Sica Monluc, 32310 St-Puy

This Vin Sauvage comes from deep in the heart of southwest France. Combined with a splash of the local Liqueur à l'Armagnac it makes a drink known as a Pousse Rapière. Blessed with a big, fat fruity character it also happens to be very good on its own. Excellent value for money.

### L. Vitteau Alberti                 MC                       ★→★★
Rue du Pont d'Arrot, Rully, 71150 Chagny

Only 20% of the grapes used in the Vitteau Alberti *méthode champenoise* come from the Vitteau family's vineyards. However the remainder, including Bourgogne Aligoté, Chardonnay, Pinot Noir and Gamay, are a definite quality notch up from the usual. The range includes a *méthode champenoise* Vin Mousseux Blanc de Blancs Brut plus a Crémant de Bourgogne Blanc. Tiny amounts of pink sparklers and a Bourgogne Rouge are also produced. *Remuage* is all by hand. Exports go mainly to the UK, Australia and Belgium. The Vitteaus are proud that several of those ultra-quality-conscious three-star French restaurants, including Taillevent in Paris and their own local Lameloise at Chagny, offer their Crémant de Bourgogne.

## Other French sparkling wine producers:

Achard-Vincent, 26150 Die; Jean Bourdy, Arlay; E. Chevalier & Fils, Charnay-les-Mâcon; A. Clape, St-Péray; Domaines Viticoles des Salins du Midi, Montpellier; Les Maîtres Vignerons de St-Tropez, St-Tropez; A. Monassier, Rully, Chagny; Pierre Sadoux, 24240 Sigoules.

# Spain

Spanish sparkling wines have improved dramatically during the last five years. In the early 1980s most Spanish sparkling wines were clearly identifiable because of their hot, sweet, earthy, peppery style. Today, although a slight sweetness is still detectable due to the ripeness of the grapes, most Spanish *méthode champenoise* or *cava* sparkling wine is fresh, fruity and very easy to drink. Indeed, top producers such as Segura Viudas are making wine that has some of the class and elegance of champagne.

This marked improvement has been due primarily to more advanced winemaking equipment including stainless steel vats, cold fermentation and the latest Willmes or Vaslin presses. Rumasa, the now defunct banking, wine and property group, certainly helped the industry by investing in its own sparkling wine operation at just the right time. And others soon followed. Spain's impressive average annual *cava* production of some 110m bottles could not have been achieved without the *girasol* ("sunflower"). This metal riddling frame containing about 500 bottles enables two men to riddle five times as many bottles in one day as they had been able to do with the old *pupitre* method.

While Spanish winemaking techniques are getting better all the time there are few changes taking place in the vineyards. 99% of Spanish *cava* sparklers come from the Catalonia region in northeast Spain and the three traditional Catalonia grapes, Xarel-lo, Macabeo and Parellada, are still used everywhere. Xarel-lo gives firmness and acidity to the blend, Macabeo supplies the fruit and freshness, leaving the superior Parellada to donate softness plus some fragrance and finesse. However several *cava* houses are experimenting with Chardonnay. This classic variety can now officially be used by *cava* producers and once it starts to appear in commercial blends another dramatic improvement in quality is expected. Many firms are now extending the time their *cava* wines spend on yeast from the minimum of nine months up to five years or more – again this will boost quality.

Within Catalonia southwest of Barcelona is the Penedès region. Here in the cooler, more mountainous Alt Penedès district that fans out from San Sadurní de Noya, dominated by the extraordinary jagged teeth of the Montserrat mountain, the *cava* producers are mostly based. Wine estates have thrived here since the early 16th century and Don José Raventós of Codorníu made the first Spanish *cava* sparkling wine here in 1872. To the north of Penedès is Alella, another *cava* region. Further north still is the Ampurdán-Costa Brava area, centred on Perelada in the Gerona province. Still in Catalonia but west of Barcelona, almost on the border with Aragón is another *cava* producer, Raimat at Lerida. Other Catalonia *cava* regions, to the south in Tarragona, include Alto Campo and Conca de Barberá. Several Rioja bodegas, most notably Muga and Bilbainas, also produce *cava* sparklers as does the odd Navarra producer. Other Spanish producers not necessarily using the *cava* method are dotted throughout the country at places such as Ainzon near Zaragoza and Carinena. There are also *méthode champenoise* producers in Valencia and Extremadura but they can only use the words *metodo tradicional* and not *cava* for their wines.

91% of all sparkling wine produced in Spain is made by the *cava* method or *méthode champenoise*, and although the odd advertisement and truck in Penedès still bears the word *champaña*,

Spain is careful not to use the jealously-guarded French name. Spanish sparkling wine laws and labelling requirements are some of the toughest and most explicit in the world (see page oo). No *cava* house for instance may have any *cuve close*, carbonated or transfer-method equipment on the premises. It therefore seems both shortsighted and unfair for the French and the EEC (backed by Italy, Germany and the UK) to insist that the term *méthode champenoise* can only be used to describe champagne. If this legislation is passed (see page oo) then Spain, as Europe's biggest *méthode champenoise* producer outside France, has the most to lose.

Apart from this difficult EEC question, Spain's sparkling wine industry appears to have few problems. The collapse of the Rumasa group in 1983 created considerable turmoil, but the responsible Freixenet group appears to have absorbed the Rumasa *cava* companies without any hiccups. With Freixenet's overseas interests in Champagne and California, their own *cava* sparklers are bound to improve and with them Spain's. The future looks good.

---

### Spanish Sparkling Labels and the Law

Spain has some of the most helpful, clear and concise sparkling wine label regulations in the world.

● "*Cava*" (the word means "cellar" in Spanish) or the words "*cava tradicional*" denote a wine that must have spent a minimum of nine months in bottle on yeast before being disgorged and re-corked. All *cava* wines must carry the word *cava* on the label and all *cava* corks are printed with this star symbol. ☆

● *Cuve close* or Charmat method sparkling wine is known as *granvas* or *grandes envases* in Spain. By law a minimum of 21 days must elapse between the addition of yeast and the actual bottling process. All *granvas* sparkling wine must have the word "*granvas*" printed on the label and carries this symbol on the cork. ○

● Transfer-method sparklers in Spain are simply described as "*fermentación en botella*" and these words must appear on the label. Like *cava* and *granvas* sparklers these wines are classified as natural sparkling wine or *vino espumoso natural*. The transfer-method process must be allowed to continue for two months before bottling takes place. *Fermentación en botella* sparkling wine carries this symbol on the cork. ▢

● Carbonated wine is denoted by the words "*vino gasificado*" which again must appear on the label. These wines carry a triangle symbol on the cork. △

● In Spain (and throughout this section) expect to see the following Spanish terms: Brut de Brut for a non-*dosage* wine, Brut Natur or Nature for a low- or non-*dosage* wine, Brut for Brut, Seco for Sec, Semi-seco for Demi-Sec, Semi-dulce and Dulce for the sweeter or Doux wines and Rosado for Rosé.

---

Albet i Noya                    MC                                        ★

Can Bendrell, San Pablo de Ordal, Barcelona

Josep M. Albet i Noya started his sparkling wine firm in 1979.

Production, of Brut Nature, Brut, Semi-seco and Rosado, is limited to just over 3,000 cases annually and the grapes (mostly Xarel-lo but with an increasing percentage of Parellada) come entirely from Señor Albet i Noya's own vineyards. The latest introduction is the Rosado made from Tempranillo and Sumoll grapes. Brut Nature is the firm's finest sparkling wine. Encouragingly future releases may well contain a proportion of Chardonnay.

| L'Aixertell | CC | →★ |
|---|---|---|

Paseo del Urumea s/n, 20014 San Sebastian

L'Aixertell are jointly owned by Savin (Spain's vast wine firm with wineries all over the country) and Freixenet, who recently bought the German firm Henkell's holding in this company. L'Aixertell produce 250,000 cases a year of sweet, inexpensive sparkling wine under Brut, Extra and Gran Cremant labels.

| René Barbier | MC | ★→ |
|---|---|---|

PO Box 57, San Sadurní de Noya

Previously part of the Rumasa group and now owned by the giant Freixenet. René Barbier was set up by phylloxera-fleeing Frenchman Léon Barbier in 1880, as were so many Rioja and Penedès wine firms. Leon died in 1934 and his son René took over. Traditionally Barbier has concentrated on table wine but at its impressive, highly-equipped Rumasa-built headquarters, which are shared with Segura Viudas and Conde de Caralt, sparkling wine is now made. Brands include a vintage and non-vintage Brut, Seco, Semi-seco and Rosado.

| Bodegas Bilbainas | MC | ★→ |
|---|---|---|

2, Particular del Norte, Bilbão

This important Rioja house produces two types of sparkling wine: the superior Royal Carlton selection and the cheaper, sweeter and more luridly labelled Lumen range. Viura and a few Malvasia grapes from Bilbainas' own 100ha (247 acres) of vineyards supply the base wine that is turned into 50,000 cases of full-bodied Bilbainas *méthode champenoise* wine every year. Royal Carlton accounts for most of the production, and Brut, Seco and Semi-seco versions of both the Royal Carlton and the Lumen brands are made. Bilbainas' most expensive sparkling wine is Royal Carlton's Brut Nature. Bilbainas are proud to reveal that after the Second World War when many Champagne vineyards had been devastated, a "prestigious Champagne house" fulfilled its orders by buying Bilbainas sparkling wine and selling it under its own label.

| Bolet | MC | ★ |
|---|---|---|

Cal Tessu, Castellvi de la Marca, Barcelona

This small traditional *cava* house produces Semi-seco, Brut and Brut Natural Bolet sparkling wines from the usual Penedès blend of Macabeo, Xarel-lo and Parellada. Lluet Brut and Brut Natural is made by the same house but it spends 2–3 years ageing as opposed to Bolet's 1–2 years.

| Bonaval | MC | ☆ |
|---|---|---|

Crta Santa Marta s/n, Almendralejo

The family firm of Bonaval was founded in 1931, its full title being Industrias Vinicolas del Oeste. The firm's first sparkling wine is due to be released in 1987. The family hope to produce

5,000 bottles of Brut and Seco every year from their 24ha (59 acres) estate. The firm claims to be the first *cava* producer in Extremadura.

| Bordeje | MC | ★ |
|---|---|---|
Carretera Borja, Rueda

Bodegas Bordeje are situated in the mountainous Zaragoza region of Aragón. This family firm own 50ha (123 acres) of vines, half the crop being turned into 10,000 cases of sparkling wine sold under a Brut label. Bordeje are also experimenting with Rosado. The firm ages its sparklers for four years on yeast and claims that it was the first sparkling wine firm in Aragón.

| Canals & Munné | MC | ★ |
|---|---|---|
6 Plaza Pau Casals, San Sadurní de Noya

The small family firm of José Maria Canals Casanovas was founded in 1930, though like many *cava* concerns the estate dates from much earlier – in this case, 1890. No less than nine different Canals & Munné sparkling wines are produced in Seco, Semi-seco and Dulce styles. Choose from Brut Nature, Brut, Rosado, Extra Especial, Extra, Cristal Dore, Gran Cremant, Carta Blanca and Reserva de l'Avi.

| Castellblanch | MC/CC | ★→ |
|---|---|---|
Avenida Casetas Mir, s/n San Sadurní de Noya

Castellblanch was once a Rumasa firm and is now owned by Freixenet. However the wines are made at a different winery from those of Segura Viudas, also owned by Freixenet. Castellblanch was founded by Jerónimo Parera Figueras in 1980. Today its ugly modern winery, although capable of storing and ageing 20m bottles, still has the air of a building site. Castellblanch only produce sparkling wine – almost 1m cases of it every year. Much of this is made from bought-in base wine but Castellblanch also own 200ha (494 acres) of vines. Castellblanch's Brut Zero (complete with red plastic seal) is good although not great, mature, yeasty, slightly dull sparkling wine whereas the Extra Brut has a similarly high alcohol level plus a pleasing, drinkable, citric, lime-juice-like taste. Also in the Castellblanch range are Gran Cremant and Cristal in various degrees of sweetness, plus Rosado, Lustros Brut, Gran Castell and Canals Nubiola. Of them all, Lustros and Gran Castell are reckoned the best.

| Els Castellers | MC | ★ |
|---|---|---|
18–24 Bisbe Morgades, Vilafranca del Penedès

397 members with 600ha (1,482 acres) between them belong to this cooperative, founded in 1933. Only 17,000 cases per annum of sparkling wine are produced here using Brut, Extra, Gran Cremant Brut Natural and Rosat labels.

| Cavas del Ampurdán | CC | →★ |
|---|---|---|
Plaza del Carmen 1, Perelada, Gerona

The sister firm of Cavas del Castillo de Perelada. According to Spanish law however, as it produces still wines and sparklers made by the *cuve close* method, it has to be housed in a different building from Cavas del Castillo, on the other side of the road. Muscantini is Ampurdán's Muscat-based sparkling wine and its Perelada *cuve close* wine is one of Spain's most popular sparklers. Ampurdán, formerly the Costa Brava Wine Co., is a name that the *Champenois* will not forget: this firm was the defendant in the

1960 London court case in which the Spanish lost the right to call their sparkling wine "champagne".

## Cavas del Castillo de Perelada    MC    ★→

P°de San Antonio 1, Perelada, Gerona

North of Barcelona and the Penedès region is the Ampurdán-Costa Brava area whose winemaking activities are centred on Perelada. The celebrated Cavas del Castillo here is definitely worth a detour. Admire the 14th century Castillo and church (with wine cellars below) plus the wine museum, library, glass and ceramic displays and the latest addition – a casino. Unlike other Ampurdán producers Perelada make only sparkling wine. The Castillo's sparklers include Brut Castillo and the well-regarded Gran Claustro that is aged for 5–6 years. The Olivella Reserva range vinified in Penedès but aged in Ampurdán, is slightly less distinguished, but the Olivella Ferrari Brut Reserva has a fresh lime-juice-like nose and a good, clean, fruity, uncomplicated, citrussy palate. The Brut Nature with its flowery nose and pleasant, fruity taste is equally enjoyable.

## Cavas Hill    MC    ★

2 Bonavista, Moja-Olerdola

Cavas Hill obviously believe in catering for each and every whim of their customers, for there are ten different sparklers from which to choose. Mr Hill was an Englishman, as his name suggests, who set up his Moja estate in 1660. A descendant of his built Cavas Hill's impressive underground cellars in 1918. Cavas Hill are fond of describing their sparklers as "masterpieces", which seems a trifle over-enthusiastic as their Gran Sec Brut Blanc de Blancs is a soft, ordinary, rhubarb-redolent sparkling wine and their 81 Brut Brutísimo is raw, green and not very nice at all. Other Cavas Hill sparklers are Brut de Brut (Gran Reserva de Artesania), Sant Manel (Brut, Extra Semi-seco, Extra Seco), Oro Negro, Rosado and Reserva Oro (Semi-seco and Seco).

## Celler Trobat    MC    ★

5 Calle Castello, Garriguella-Girona

Celler Trobat's distinctively bottled sparkling wine hails from the Empordà-Costa Brava region. 20,000 cases of Brut, Seco Extra, Semi-seco and pink Rosat are produced here, but so far they are only available in Spain.

## Paul Cheneau    MC    ★→

Segura Viudas, San Sadurní de Noya

This delightfully inexpensive Spanish sparkler is made at Segura Viudas to leading wine writer and merchant Gerald Asher's own specifications. Mr Asher clearly understands the American palate. This soft, drinkable predominantly Parellada *méthode champenoise* wine, aged for about three years, goes down well both with the public and even competitive California sparkling wine producers. Americans consume an impressive 200,000 cases every year.

## Conde de Caralt    MC    ★

Ctra de San Sadurní a la Llacuna, San Sadurní de Noya

Conde de Caralt wines are made at Segura Viudas's impressive headquarters and like that other ex-Rumasa firm René Barbier, this concern is now owned by the ever-expanding Freixenet group. Like other Penedès wine firms, Conde de Caralt now have a range of table wines in addition to their sparklers. Conde de

Caralt made sparkling wine first, though. The wines are good rather than great. The non-vintage Brut is warm, rich, sunbaked and easy to drink. The 80 Brut Nature is pleasing, intense, biscuity and yeasty, albeit with a strange, sour finish. A numbered Brut Reservada, Blanc de Blancs, Rosado Extra Seco and Extra Semi-seco are also produced here.

| Codorníu | MC | →★ |
|---|---|---|

644 Avenida Gran Via, Barcelona

Visiting Codorníu is an experience, not just for the gardens, lake, ancient oak tree, the century-old house with tower, the museum and bizarre cathedral-like Puig and Cadafalch reception salon (now a national monument), but also for the cellars below. There are 18km (11 miles) of man-made caves on five levels beneath the surface containing 100 million bottles of sparkling wine, which must make Codorníu's cellars among the largest in the world. To become this big takes time and Codorníu dates back to 1551. The year 1872 was an even more auspicious date, perhaps, as that was when Don José Raventós made the first Spanish *méthode champenoise* wine in Codorníu's cellars. Codorníu use the first four gentle pressings of their Penedès grapes, most of which are bought in, with only 25% from their own vineyards. With an annual production of more than 5m cases Codorníu, like their greatest competitor Freixenet, have to use *girasols* to *remuage* their sparkling wine. Unidad 504, the Codorníu variety of *girasols*, look like rocking chairs with 504 bottles of sparkling wine in the "seat". To ensure continuity and to improve quality Codorníu keep back mostly three year old reserve wines for blending, storing them in large stainless steel vats. The basic quality sparkling wines, Première Cuvée and the similar Extra, have a musty nose and dull, yeasty-sulphury taste. Similarly the 80 Gran Codorníu, with five or so years on yeast, is a sour, vaguely biscuity wine. Codorníu's other brands of Non Plus Ultra, Rosado, Gran Cremant and the new Anna de Codorníu could also be better. It is sad to have let quality slip in this way.

| Delapierre | MC | ★ |
|---|---|---|

644 Avenida Gran Via, Barcelona

Delapierre, owned by Codorníu, produce a Blanc de Blancs as well as a partly Chardonnay-based Etiqueta Nera sparkling wine.

| Ferret | MC | ★ |
|---|---|---|

Avgda Cataluña, Guardiola de Font-Rubi

Parellada plays an important part in the manufacture of the sparkling wine produced at this small house. Cavas Ferret make a Semi-seco, Seco, Brut and Brut Nature.

| J. Freixedas | MC | ★→ |
|---|---|---|

87–89 Calvo Sotelo, Vilafranca del Penedès

J. Freixedas, almost 100 years old, is a respected name in the Penedès region. Despite its 69ha (170 acres) San Cugat Sasgarrigues estate, this big producer also buys in grapes. Among their sparklers are Gran Cremant, Gran Brut Nature and the higher-quality Special Reserva Castilla La Torre.

| Freixenet | MC | ★→★★ |
|---|---|---|

PO Box 1, San Sadurní de Noya

*Star buy 81 Brut Nature*

It is difficult to keep up with Freixenet. In 1983 a new winery at

Ezequiel Montes in Mexico was completed. In 1984 they took over the Rumasa sparkling wines (Segura Viudas, Conde de Caralt, Castellblanch, René Barbier and Canals Nubiola). In 1985 they bought the French champagne house Henri Abelé. In 1986 the new Freixenet Gloria Ferrer winery opened in Sonoma, California. The Freixenet group is now one of the biggest sparkling wine producers in Spain and indeed the world, with an annual total production of some 5m cases. This figure puts it alongside its greatest competitor, Codorníu, and dwarfs that of any champagne house. Freixenet, founded after Codorníu in 1889, is still a family firm run by the Ferrers. 100ha (247 acres) supply a tiny percentage of their total needs and their sparkling wine is riddled on *girasols* whose design – a cage of bottles on a pointed octagonal base – differs from that of Codorníu. Freixenet's recently much expanded cellars also look distinctly different to those of Codorníu with the builders barely able to keep up with production in this enormous, dusty, concrete jungle complete with vast, stainless-steel cold-fermentation tanks. Freixenet's most popular sparkling wine is the clean, fruity and acceptable Carta Nevada Brut in its frosted yellow livery. More distinctive still is the black and gold Cordon Negro bottle whose 81 vintage is bland, fruity and a touch raw but nonetheless a reasonable sparkler. The 81 Brut Nature is finer and has a lovely freesia-like bouquet plus a good, clean, flowery taste. Blanc de Blancs (also sold as Extra), Brut Rosé and Brut Barroco are other sparkling wines by Freixenet. The finest of all, made from their best grapes and vinified in wood, is the Cuvée DS, named after courageous Dolores Sala who continued to run Freixenet after her husband (who founded the company) and son had been killed. Donna Sala had a fine palate and created the first vintage, the 69, herself and stipulated exactly what should go into the 77 *cuvée* before she died. This cuvée, with its light, fresh, pineappley nose and hefty palate, is a shade disappointing.

| Gramona | MC | ★→ |
|---|---|---|

Industria 36, San Sadurní de Noya, Barcelona

Another small *cava* firm that produces Brut and Nature sparkling wine. Gramona sparklers spend a considerable length of time ageing on yeast, often as long as 7–8 years.

| Guilera | MC | ★ |
|---|---|---|

Masia Artigas, Lavern-Subirats

This firm produces limited amounts of mostly four-year-old Extra Seco, Extra Semi-seco, Brut and Nature sparklers.

| Juvé y Camps | MC | →★ |
|---|---|---|

14 Apartado de Correos, San Sadurní de Noya

Three different estates with 152ha (375 acres) between them account for about one-third of Juvé y Camps' requirements. The rest of the grapes are supplied by local growers. Annual production is 84,000 cases of Reserva, Reserva de la Familia and fancy-bottled Gran Cru Juvé y Camps Rosada in various styles. Neither the sweet, overblown fruit character of the Reserva Brut, nor the marginally better but raw, beery and astringent 81 Reserva de la Familia are likely to win many fans.

| Lavernoya | MC | ★→ |
|---|---|---|

17 Calle San Pedro, San Sadurní de Noya

This *cava* house is owned by the Raventós Poch family with

estates close to the Lavernó and Noya rivers. Lácrima Baccus is Cavas Lavernoya's brand name and every year up to 84,000 cases of some seven different Lácrima sparklers are made. Lavernoya obviously specialize in inexpensive bulk sales for they do not own any vineyards and most of their sparkling wine is made by the automatic *remuage* method. Lácrima's Brut Nature is disappointing. The Extra Reserve is drinkable but somewhat undistinguished, warm, yeasty and vanilla-like. Other Lácrima sparkling wines include Super Semi-seco, Gran Cremant Seco, Rosado and Primerisimo Grand Cru and Summum, the latter in strange, skittle-shaped bottles.

| Masachs | MC | ★ |
|---|---|---|

20 Calle Poniente, Vilafranca del Penedès

The Masachs family made sparkling wine for themselves and their friends as early as 1920, though commercial production did not begin until 1940. Since then the annual output has increased to 120,000 cases and Masachs are now a limited company. Grapes from their own vineyards currently supply about one-third of the firm's needs but this is likely to be increased soon to 50%. Future production, if the Masach's hopes and predictions are correct, will leap from about 168,000 cases in 1986 to half a million cases by 1992. Whether they will be able to manage quality as well as quantity at their big new plant is a moot point. Still, the raw, yeasty, Masachs Brut and the fresh, young, straightforward, appley Gran Reserva Brut are both currently palatable enough. Other Masachs labels include Nature, Rosé, Semi-seco and Seco versions as well as the cheaper Louis de Vernier sparkling wines which are available in Brut Nature Reserva, Brut, Rosé, Seco and Semi-seco styles.

| Mascaró | MC | ★→ |
|---|---|---|

Casal 9, Vilafranca del Penedès, Barcelona

Antonio Mascaró's small, traditional family firm, founded in 1946, produces some good white and red Penedès still wines besides 34,000 cases of Mascaró sparklers every year. Automatic *remuage* creates a stylish well-made Blanc de Blancs Brut available in Semi-seco and Seco styles, and Mascaró also produce a Reservada Rosé in various styles plus Grand Brut and Natur. They use a high proportion of the Parellada grape in their blends which accounts for their finesse and bouquet, and encouragingly are experimenting with Chardonnay.

| Masia Vallformosa | MC | ★ |
|---|---|---|

Lasala 45, Vilovi del Penedès

Little known outside Spain, Masia Vallformosa sparkling wines are admittedly not really worth writing home about. The Masia Vallformosa Brut with its raw, appley fruit is no more than acceptable and the Brut Nature, with its soft, ripe, slightly earthy fruit, is drinkable but not special.

| Cooperativa de Mollet de Perelada | MC | ★→ |
|---|---|---|

Alt Empordà, Perelada, Gerona

This cooperative with 50ha (123 acres) was founded in 1975 and is associated with the Castillo de Perelada. It has a French-trained winemaker. This expertise shows in the cooperative's well-made sparkler sold under the Rapsodia Brut, Extra Semi-seco and Extra Seco labels. Usually all of the sparkling wines are made from one grape, the Macabeo.

## Mont Marcal                    MC                    ★★ →
### Castellvi de la Marca, Penedès
*Star buy Mont Marcal Brut*

Manuel Sancho y Hijas is the family behind the well-designed
label. Manuel Sancho founded his company in 1975. A decade
later, 42ha (104 acres) of vines produce an impressive annual crop
of 50,000 cases. Happily Mont Marcal sparklers are as impressive
as their sales: the straight Mont Marcal Brut has a lovely fresh,
racy, flowery nose and taste, and only a slight touch of *cava*
earthiness on the finish gives its origins away. The Mont Marcal
Nature, with its aggressively clean, young, yeasty taste will
appeal to low-*dosage* lovers when drunk young, but other palates
will want to give it more time. Mont Marcal also produce Semi-
seco, Seco and Gran Reserva wines. The most exciting develop-
ments here are experiments with Chardonnay. The 1984 base
wine is of 30% Chardonnay. We can thus expect even more
distinguished Mont Marcal sparklers in a few years' time.

## Mestres                    MC                    ★★ → ★★★
### 8 Plaza del Ayuntamiento, San Sadurní de Noya
*Star buy 1312 Brut*

Mestres is one of the most historic *cava* houses: the Antonio
Mestres Sagués house and vineyards date from 1312; some even
say from 1243. Sparkling wine, however, was not produced here
until 1928. Today 80ha (198 acres) of vines produce almost all the
grapes needed to create the 10,000 cases of sparkling wine,
production of which is increasing at the rate of 800 cases a year.
Methods are traditional: all the sparklers are aged for at least three
years, with the Clos Nostre Senyor and Clos Damiana enjoying
five years in the cellar, and the Mas-Via a lengthy seven-year
spell. Mestres' winemaker is keen on making 90 different *cuvées*
every year to give him the blending tools he requires, and many
different young blends are sold to Spain's top restaurants every
year under the new Los Cupages de Mestres label. Such detail and
care certainly pays off, for the 1312 Brut with its deep gold colour
and big, mature, toasty-biscuity, yeast-influenced character is a
beautifully made three-star wine. Other sparkling wines produced by Mestres include Coquet Brut, Brut Nature and Rosado
Brut Nature.

## Marqués de Monistrol                    MC                    → ★
### P. Esglesia s.n., Monistrol de Noya

Recently bought out by Martini & Rossi, Marqués de Monistrol
own 300ha (740 acres) of vines and make a wide range of
sparklers. Monistrol styles include Extra and Gran Cremant,
Brut, Rosado, Reserva Gran Coupage, Brut Selección, Brut
Nature and Brut Gran Tradición. The straight Monistrol non-
vintage is an acceptable if soft and bland wine. The 79 Monistrol
Brut Nature is not a success.

## Muga                    MC                    ★ →
### Barrio de la Estación, Haro

This well-known but small family bodega has one of the best
reputations in Rioja. Just 4,000 cases are made annually of their
vintage-dated Conde de Haro (previously sold under the curious
name Mugamart) in both Brut Nature and Brut versions. The
non-*dosage* Brut Nature accounts for most of Muga's production
and this firm uses just one grape, the Viura, for its sparklers.

## Nadal                    MC                                →★
El Pla del Penedès (Barcelona)

The Nadal family estate dates back to 1510 but Cavas Nadal was
founded by Ramón Nadal Giró in 1945. Today he is one of the
very few *cava* producers whose own grapes supply all their needs.
With 100ha (247 acres), production could be increased by 40%
before grapes would need to be bought in. Due to public demand
Nadal sparkling wine has become noticeably drier recently.
Despite this, neither the current bottlings of the Nadal Brut, nor
the premium 80 Brut Especial, are particularly enjoyable.

## Parés Baltà                                            ★→★★
Afueras s/n, Pacs del Penedès
*Star buy Brut Nature Privée Cuvée*

Parés Baltà is not a name that even the most dedicated *cava* drinker
comes across regularly. A pity, for although the Brut de Pacs,
Cuvée Privée is not special, with slight, raw fruit and a dull finish,
the Brut Nature Privée Cuvée is a two-star delight with its clean,
refined, flowery bouquet backed up by an elegant, flowery taste
and finish. Worth seeking out.

## Parxet                   MC                             ★→★★
38 Torrente, Tiana

Cavas Parxet was founded in 1918 by the Suñol family at Tiana
just to the northeast of Barcelona. Just over 40,000 cases are
produced annually here of five different *méthode champenoise*
Parxet sparklers. Most of these are drunk in Spain but exports go
to Italy, America, and the UK. Parxet's production is mostly
divided between the gold-label raw, musty, almost rosehip-like
Reserva Brut and the infinitely better black label Brut Nature
which also has a curious, though pleasing flowery, rosehip-like
flavour. Seco, Semi-seco and Rosé sparklers are also made. Parxet
sparkling wine does not carry vintage dates.

## Jean Perico                MC                            ★→
C. Can Ferrer del Mas, San Sadurní de Noya

Jean Perico's label has Gonzalez y Dubosc firmly stamped at the
bottom (a *sous-marque* of Gonzalez Byass, the sherry people) but
this sparkling wine is actually made by Segura Viudas. Its greeny-
gold, full-flavoured, pleasant style does well in blind tastings.

## Raimat                    MC                             ★→
Raimat, Lérida

Now owned by Codorníu, Raimat is situated at Lérida way
inland from Barcelona, almost on the border of Aragón. Here
Manuel Raventós from Codorníu has revamped an old operation
and set up a spectacular new winery with high-tech equipment
and extensive new vineyards surrounding the Castle of Raimat.
Raimat have been making sparklers since 1930 and today they are
sold under the Carta Dorada and Rondel labels. Their premium
*cuvée* Rondel Gran Brut spends 5–6 years on yeast. Annual
production is 1.5m cases, making Rondel Spain's third largest
sparkling wine producer after Codorníu and Freixenet.

## Recaredo                  MC                             ★
Tamarit 7, San Sadurní de Noya

This house, founded in 1924, specializes in the driest of styles
which it sells under Brut de Brut and Brut Nature labels.

| Rovellats | MC | ★ |
| --- | --- | --- |

La Bleda, Sant Marti Sarroca

Rovellats own 210ha (519 acres) of vines and their annual
production is almost 42,000 cases. With 3–4 years of ageing on
yeast, the aim is a traditional high-quality sparkling wine.
Unfortunately, Rovellats still have some way to go before they
achieve their aim. The Brut Natural Gran Reserva is soft, almost
rhubarb-like and the superior Grand Cru Brut, Gran Reserva
Masia s.XV, has a pleasant but bland and vaguely fruity flavour.

| Segura Viudas | MC | ★★★ |
| --- | --- | --- |

Ctra de San Sadurní a la Llacuna, San Sadurní de Noya

*Star buys Blanc de Blancs non-vintage Brut, 1978 Brut*

Segura Viudas was founded in 1954 when Señor Segura Viudas
planted the first 110ha (271 acres). The old Segura Viudas house
with the magnificent Montserrat mountain behind it soon had a
modern, handsomely-designed winery tacked onto it by
Rumasa. Now owned by Freixenet, Segura Viudas make
sparkling wine for sister firms René Barbier and Conde de Caralt
plus Gonzalez Byass's Jean Perico and Gerald Asher's Paul
Cheneau. Wisely, Segura Viudas has learnt to keep the best for
itself, for grapes as well as finished base wine are received here to
be turned into sparkling wine by obviously well-trained
winemakers. Visitors to Segura Viudas's five levels of subterra-
nean cellars will note that virtually all of this firm's production is
racked by hand. Segura's three-star sparkling wine represents
some of the finest, cheapest and most delicious drinking in Europe
at the moment. The Blanc de Blancs non-vintage Brut is big, rich
and biscuity and the truly superb 78 Brut is deep, rich and intense
– a wine of real distinction and class. Segura sparklers spend
between 2–6 years on yeast and the firm feels that part of their
style stems from this along with their specially-chosen yeast. Also
in the range are a Seco, Semi-seco and Rosado and the premium
Reserva Heredad in its bizarre pot-bellied, encrusted, bottle.

| Torre Oria | MC | ★ |
| --- | --- | --- |

Pequena, Valencia

This 110ha (271 acres) strong cooperative owned by six families
was founded in 1977. The cooperative's own grapes supply most
of its needs and current production at the modern *bodega* is almost
30,000 cases of Semi-seco, Brut, Nature and a popular Rosé made
from the red Bobal grape.

# Other Spanish
# sparkling wine producers:

Cavas Blancher, San Sadurní de Noya; Canals y Nubiola, San
Sadurní de Noya; C. Colomer Bernat, San Sadurní de Noya;
Jaime Serra, Alella; J. Llopart, San Sadurní de Noya; Taraga
Lopez, Vallbona d'Anoia.

# Portugal

Wine has been made for 5,000 years on the northwest Iberian peninsular, but Portugal has only been making sparkling wine commercially for just over a century. Her *méthode champenoise* wines are not on a par with those of neighbouring Spain despite similarities in climate and grape variety. This discrepancy in quality is largely due to Portugal's lack of modern sparkling wine technology and equipment. Most firms use the *méthode champenoise* for want of an alternative: automatic *remuage* and cold-fermentation tanks (necessary given Portugal's high temperatures at vintage time) are relatively rare.

The majority of Portugal's sparkling wines are produced in the Bairrada – a demarcated region that lies to the north of Coimbra, roughly half-way between Lisbon and Oporto. Most Bairrada producers buy in wines to turn into sparklers (another reason for the quality shortfall, perhaps?). The Maria Gomes is the chief grape, followed by the Bical, Rabo de Ovelha and to a lesser extent the Arinto, Sercial and Sercialinho. Encouragingly, plantings of Bairrada Chardonnay appear to be on the increase. The Lamego region, planted with some Chardonnay and Pinot Noir, also produces sparkling wine, as do other areas occasionally. It is difficult to obtain a wide range of Portuguese sparklers anywhere else in the world. Exceptions are Brazil, Angola, Mozambique and other African nations that have historical trade connections with Portugal.

---

### Portuguese Sparkling Labels and the Law

● *"Método Champanhês"* is Portuguese for *méthode champenoise* and any sparkler with these words on the label has indeed been made by the classic champagne method. Similarly, labels printed with "champagne method" or "fermented in *this* bottle" are also true *méthode champenoise* wines.

● Beware of *"Espumante Natural"* on a label for it is a general term that can be attached to any sparkling wine except those sparklers that are made by the carbonated method.

● *"Fermentação em Cuba Fechada"* indicates a sparkler made by the *cuve close* or tank method.

● *"Espumante Método Continuo"* is a legally-approved Portuguese wine term used by Lancers to indicate that their wines are made by the continuous flow method.

● In Portugal (and throughout this section) the following terms are used, listed here with their more familiar French equivalent: Bruto for Brut, Seco for Sec, Meio Seco for Demi-Sec and Doce for Doux.

---

| Aliança | MC | ★→ |
|---|---|---|
| Apartado 6, Sangalhos, Anadia | | |

Unlike most Bairrada firms, Aliança, founded in 1920, has planted Chardonnay alongside its Bical and Maria Gomes, the more usual grape varieties of the region. The firm's own grapes supply only a quarter of this company's sparkling wine requirements and the rest are bought in. Aliança's deliberate change of style a few years ago and their 1986 installation of a new cold-fermentation unit are significant efforts aimed at producing high quality *méthode champenoise* wines – not an easy thing to do in Portugal. 50,000 cases of five different sparklers are sold annually under the Danúbio, Super Reserva, Extra Reserva, Rosé and Tinto Brut (a red sparkler) labels. Extra Reserva is their best wine.

| Barrocão | MC | ★ |
|---|---|---|
Fogueira, Anadia

The large Caves do Barrocão are still family-run and, like most Bairrada producers, use the *méthode champenoise* to make their sparkling wines, the most popular brand of which is Diamante Azul. This goes down well on the home market, accounting for 8% of the total domestic sparkling wine sales, and some is exported. Barrocão also make a pink and red (Tinto) sparkler by the traditional method.

| Borges & Irmão | MC | ★ |
|---|---|---|
796 Avenida da Republica, 4400 Vila Nova de Gaia

Borges are better known for their Gatão Vinho Verde than for their sparkling wines. However, their reasonable, yeasty-fruity *méthode champenoise* Fita Azul sells well in Portugal and in Brazil and the other traditional Portuguese export markets.

| Borlido | MC | ★ |
|---|---|---|
Sangalhos, Anadia

Founded in 1930 by the Borlido family, Caves Borlido make three different sparklers in both Bruto and Meio Seco styles: Borlido, Borlido Reserva and the best of the bunch – Borlido Extra Reserva. The traditional Bairrada grapes, Maria Gomes and Bical, are used. Most of the production is sold in Portugal.

| Caves Monte Crasto | MC | ★→ |
|---|---|---|
Justino de Sampaio Alegre Filho, 3780 Anadia

Justino de Sampaio Alegre Filho are the producers of this sparkling wine and, like many other Portuguese sparkling wine houses, they also produce a wide range of table wines and brandies. Second only to Raposeira in terms of home sales, Monte Crasto has cornered 9% of the total domestic sparkling wine market. Made from the usual Bairrada blend, an aged bottle of Monte Crasto's Paris 1900 Brut, despite its lurid, multi-coloured livery, had a pleasing mature, buttery, burnt-caramel nose and taste – a good advertisement for the rest of the range.

| Conselheiro | MC | ★ |
|---|---|---|
Aguága de Baixo, 3750 Aguéda

Caves Primavera's unexciting trio of sweet, medium-dry and Brut sparklers is unlikely to impress any international palates. Of the three the Brut is the best – remarkable for its pale golden colour, its curiously rich, over-ripe, almost cologne-like smell and taste and its aggressive finish. Caves Primavera also produce a Célebre Data Brut which is uninspiring.

| Império | MC | ★ |
|---|---|---|
Sangalhos, 3783 Anadia

Founded in 1942 by five families (and joined in 1945 by one more), Caves Império first made sparkling wine in 1943. Today they make a wide range of wines and brandies with at least five different sparklers, mainly in the Meio Seco category. Distinguishing the Extra from the Super, the Império from the Principe Real and Principe Perfeito can be testing as all are *méthode champenoise* wines made from the usual Bairrada mix of Bical, Maria Gomes, Sercial and even the Arinto grape. All five come in a variety of styles from Bruto to Meio Seco and there is a Rosé version of Principe Real and Império. The Extra Reserva followed by the Super Reserva are Império's best. The Principe Real Brut, a lesser wine, is much fancied by locals.

| João Pato | MC | ★→ |
|---|---|---|
| Amoreira de Gandara, 3780 Anadia | | |

In addition to being the Bairrada region's only sparkling wine operation, João Pato produce a range of table wines and brandies. Although this family-owned firm has been making wine for more than two centuries at its Quinta do Ribeirinho estate (the house is depicted on the sparkling wine label), it has only been producing sparklers since 1982. The distinctly Portuguese Maria Gomes, Sercial, Bical and Sercialinho grapes provide the base wine for their annual 7,000 cases of vintage-dated Bruto and Meio-Seco sparklers, with future production likely to contain increased proportions of Sercialinho. Currently, their greeny-gold João Pato Brut is a drinkable, ripe, fruity wine with a slightly bitter finish. Portugal takes most of Pato's sparkling wine but a little is exported to Great Britain.

| José Marques Agostinho | CC | →★ |
|---|---|---|
| 2331 Entroncamento | | |

Senhor Agostinho founded this firm in the Ribatejo region of Portugal in 1900 and today it is still a family company, owned by five female descendants. With such a mouthful of a name the family has wisely decided to adopt the rather more manageable brand names of Famoso, Conde d'Arcos and Magos. All three wines are made by the *cuve close* method and these inexpensive sparklers are mainly sold as Meio Seco wines.

| Lancers | CM | →★ |
|---|---|---|
| Vila Nogueira de Azeitão, 2925 Azeitão | | |

Lancers is a famous brand name in America but is not as well-known elsewhere. Heublein, together with their Portuguese partners, J. M. da Fonseca, are the driving forces behind this big brand and the sales of their sparkling non-vintage Lancers Brut and Lancers Extra Dry add up to 150,000 cases annually. This market success is due in part to Lancers' continuous method unit, installed in 1984 (bought from Seitz in Germany and modelled on a Russian original) which facilitates high-volume production. The ingenious process enables Lancers to pour their base wine continuously into the first tank of a multi-tank unit and 30 days later to remove the sparkling wine from the final tank, ready for immediate bottling and shipping. Quality, alas, does not go hand-in-hand with such technology and winelovers are unlikely to rave about these sweet sparklers. The base wine is made from local decolourized black Periquita grapes – fine for producing red wine but lacking sufficient character to make good sparkling wine.

| Messias | MC | ★ |
|---|---|---|
| 796 Avenida Marechal Carmona, Mealhada | | |

This traditional Portuguese house, based in the heart of the

Bairrada region, has a 3% share of the domestic sparkling wine market and also exports to Portugal's longstanding trade partners in Africa. Messias produce a curious cologne-like Bruto.

| Montanha | MC | ★ |
|---|---|---|
| 14 Rua Adriano Henriques, 3781 Anadia | | |

Montanha is the winner of gold medals in places such as Bucharest and Bratislava. Caves da Montanha buy in wine every year from the same Bairrada farmers. Most of these base wines are made from that familiar Bairrada blend of grapes – mainly Maria Gomes with a little Bical and Rabo de Ovelha. Five different sparklers are available; the firm considers the Montanha Real and the gaudily-labelled A. Henriques in Bruto, Seco and Meio Seco versions their best. They also make a Super Reserva, a Reserva and a straight Montanha. Montanha Real Brut's lively, fresh, fruity green nose shows initial promise but the wine has a disappointingly harsh and rubbery finish. Montanha are likely to launch a new sparkling wine sometime in 1987.

| Raposeira | MC | ★→★★ |
|---|---|---|
| 5100 Lamego | | |

Lamego at the entrance to the hot Douro region across the river from Regua is the rather unlikely site of the largest Portuguese sparkling wine producer. Yet, in cellars hewn out of the hillside, 600 metres (2,000 feet) above sea-level, this new Seagram-owned firm produces Portugal's finest sparkler – the vintage-dated Velha Reserva Brut. Raposeira specialize in sparkling wines and all are made by the *méthode champenoise*, but Velha Reserva stands out with its classy 50/50 blend of Chardonnay and Pinot Noir. Certainly the 78 Velha Reserva had an almost champagne-like rich, biscuity nose, let down by a less inspiring sulphury palate. Raposeira annually produce about 166,000 cases of sparkling wine, made from mostly bought-in grapes such as Malvasia and Sercial as well as Pinot Noir and Chardonnay. The fresh, yeasty Super Reserva and Super Reserva Rosé, in Brut through to the sweet versions, contain some Pinot Noir and Chardonnay in their mix, and are next in quality to the Velha Reserva. Next comes the Reserva range which, as the firm's cheapest sparkler, accounts for the vast majority of sales. In addition to home sales, Raposeira also export to Venezuela, Brazil and Angola.

| Real Companhía Vinícola do Norte de Portugal | MC | ★ |
|---|---|---|
| 314, Rua Azevedo Maglhaes, Vila Nova de Gaia | | |

Now owned by mysterious Portuguese dynamo Senhor da Silva Reis, Real Vinícola, as they are known for short, produce a vast range of table wines, brandies and ports. Their sparklers have 6% of the local market and are exported, in the main to France.

| São Domingos | MC | ★→ |
|---|---|---|
| Caves do Solar, Ferreiros, Anadia | | |

Yet another Bairrada sparkling wine, this time from Caves do Solar who make a wide range of table wines as well as São Domingos, their sparkling wine. Unlike some other Bairrada sparklers however, the São Domingos wines are in the main clean, lively and well-balanced. The pale golden, straight Meio-Seco (half dry for once, instead of half sweet) is surprisingly the best in the range with a bland, fruity nose followed by a pleasingly clean, flowery, fruity palate. The Extra Reserva Brut by comparison has a deeper greeny-gold colour, a mature vanilla yeast-influenced bouquet – but a disappointing palate. Rosé fans may not necessarily enjoy the exotic Grande Reserva Rosé with its pale colour and slightly artificial strawberry flavour. Nevertheless, São Domingos is one of the better Portuguese sparkling wines.

## Other Portuguese
## sparkling wine producers:

C. da Silva, Vila Nova de Gaia; Caves Neto Costa, Anadia; Caves del Rei, Anadia; Caves São João, Anadia; Ferreira & Santiago, Anadia; Quinta de San Miguel, Mealhada; Sociedade Vinhos Irmãos Unidos, Anadia; Vinicola Castelar, Anadia.

# Italy

Tasting all the Italian *spumanti* could take a lifetime, perhaps even two, for there can be few Italian winemakers who do not produce a sparkling wine. Foreigners note with envy that in addition to drinking some 185m bottles of their own sparkling wines annually (an increase since 1979 of more than 40%) Italians are also keen consumers of French champagne. During the past decade Italy has been the leading champagne drinking country for four years out of ten. Italy is clearly *spumante* crazy.

The sweet, grapey Asti Spumante can be found worldwide; it accounts for just over half the sparkling wine production. But the finest Italian sparklers can be very elusive: outside Italy only a few specialist Italian wine merchants and restaurants sell them.

The *spumanti* hunt is a worthwhile one, however, for the quality of these sparkling wines has much improved during the past five years or so. While the sweet and somewhat simple delights of Asti Spumante may not suit everyone, the drier wines are often as good as much that France can produce. This is a tremendous achievement given Italy's considerably hotter climate. Admittedly about 88% of the sparkling wine is made by the *cuve close* method.

Most of Italy's finest sparkling wines are produced in the most northerly regions of Piedmont, Lombardy, Trentino-Alto Adige and Veneto. Piedmont accounts for the majority. Within this region's borders lies the Asti Spumante zone with Canelli at its centre plus its southwesterly offshoot of Serralunga d'Alba. Also made here are the low-alcohol, often slightly sparkling, enchantingly fresh and grapey Moscato d'Asti or Moscato d'Asti Naturale. Lombardy, Piedmont's next door neighbour, has two sparkling wine areas, the Oltrepò Pavese zone in its southwest corner and Franciacorta in the centre, close to Lake Iseo. Italy's increasingly fashionable Trentino-Alto Adige region, cool and mountainous, produces some impressive sparklers as does the Veneto's aromatic Prosecco grape grown between Valdobbiadene and Conegliano north of the Piave river.

The sparklers produced in these four regions can conveniently be divided into five different taste groups. The most important in terms of quality are the *méthode champenoise* Pinot-based wines made in Serralunga d'Alba, Franciacorta, Oltrepò Pavese and throughout the Trentino-Alto Adige region. Pinot-based could mean any one of the Pinot Nero (Pinot Noir), Pinot Bianco (Pinot Blanc) plus Chardonnay and Pinot Grigio (Pinot Gris). Expect these sparklers to range in flavour, just as they do in France, from the fresh, young, fruity and pineapple-like Pinot Bianco and Chardonnay-dominated wines through to the biscuity, full-bodied and mature Pinot Nero styles.

Many of these Pinot sparklers are produced by members of the Istituto Spumante Classico Italiano founded in 1975. Istituto sparklers are well worth seeking out for they must be made from at least 80% Pinot-family grapes and have been produced via the *méthode champenoise*. In addition non-vintage Istituto sparkling wine will have been aged for two years after the harvest of which 10 months will have been spent on yeast. Vintage Istituto *spumante* is made to even more quality-conscious regulations: the wines age for 28 months, with at least 18 months on yeast.

The most popular Italian sparkler, and probably the country's most famous wine, is the sweet, grapey and gulpable Asti

Spumante. All Asti boasts the unmistakable seductive, musky fragrance of the Moscato grape. In the early days when the *méthode champenoise* was the only system the Italians had of putting bubbles into a wine, preserving the Moscato's distinctive character was difficult. Today all Asti Spumante is made via the *cuve close* system. The slow cool fermentation is arrested early on before all of the natural sugar in the grape has been turned into alcohol, which accounts for both its low alcohol content and luscious, grapey freshness.

The third group consists of Moscato d'Asti or Moscato d'Asti Naturale. It is in fact the base wine for Asti and is mouthwateringly fresh and fruity with all the youthful charm of the Moscato grape at its very best. It usually acquires its sparkle from a light secondary fermentation in bottle. Asti lovers who like to watch their alcohol intake will be glad to know that Moscato d'Asti is often as low as 5% alcohol.

The fourth category is the Prosecco-based range of wines made from the grape of the same name. This traditional Italian variety is grown chiefly in northern Veneto in the province of Treviso and to a lesser extent it is also grown in Trentino-Alto Adige and Friuli Venezia Giulia. Its strong, aromatic, tutti-frutti quality will not be appreciated by everyone. However it makes good sparkling wine, mostly via the *cuve close* in this part of Italy. Originally the *méthode champenoise* was used.

The fifth category will usually be encountered only in Italy. These sparkling wines are made all over the country from any of Italy's hundreds of grape varieties. Many of them will have been made by small producers who will have simply turned part of their white grape production into sparkling wine. Discovering a good one has increased the enjoyment of many an Italian holiday.

Modern Italian winemakers are fond of describing their exciting new wave of good quality wines as the renaissance of Italian wine. Certainly a renaissance has taken place with *spumanti*.

---

### Italian Sparkling Labels and the Law

● Most Italian sparkling wine is made by the *cuve close* or Charmat method. However, *cuve close* bottles will not usually have these words on the label. Occasionally *cuve close* wines carry the words "*fermentazione naturale*" or "*metodo charmat*". The production time for *cuve close* sparklers including ageing must not be less than six months.

● True *méthode champenoise* wines are denoted by the words "*metodo champenois*", "*metodo classico champenois*", "*champenois d'Italia*" and "*méthode champenoise*". The production time for *méthode champenoise* wines including ageing must not be less than nine months.

● Artificially carbonated wines will carry the words "*vino addizionato di anidride carbonica*" clearly on the label. Carbonated wines cannot be produced or even stored on the same premises as *cuve close* or *méthode champenoise* wines.

● Sweetness levels range from Extra Brut, the driest, followed by Brut, Extra Dry, Secco (or Sec), Abboccato (or Demi-Sec) to the sweetest, Dolce (or Doux).

## Marchese Antinori    MC    ★→

Palazzo Antinori, 3 Piazza Antinori, 50100 Firenze

The current generation of Antinori's, Marchese Piero Antinori and his brother Lodovico, are the heirs of 600 years of winemaking and are obviously every bit as capable as their ancestors. They may well be rather more interested in producing great red wines, but this does not stop them from making a good *méthode champenoise* Brut Nature. This wine is made from a blend of Pinot Noir and Chardonnay grapes from Lombardy. The first fermentation takes place in stainless steel and the second fermentation and ageing on yeast extends over a 20-month period. The result is a pleasant, warm, fruity sparkling wine.

## Arunda    MC    ★

1–39010 Mölten, Alto Adige

This firm produces two *méthode champenoise* sparklers, the non-*dosage* Extra Brut and Brut. The grapes are mostly Chardonnay, Pinot Blanc and Pinot Noir grown on hillside vineyards around Terlan and Girlan in the South Tyrol and vinified in what Arunda claim is the highest winery in Europe, if not the world, at 1,150 metres (3,772 feet). Both types are matured for two years in bottle. The Extra Brut is excessively green and herbaceous.

## Villa Banfi    CC/MC    ★→★★

Montalcino, 53024 Siena

*Star buy Brut Pinot Oltrepò Pavese*

Villa Banfi must represent the international blueprint for what every winemaker would like to own if only they had the capital: 2,874ha (7,100 acres) of fine Montalcino land, a vast, computerized, high-tech winery, enormous cellars and the handsome Castello Banfi dating back to 800AD. Riunite lambrusco provided the wherewithal for all this and Banfi's clever winemaker Dr Ezio Rivella has certainly made the most of the opportunity. Banfi sparklers include Riunite Spumante, (Sauvignon- and Sémillon-based) the red Brachetto d'Acqui Asti Banfi and the excellent, big, biscuity, aged Brut Pinot Oltrepò Pavese (Pinot Noir and Chardonnay-based). Banfi's *méthode champenoise* Brut is their best sparkler made from Chardonnay and Pinot Noir grapes plus a little Pinot Bianco. Its tinny, metallic taste will not appeal to everyone, however.

## Barbero    CC/MC    ★

Frazione Valpone, 12043 Canale

The six Barbero brothers all work for the family firm, which must make it rather confusing for the staff. Everyone, however, is kept busy here, making 700,000 cases annually of sparkling wine which is sold under nine different labels. Barbero Asti Spumante accounts for most of this, but the multi-variety Conte di Cavour also sells well as does the Moscato Spumante. The sweet Barbero Gran Dessert is the next best seller, followed by the Pinot Crémant, Chardonnay and the medium-dry Prosecco made from the grape of the same name. Much smaller quantities are made of Pinot Brut Rosé, and Barbero's best sparkler, the vintage-dated *méthode champenoise* Stefano Barbero.

## Cantine Bava    CC/MC    ★

Borgo Stazione, 14023 Cocconato d'Asti

For three generations the Bava family have been making

sparkling wine at this *cantine*, or cellar, situated halfway between Montferrato and Asti. All their sparkling wine grapes are bought in from local farmers and are turned into Asti Spumante, a Malvasia di Castelnuovo don Bosco Rosé and the superior *méthode champenoise* Brut Cà Traversa. The Bava family also own the major part of Giulio Cocchi *spumante*, founded in 1891 and which they claim is the oldest *spumante* house in Asti.

| Berlucchi | MC | ★→ |
|---|---|---|

4 Via Don Secondo Duranti, 25040 Borgonato

Most unusually this young firm founded in 1966 by Guido Berlucchi only produces sparklers via the *méthode champenoise*. With the help of Franco Ziliani, fresh from the oenology school at Alba, today Berlucchi's impressive old cellars beneath the Castello di Borgonato produce 250,000 cases of sparkling wine a year, making the firm the leading Italian *méthode champenoise* producer. Chardonnay and its distant relative Pinot Bianco, plus Pinot Nero and, intriguingly, Pinot Meunier are the grapes used. The sweet, peppery Cuvée Imperiale Brut is Berlucchi's most popular sparkler, made from a blend of all the grapes. It also comes in a non-*dosage* or *Pas Dosé* version, which was previously sold as "*dosage pas opéré*". A gently sparkling *crémant*, the Cuvée Imperiale Grand Crémant, is also made here as is the Cuvée Imperiale Max Rosé, a Pinot Nero-dominant rosé. In great years such as 1981 a vintage-dated Cuvée Imperiale Millesimata Brut, aged for three years on yeast, is also produced.

| Bisol | MC | ★ |
|---|---|---|

31040 Santo Stefano di Valdobbiadene

Eliseo Bisol's wine estate and distillery was destroyed in the First World War. His son Desiderio started the business again after the War, buying up vineyard land at Cartizze and Fol in the heart of the Prosecco region. Today the Bisol family produce mainly Brut Nature and Brut Riserva from Chardonnay, Pinot Blanc and Pinot Noir. Some Bisol Rosé is also produced from Pinot Noir grapes. The Bisol Brut Riserva is their best wine.

| Bonardi | CC | ★ |
|---|---|---|

57 Corso Piave, Alba

This small Asti Spumante house produces only Asti, made of course from the Moscato d'Asti grape. 20,000 cases of this sweet, grapey sparkling wine are produced here every year and a little is exported to the UK and France. A trial batch of a drier Gran Spumante Secco has also been made recently.

| Luigi Bosca & Figli | CC/MC | ★→ |
|---|---|---|

2 Via L. Bosca, 14053 Canelli

The Bosca family have owned this firm since they founded it in 1831. Apart from a classical Asti Spumante, Luigi & Figli make a finer *méthode champenoise* Brut Nature and Riserva del Nonno.

| Braida | CC | ★→ |
|---|---|---|

Rocchetta Tanaro, 14030 Asti

Giacomo Bologna is Braida's clever winemaker. Many regard his Moscato d'Asti as the quintessence of this sparkler.

| Bruzzone | CC/MC | ★→ |
|---|---|---|

22 Via Vittorio Veneto, 15019 Stevi

Bruzzone are connected with Villa Banfi and also share their

capable winemaker, Dr Ezio Rivella. Sparkling wine production
here consists of Asti Spumante, the red Brachetto d'Acqui and a
*méthode champenoise spumante* of which just 4,000 cases are made
annually. Some of these come from Bruzzone's own 40ha (100
acres) of vines and the rest are made from bought-in grapes.

## Ca' del Bosco    MC    ★→★★
11 Via Case Sparse, 25030 Erbusco

Ca' del Bosco, situated in Lombardy's Franciacorta region, rate
themselves as the most highly-respected of Italian *spumanti classici*
and it would be hard to disagree. Their prices are outrageous –
about the same as French champagne. But Maurizio Zanella is a
perfectionist and the combination of his Moët & Chandon-
trained winemaker plus a vast, no-expense-spared, custom-built,
temperature-controlled winery and deep underground cellars is
formidable. Such attention to detail does not come cheap and
perhaps the eventual Ca' del Bosco bottle price is justified. The
34ha (86 acres) of vineyards supply almost all their needs and are
mostly planted to Chardonnay, Pinot Bianco and Pinot Nero.
They buy in an additional 10ha (26 acres) planted to Pinot Bianco.
The Ca' del Bosco *cuvées* contain 15% of older barrel-aged wines,
gentle basket presses are used, and all the wines are aged for three
years prior to sale. Despite all this, perhaps the most impressive
fact about Ca' del Bosco is that the grapes are processed within 30
minutes of being picked. Current production is only 14,000 cases,
mostly the white grape-dominated Dosage Zero and Brut, which
is big, yeasty, full-bodied and redolent of champagne. The *pelure
d'oignon*-coloured Rosé, which is from Pinot Nero, has a yeasty,
fruity character. It is made in small quantities, as is the Crémant.
Just 416 cases of Ca' del Bosco's best sparkling wine, a vintage-
dated Millesimato, are also produced.

## Luigi Calissano    CC/MC    ★→
Alba, 12051 Cuneo

Just over 4,000 cases of both *méthode champenoise* and Charmat-
method sparkling wines are made here annually. Pinot Brut is the
tank-method sparkler and the Duca d'Alba Brut and Real Brut
are the two *méthode champenoise* wines.

## Cantina Sociale di Canelli    CC    ★
12 Via Loazzolo, 14053 Canelli

This cooperative celebrated its 50th anniversary a few years ago.
It has 400 members with 500ha (1,235 acres) between them,
planted mostly to Moscato d'Asti but with a little Brachetto.
125,000 cases of sparkling wine are produced here every year,
mostly of the Cantina's Asti. Moscato Piemonte Spumante and
Gran Spumante Riserva Brut (with Riesling and Pinot as the base)
are also made from the grape of the same name.

## Carpenè Malvolti    MC/CC
1 Via a Carpenè, 31015 Conegliano

Antonio Carpenè, who founded this firm in 1868, was one of the
first to bring the *méthode champenoise* to Italy. Today Carpenè Malvolti use Pinot Noir, Pinot Blanc and Chardonnay grapes grown
in the Alto Adige to make Malvolti Brut and Brut de Brut.

## Càvit    CC/MC    ★→
31 Via del Ponte, 38100 Trento

This important group of cooperatives is one of the largest in the

Alto Adige. It consists of 15 different cooperatives scattered throughout the region with some 4,500 members. The emphasis here is therefore on quantity (some 125,000 cases of sparkling wine are produced per annum) but the quality is better than one might suppose. All the sparklers here are *cuve close* wines, but the vintage-dated Chardonnay-dominated Graal Ducale launched in 1984 is a *méthode champenoise* wine. Most of Càvit's members have hillside vineyards planted to Chardonnay and Pinot Bianco with a little Pinot Nero and Pinot Meunier. Other Càvit sparklers include a Chardonnay Brut plus a Pinot (Bianco) Spumante as well as a Chardonnay-dominated Gran Càvit Brut. Case sales of all four sparklers add up to roughly 25,000 cases annually.

---

| Cinzano | CC/MC | ★→ |
| --- | --- | --- |

7 Via Gramsci, 10121 Torino

Cinzano was set up in the mid-18th century by the Cinzano brothers as a distiller and bitters producer in the best Torino traditions. A century later Cinzano's vermouth had become popular throughout Europe. In 1893 Cinzano built a new winery and expanded the rock-hewn cellars at Santa Vittoria d'Alba – still a Cinzano base today. In 1925 the ever-expanding Cinzano empire had designed the perfect logo – the famous red, white and blue rectangle. Enterprising Cinzano now have 28 affiliated companies scattered throughout the world producing and importing vermouth, sparkling and other wines, with annual sales adding up to a formidable £240m ($360m). In addition to the tank-method soft, frothy Asti Spumante Brut Pinot Nature and Principe di Piemonte Blanc de Blancs, Cinzano now produce a *méthode champenoise* Brut and a non-*dosage* Marone sparkler.

---

| Giulio Cocchi | CC/MC | ★ |
| --- | --- | --- |

17 Via Malta, 14100 Asti

Cantine Bava now own the major share in this firm, reputed to be the oldest *spumante* house in Asti. Giulio Cocchi, a Florentine, founded the firm in 1891 and by 1927 he was exporting to New York, Europe and Venezuela. Today Cocchi produce Asti, Cocchibrut 91 and a Cuvée Juventos *méthode champenoise* wine.

---

| E. Collavini | CC/MC | ★→ |
| --- | --- | --- |

33040 Corno di Rosazzo

Three generations of Collavinis have looked after this company, now producing 62,000 cases of sparkling wine annually. Short-sighted fans will find it hard to track down Collavini sparklers, for the company's name is usually reproduced in minute lettering on the back label. Cavieco appears to be another Collavini company, and both a dry Prosecco and Demi-Sec Verduzzo are produced under this name. The Beardsley-inspired appley, perfumed Extra Dry Il Grigio is Collavini's biggest seller (41,000 cases). Applause Nature, also made from the Chardonnay grape, is their only *méthode champenoise* wine.

---

| Giuseppe Contratto | CC/MC | ★→ |
| --- | --- | --- |

Canelli, 14053 Asti

Giuseppe Contratto was established in 1867 and is still a family firm today. Alberto Contratto is now in charge. Contratto sparklers are made mostly from bought-in grapes. The range includes the red Freisa d'Asti and the Grignolino d'Asti. The *méthode champenoise* Contratto Brut, Riserva Bacco d'Oro and the sweet Imperial Riserva Sabauda are more expensive.

## Cora                    CC/MC                    ★★

14055 Costigliole d'Asti

*Star buy Cora Asti Spumante*

Founded in 1835, as each bottle of their Asti Spumante tells you 3
times over, Cora also produce a Pinot del Poggio Spumante plus a
Royal Ambassador Brut *méthode champenoise* wine made from
Pinot grapes. The straight Asti is gloriously fresh, floral and
grapey. Definitely one of the best *spumantes* available.

## Corvo                   CC                       ★

Casteldaccia, 90014 Palermo

Established in 1824 by the Duca di Salaparuta. Quality may not
outshine that of other Italian firms but the wines are usually
reliable. 12,000 cases of Corvo sparklers are produced annually.
The range includes a Brut and Demi-Sec multi-variety Riserva
del Duca di Salaparuta, made by the Charmat method.

## Equipe 5                MC                       ★→

92b Viale Vittoria, Rovereto

Equipe Trentino Spumante is the firm behind Equipe 5, a well-
known *méthode champenoise* house in Trentino. (Five friends
founded the firm, hence the name, in 1964.) It buys in Pinot
Blanc, Pinot Nero and Chardonnay grapes from the Oltrepò
Pavese district in the southwest corner of Lombardy. Five
different sparklers are made here (of course) including Brut, Extra
Brut, Sec, Brut Rosé and Brut Riserva. Worth seeking out.

## Fazi-Battaglia          CC                       ★→

175 Via Clementina, 60032 Castelplanio

Fazi-Battaglia Titulus (their full title) produce a clean, refreshing, pepperminty Charmat-method Spumante Brut.

## Ferrari                 MC                       ★→

15 Via del Ponte di Ravina, 38040 Trento

Almost as famous in Italy as the eponymous racing car, Ferrari is
now owned by the Lunelli family. Giulio Ferrari, who founded
the firm in 1902, is acknowledged as the father of sparkling wine
in Trentino and was specifically responsible for cultivating and
introducing the Chardonnay grape here. Ferrari own 40ha (100
acres) of hillside vineyards in Trento, which provide 20% of their
needs with the rest of their Chardonnay being bought in.
Production is currently just over 100,000 cases, most of which is
taken up by the Ferrari Brut. Unlike most Italian sparkling wine
producers Ferrari only produce *méthode champenoise* wines and
riddle all of them by hand. Quality above all is obviously what
Ferrari are aiming at and the Lunelli's own Chardonnay grapes
always go into their vintage-dated sparklers. Apart from the
Ferrari Brut, the non-vintage range includes a curious, intense
green Pinot Nero-dominated Brut Rosé, a Nature and an Extra
Dry sparkler. The premium vintage-dated Ferrari sparklers are
worth trying. The incense-redolent 81 Brut de Brut is made in
limited quantities, using gentle pressings and grapes from selected
vineyards. The 78 Giulio Ferrari Riserva del Fondatore with
seven years on yeast is also highly thought of.

## Fontanafredda           CC/MC                    ★→

PO Box 29, 12051 Alba

One of the largest and best known Piedmont houses,

Fontanafredda, as befits their position, make a wide range of sparkling wines. Fontanafredda were founded in 1878 by Conte Emanuele Guerrieri, son of King Vittorio Emmanuel II and Contessa Rosa di Mirafiori. Today Fontanafredda sparklers include an Asti plus the Noble Sec Spumante and Pinot Bianco. Fontanafredda's finest sparkler is the non-*dosage* Contessa Rosa Brut Nature, a *méthode champenoise* wine made from Pinot grapes grown at Serralunga d'Alba and also available in Brut and Rosé styles. At a recent tasting the Asti was an intense green, floral wine whereas the Contessa had a perfumed, earthy character.

---

| Fratta | MC | ★ |
| --- | --- | --- |

7 Via Fontana, 25040 Monticelli Brusati

The Antica Cantina Fratta, to use their full name, have been closely associated with the Berlucchi firm since 1979. Today, as their labels proudly state, Fratta is under the direction of Berlucchi's oenologist Franco Ziliani. Fratta sparkling wines include Cuvée Antica Fratta Brut made from early-harvested Pinot Blanc and Pinot Noir grapes and the Pinot Noir-dominant Cuvée Antica Fratta Rosé. The best Fratta wine, the vintage-dated Cuvée Antica, comes in Brut and non-*dosage* versions.

---

| Marchese de' Frescobaldi | MC | ★→ |
| --- | --- | --- |

11 Via Santo Spirito, 50125 Firenze

The distinguished Frescobaldi family only make one sparkling wine – the biscuity, foamy *méthode champenoise* vintage-dated Brut. The Chardonnay and Pinot Nero grapes used are all bought in from farmers whose vines carpet the Trento hillsides. Given Frescobaldi's giant production of still wines, the 16,000 cases or so of this sparkler seem modest but it is currently all hand riddled and increased production could be on the way. Ancestor Vittorio degli Albizi, born in France, first brought Chardonnay and Pinot Noir vines to Italy in 1855.

---

| Gallo d'Oro (Cantina Duca d'Asti | CC | ★→★★ |
| --- | --- | --- |

Strada Nizza-Canelli, 14042 Calamandrana

*Star buy Gallo d'Oro Moscato d'Asti*

Bottled at Calamandrana near Asti this amazingly fresh, fruity DOC Moscato d'Asti shows how glorious these seductive, sweet, grapey wines can be. Most Moscato d'Asti is sweeter and lower in alcohol than Asti Spumante.

---

| Gancia | CC/MC | ★→★★ |
| --- | --- | --- |

16 Corso Liberta, 14053 Canelli

*Star buy Pinot di Pinot*

Gancia, along with Martini, Cinzano and Riccadonna, is one of the world's big *spumante* names. Carlo Gancia founded the firm in 1850 and visited Reims to study the classical sparkling wine method. He was soon convinced that his own Asti region's Moscato grapes could make good sparkling wine and by 1865 the first Gancia sparkler was launched. (Some sources credit this wine with being the first Moscato-based sparkler.) Carlo and his brother Edoardo were also among the first to turn the Pinot grapes grown in the Oltrepò Pavese into sparkling wine. With both the firm's sparkling and vermouth trade doing well, Gancia expanded their Canelli winery and set up other branches in Italy, Argentina and France. Today the Gancia family still own the company and more than 1m cases of sparkling wine are made every year. Most markets only receive Gancia Asti Spumante, the

Demi-Sec grapey, muscatty Gran Spumante, and the excellent zippy, pineapple-like Pinot di Pinot, based on Pinot Nero and Pinot Bianco in addition to the refreshing, elegant and classic Gran Crémant Riserva Vallarino Gancia made from Trentino Pinot grapes via the *méthode champenoise*. But Gancia also make an Extra Brut from Pinot Bianco plus a Chardonnay Brut and Sauvignon Brut, both of which are made from Veneto grapes. The USA and UK are Gancia's chief export markets.

| Conte Loredan Gasparini | CC/MC | ★→ |
|---|---|---|

Venegazzù del Montello, 31040 Treviso

Better known for the red Venegazzù wines, Conte Loredan Gasparini do produce some well-made sparklers too. The range includes the Charmat-method intense, big, citric Prosecco Brut and the fancier flat, biscuity *méthode champenoise* Loredan Gasparini Brut made from Pinot grapes.

| Martini | CC/MC | ★→ |
|---|---|---|

42 Corso Vittorio Emanuele, 10123 Torino

The one Italian sparkling wine firm that everyone knows. Martini & Rossi were founded in 1863. Better known for vermouth, Martini produce three different sparklers: the lively, grapey Moscato-based Asti, a big seller in Italy, the Riesling Italico-based Riesling Oltrepò Pavese Brut and the Pinot Nero-based Riserva Montelera Brut. Production is vast, as is to be expected, with more than 1m cases of sparkling wine made here. Most of that, of course, is the sweet Asti but the 150,000-case sales of the two Bruts are not to be sneered at. The recently-introduced Riserva Montelera is a *méthode champenoise* sparkler, two-thirds of which is currently riddled by hand and the rest by gyropalette.

| Monte Rossa | MC | ★ |
|---|---|---|

8 Via L. Marenzio, 25040 Bornato, Brescia

This estate winery with vineyards in the Franciacorta hills originally made sparkling wine for family and friends. Three different wines are made, including a Brut, Rosé and non-*dosage* sparkling wine. Pinot and Chardonnay grapes are used.

| Azienda Vinicola Montorfano | MC | ★→ |
|---|---|---|

Brescia, Lombardy

This estate produces fine *méthode champenoise* wines sold under the Bellavista label that have a prestigious reputation both in Italy and abroad. Pinot Bianco, Nero and Chardonnay are the grapes used here. They are turned into either the inexpensive and well-thought-of non-vintage Cuvée Brut, or the vintage-dated Gran Cuvée Pas Operé or Franciacorta Cuvée Brut.

| Montresor | CC | ★ |
|---|---|---|

16 Ca di Cozzi, 37100 Verona

The Cantine Giacomo Montresor is still owned by the Montresor family who originally came from France and settled in Italy at the end of the 16th century. The Montresors have been vineyard owners for several centuries and today their own estates close to Lake Garda supply almost all of their needs. The Chardonnay grape provides the base wine for more than half of their production, with the local white grapes of Verona accounting for the rest. About 20,000 cases of a Chardonnay Brut Extra, a Pinot Bianco Brut, the multi-variety Bianco di Custoza and a sweet red Recioto della Valpolicella sparkler are produced here every year.

## Neirano                      MC                          ★→
39 Via San Michele, Mombaruzzo, Asti

Giacomo Sperone and his sons Paolo and Antonio are the forces
behind this firm situated at Mombaruzzo in the Alto Monferrato
hills south of Alessandria. The restored cellars with ultra-modern
equipment are capable of ageing about 40,000 cases at any one
time. Although the Sperones produce both still red and white
wines, their pride and joy is the *méthode champenoise* Neirano
Brut. This sparkler, aged for three years on yeast, is made from a
blend of mostly Pinot Noir plus a little Chardonnay and current
production is only 2,500 cases annually, but the cellars have the
capacity to produce about four times as much.

## Riccadonna                  CC/MC                        ★
15 Corso Liberta, 14053 Canelli

Ottavia Riccadonna founded this famous Asti firm in 1921.
Today its vast Asti plant has a tank capacity of 22m litres and
Riccadonna is one of the leading Asti firms (Martini, Gancia and
Cinzano are the other three). Annual production of Riccadonna's
main sparkling labels is almost 1m cases including the sweet,
grapey Asti Spumante, Gran Dessert, the lively, lime-juice-like
President Brut and Demi-Sec, Nature de Pupitre and C.
Balduino. 25% of Riccadonna's production is exported. Presi-
dent Reserve is made from Pinot grapes and enjoys a long cool
fermentation. The vintage-dated Angelo Riccadonna Brut
Riserva Privata is made by the *méthode champenoise*.

## Romagnoli                   CC/MC                        ★→
5 Via Provinciale, Villo di Vigolzone

This winery and estate owned by the Romagnoli family has some
50ha of vineyards in the hills of Piacenza surrounding their
property. The Romagnolis produce about 18,000 cases of
sparkling wine every year, most of which is taken up by
Romagnoli Brut whose base wine is made from the local Ortugo
grape topped up with a little Pinot Nero. The rather better Il
Pigro made from Chardonnay plus a little Pinot Nero sells well
too. Small amounts of a sweet, grapey Malvasia Nature Secco and
Malvasia Demi-Sec, plus the Romagnoli's finest sparkler, a
*méthode champenoise* Pinot Naturale made from a blend of Pinot
Meunier and Chardonnay grapes, completes the range.

## Rotari                      MC                          ★
13 Corso IV Novembre, 38016 Mezzocorona

The Cantine Mezzocorona is the group of wineries behind Rotari
sparkling wines. The group made their first sparkling wine in
1976: 520 cases from their own grapes via the *méthode champenoise*.
Today, 33,000 cases are made, mostly from Chardonnay grapes
but with some Pinot Noir too. Only two sparklers are made here,
the Rotario Brut and Rotario Brut Rosé.

## Santa Margherita            CC                          ★
8 Via I. Marzotto, 30025 Fossalta di Portogruaro

Santa Margherita have some of the most stylish labels in all Italy
gracing their sparkling wine bottles, depicting the Villa Marzotto
in Portogruaro. The Marzotto family still own the firm and
Conte Umberto Marzotto is the current President. The original
Santa Margherita vineyards have now been ceded to tenant-
farmers from whom the estate buys only the best grapes. About

20,000 cases of non-vintage sparklers are produced here every year. Most are sold under the Prosecco di Conegliano-Valdobbiadene label in Secco (black capsule) and Amabile (gold capsule) styles. The black-label Pinot Brut (a Pinot Blanc wine) and Rosé Brut sparklers also sell well. Smaller quantities of a Superiore di Cartizze (made from the Cartizze grape) and a white-label 100% Chardonnay Crémant are made. The Alto Adige Chardonnay, in particular, is a Santa Margherita speciality.

## Cantina Sociale di Santa Maria della Versa    CC/MC    ★→
15 Via Crispi, 27047 Santa Maria della Versa

This cooperative was founded in 1905 in the heart of the Oltrepò Pavese region in southwest Lombardy. Its members own about 1,000ha (2,471 acres) planted to Pinot Nero, Pinot Grigio, Riesling Italico and Moscato. Production is an impressive 50,000 cases of Gran Spumante La Versa Brut *méthode champenoise* and 166,000 cases of Charmat sparklers. The Cantina sells very little under its own label. The Pinot Nero-dominated Pinot Spumante accounts for most of the production but the *méthode champenoise* La Versa Brut (also Pinot Nero-dominated) has handsome sales too. Riesling Italico and Moscato respectively are the grapes behind the Riesling Spumante and Moscato Spumante produced here.

## I Vignaiolo di Santo Stefano    CC    ★
12 Frazione Marini, Santo Stefano Belbo

This recently founded firm specializes in Asti Spumante, of which they produce 2,000 cases a year. Only 20% of their own Moscato d'Asti grapes are used in their vintage-dated sparkler. The rest are bought in.

## Cesarini Sforza    CC/MC    ★→
38100 Trento

Sforza specialize exclusively in sparklers, both by the tank method and *méthode champenoise*. Their everyday sparkling wine is sold under the Riserva dei Conti and Riserva Nature labels. Confusingly the special occasion *méthode champenoise* non-*dosage* Sforza is also sold under the Riserva dei Conti label with only the words "*metodo champenois*" to alert consumers to the difference. 25,000 cases of this are sold annually.

## Villadoria    CC    →★
65 Via L. Bosca, 14053 Canelli

Villadoria is the Asti Spumante brand name of AZ.I.VI.S.I., an important bottler and shipper of a range of Piedmont wines. Their unpleasant Villadoria Brut Spumante is not to be recommended.

## Zardetto    CC    ★
Conegliano, 31015 Treviso

Zardetto, like other quality-minded producers, gives his Charmat sparklers extended ageing time in tank on the yeast, with the result that Zardetto Brut has some *méthode champenoise* characteristics. 7,500 cases are made every year.

# Germany

It is hard to love Sekt. This is principally because most German sparkling wine is made from tanker-loads of base wine that come from all over Europe but rarely from Germany's own vineyards.

Riesling grown in the cool German vineyards can make good sparkling wine, as a few producers prove. But line up 20 of Germany's best-selling sparklers and only five are likely to display any Riesling – or even German – characteristics at all. The rest will reek of whatever wine happens to be going cheap at the time – those low-quality white varieties that are all too familiar components of the EEC wine lake.

Until recently the German wine laws have compounded the confusion by allowing these mixtures to be labelled "*Deutscher*", or German, Sekt. Now Germany has at least done the decent thing: see EEC Directive No 3309/85. This requires that Deutscher Sekt must be made exclusively from German wine or German grapes. Previously most Deutscher Sekt was made from imported foreign wine and was only German by virtue of experiencing a second fermentation on German soil. Hopefully this change in the rules will encourage more Sekt producers to make fine Deutscher Sekt from Deutscher Wein.

The new regulations that took effect from September 1986 mean that there are four categories of German sparkling wine or Sekt. The first or lowest quality will simply be labelled as Schaumwein. Next comes Qualitätsschaumwein, or Sekt, both of which will generally be made from imported wine and merely processed and fermented in Germany. The next level up is Deutscher (German) Sekt, which will now originate entirely from Germany and will therefore be on the same quality level as that of still Deutscher Tafelwein. The fourth or highest sparkling wine category is Deutscher Sekt bA which now follows the same regulations as German still QbA wines: that is, they are quality wines with defined geographical origin.

At the time of writing, Deutscher Sekt amounts to only a tiny proportion of Germany's annual production of 22m cases of sparkling wine. Henkell for instance, one of Germany's largest Sekt producers, are rather coy about revealing which varieties go into which blends. But nonetheless they are content to state that they utilize the following grape varieties: Riesling, Silvaner, Chardonnay, Sauvignon, Chenin Blanc, Colombard, Folle Blanche, Pinot Noir and Trebbiano. The rest of the industry use most if not all of these grapes. The Loire supplies most of the Chenin Blanc and possibly some Sauvignon, southwest France the Colombard and Folle Blanche, Bordeaux some Sauvignon too while northern Italy is probably the source of the Chardonnay, Pinot Noir and Trebbiano. Perhaps there is an excuse for using the more neutral of these varieties, but when Sekt smells strongly of the gooseberry-redolent Sauvignon, it is difficult to see the sense in it.

Germany consumes the vast majority of its Sekt production, which is perhaps just as well. But in 1984 about 1m cases of Sekt were exported, mostly by the big firms such as Henkell, Deinhard, Fürst von Metternich and Kupferberg. With production so large it is understandable that the bulk of Germany's sparkling wine is made by the *cuve close* system with a little also made by the transfer method and *méthode champenoise* (4% of the total). Contract bottlers put the sparkle into much of Germany's

Sekt. Virtually every firm makes a wide variety of different wines with varying degrees of sweetness. These numerous brand names and styles are an attempt by each Sekt house to cater for all tastes.

Encouragingly the *méthode champenoise* appears to be growing in popularity. So too is the production of the regional or even single-vineyard, vintage-dated sparklers which, as part of the Qualitätsschaumwein or Sekt bA category, account for a tiny yet increasing 5% of the total. For those interested in drinking top-quality sparkling wines this is one of the most optimistic trends in the German Sekt industry.

---

### German Sparkling Labels and the Law

- *Schaumwein* made from imported wine is the cheapest German sparkler. Bubbles stem mostly from the Charmat method. *Schaumwein* will not show any vintage or grape variety on the label. Its alcohol level must be at least 9.5%.
- The next level up is *Qualitätsschaumwein* or Sekt, again made mostly from imported wine but occasionally from German wine too. Sekt acquires its sparkle from a second fermentation – usually via the Charmat method. It must be cellared for at least six months prior to sale, and have an alcohol level of 10% or more. Previously this category of Sekt made from imported wine could be sold as Deutscher Sekt.
- Deutscher Sekt is now exactly what it sounds like – German sparkling wine made from German grapes. It is therefore on the same German quality level as Deutscher Tafelwein. Like Sekt it gains its bubbles from a second fermentation, mostly by the Charmat process. It must also be cellared for six months prior to sale and have an alcohol level of 10% or more.
- Deutscher Sekt bA is the finest German Sekt and is on the same German quality level as still QbA wines. It must be made entirely from the grapes of one specified region such as the Mosel or Rheingau. If a more specific area is quoted, such as Bernkastel or Johannisberg, at least 85% of the grapes must come from this area and the remaining 15% must be of the same quality. The grape variety may only be stipulated if the Sekt is made entirely from 85% or more of the same variety. Two grape varieties may appear on the label provided the wine comes exclusively from these varieties. Similarly a vintage may only be quoted if 85% or more of the Sekt comes from that vintage. It must be cellared for six months before sale and have an alcohol level of 10% or more.
- Deutscher Sekt made by the *méthode champenoise* will generally bear these words or "*Flaschengärung im champagnerverfahren*". Both phrases may only appear on the label until 1994.
- Transfer-method sparklers are usually identified by the word "*Flaschengärung*" appearing on the label.
- German sweetness levels correspond roughly to those of the French. They range from Extra Herb for the driest styles through to Herb for Brut, Extra Trocken for Extra Dry, Trocken for Sec, Halbtrocken for Demi-sec and Mild or Doux for the sweetest.

## Bernard-Massard  CC/TM  ★→
6–8 Jakobstrasse, Trier, Mosel

Bernard-Massard's historic building in the middle of Trier is the headquarters of an operation that produces 400,000 cases of sparkling wine a year. The most upmarket of these (transfermethod and vintage-dated) are the Brut Riesling from the Mosel-Saar-Ruwer and the Herrenklasse Trocken. Tank-fermented wines include the silver-labelled Silver Cabinet Extra Dry plus the Graf von Luxemburg Halbtrocken. In addition to these brands Bernard-Massard have the Royal, Elbling, Diamant and Grand Rouge sparklers – the latter made from the red Spätburgunder grape. Caves Bernard-Massard in Luxembourg is a sister company. Bernard-Massard also turn some of the fine Friedrich Wilhelm Gymnasium estate's base wine into sparkling wine. Their 82 Scharzberger Riesling Trocken with its warm, over-ripe fruit taste backed up by some lime-juice-like Riesling character is a good rather than great Sekt.

## Black Tower  CC  ★
57 Mainzerstrasse, Bingen-Rhein, Rheinhessen

Black Tower is an internationally-famous brand of (still) Liebfraumilch, but the sparkling version is less well known. This export house was founded in 1947 and is still owned by the Kendermann family. Sparkling Black Tower is an acceptable, sweet, bland wine.

## Brenner'sches Weingut  CC  ★→
20 Pfandturmstrasse, 6521 Bechtheim, Rheinhessen

This traditional, family-owned estate makes a dry Riesling Sekt. It has 24ha (59 acres), all in Bechtheim.

## Brogsitter's Zum Dom Herrenhof  CC/MC  ★
125 Walporzheimerstrasse, Walporzheim im Ahrtal, Ahr

This historic wine house complete with its equally historic Sankt Peter restaurant has vineyards dating back to 1600. The Brogsitter family bought the establishment after the Second World War. Today they use base wine bought in from elsewhere to make the majority of their 25,000 cases of sparkling wine. The tank method is used for most Brogsitter Sekts, but a few are made by the *méthode champenoise*. The range of sparklers is wide. The vintage-dated red Rotsek Brut and Blauer Spätburgunder are made from Ahr Spätburgunder grapes. The firm make Astoria Brut, a Blanc de Blancs Sekt, from Loire wines, and there is also a red Halbtrocken Sekt, Sankt Peter. The Dosage Zero Scharzberger Riesling comes from Saar grapes, and there is a vintage-dated Riesling.

## Burgeff  CC  ★
6203 Hochheim/Main, Rheingau

International drinks giant Seagram now own Burgeff & Co, which was founded in 1836. Their leading brands include Schloss Hochheim and Burgeff Grün.

## Fürstlich Castell'sches Domänenamt  CC  ★
8711 Castell Unterfranken, Franken

Two princes own this immaculately-kept estate. It is rare to find Sekt in Franconia but this castle on a hill makes one called Casteller Herrenberg.

| Deinhard | CC | ★ → ★★ |
|---|---|---|

3 Deinhard Platz, 5400 Koblenz, Mittelrhein

*Star buy 79 Deinhard Lila Imperial Brut*

Deinhard like to make much of the fact that they are the only Sekt firm with vineyard estates in three different areas – Oestrich, Deidesheim and Bernkastel. It is difficult to see the advantage this confers, for apart from a bit of estate wine in the *dosage*, the base wines for most of Deinhard's sparkling production come from the Mittelrhein's four valleys area. But where Sekt is concerned sparkling wine lovers should be grateful for anything, however small, which betokens quality. Ten different wines are made at Deinhard's ultra-modern Wallersheim winery close to Koblenz, which has a capacity of 23.5m litres. The downmarket Cabinet is the main Deinhard sparkler, much admired on the local market but not exported. The non-vintage Lila Imperial is next in line. It has a deep straw-gold colour, a cheap, sweet Sauvignon-like nose and an overblown palate. At this non-vintage level Deinhard Moselle Dry, with its sweet, appley freshness is a rather better buy. The top sparkler is the vintage-dated Deinhard Lila Imperial Brut. The 79 was clearly a Riesling wine, blessed with a lovely, classic, aged Riesling lime-juice-and-petrol nose plus a clean, racy, Riesling taste. A good buy. All Deinhard sparklers are made by the *cuve close* method and aged for 6–8 months on the yeast.

| Deutz & Geldermann | MC/CC/TM | ★ → |
|---|---|---|

26 Muggens-Turmstrasse, 7814 Breisach, Baden

This famous Champagne house opened a sparkling wine cellar in 1904. By 1925 Deutz & Geldermann's Sektkellerei had moved to Breisach. Today the Breisach operation (still owned by the French Lallier-Deutz family) produces 166,000 cases of Sekt, of which most is sold under the Carte Blanche and Buyers' Own Brand labels. Their other *méthode champenoise* sparklers include Carte Noire, Rosé and a widely-admired Brut. Deutz have a cheaper transfer-method sparkler which is sold under the Wappen von Breisach Grande Classe (Extra Trocken), Privat Cuvée (Halbtrocken), and Superb (Trocken) labels. Carte Rouge is also made by the transfer method. Somewhat disappointingly perhaps the base wine for most of Deutz & Geldermann's production comes from the Loire, topped up with a little Pinot Noir and Chardonnay from Trentino in northern Italy. Deutz & Geldermann claim to be the only Sekt house that is using the *méthode champenoise* on such a large scale.

| Ewald Theod Drathen | CC | → ★ |
|---|---|---|

Auf der Hill, 5584 Alf-Mosel, Mosel

Cheap and cheerful is obviously Herr Drathen's motto for this house's specialities are Liebfraumilch, EEC blended wines and the like. This firm was founded in 1860 and is still family-owned. The best bet in the Drathen range is the Schloss Avras Halbtrocken, where the extra sweetness covers up what is obviously low-grade base wine to make a sweet and reasonably agreeable Sekt. Mosel Trocken is not pleasant, nor is the sweet Deutschherren Cuvée.

| Faber | CC | ★ |
|---|---|---|

27 Niederkircherstrasse, 5500 Trier, Mosel

Most German Sekt firms use lots of brands, but Faber manage to sell over 4m cases per annum of just two wines. Krönung Halbtrocken, made from Trebbiano/Ugni Blanc, is the biggest seller. The other wine, Rotlese Halbtrocken, is a red sparkler made from Merlot.

## Ernst Gebhardt    CC    ★
21–23 Hauptstrasse, 8701 Sommerhausen, Franken

Gebhardt produce 10,000 cases of tank-method Rubin Privat, Privat Extra, Privat Edel and Franken Privat. The first three are mostly made from Italian base wine. Discerning drinkers should choose the Privat Edel Brut, which is made from Rheinpfalz Riesling, or the Franken Privat Brut made from Franconian Silvaner. No exports.

## Georges Geiling    CC/MC/TM    ★
18–33 Mainzerstrasse, 6533 Bacharach, Mittelrhein

Georges Geiling has a long and interesting history dealing with both French and German sparkling wines. In 1890 the firm supplied base wines in cask from Champagne to the German Sekt industry. Today the family-owned firm produces 41,000 cases of Sekt a year, most of it made by the transfer method although a few special *cuvées* apparently stem from the *méthode champenoise*. Riesling from the Mittelrhein is the basis for most Geiling *cuvées* but wines from elsewhere, including Chardonnay and Pinot Noir, are also used. Geiling is non-vintage as the firm wish to produce consistent blends year in, year out. The silver-labelled Austern or oyster Sekt is Rheingau Riesling, as is the Geiling Brut and the upmarket Geiling 1890 Chardonnay. There is also a red Spätburgunder sparkler. The cheaper Geiling wines such as the Hochgewächs use a mix of Loire wine plus Rheinpfalz Riesling. Privat uses Nahe Riesling plus wine from Bordeaux, and Krone von Rheinhell uses a blend of unspecified German and French wines. Special Cuvée and Cuvée Ultra Brut are two other Geiling brands.

## Adam Gillot & Söhne    CC    ★
84 Wormserstrasse, 6504 Oppenheim, Rheinhessen

6ha (15 acres) of Riesling and Silvaner vines provide a quarter of the requirements at this medium-sized concern which makes 42,000 cases of sparkling wines a year. The tank-method sparklers include vintage-dated Riesling, Silvaner, Müller-Thurgau and Spätburgunder. Tastings are held in their 1,000-year-old Huguenot cellar, with receptions in an old ice cellar deep in the Oppenheim hill. Gillot have a sister company in Champagne – Dominic Gillot.

## Friedrich Wilhelm Gymnasium
*See* Bernard-Massard.

## Hausen-Mabilon    MC    ★→
114–124 Im Staden, 5510 Saarburg, Saar

5ha (12 acres) of vines give this 80-year-old firm a third of its total needs. Mabilon Brut, Elbling and Extra Dry are the three different sparklers made here via the *méthode champenoise*. With sales of only 12,500 cases most of this firm's production is drunk in Germany although 10% has been exported to Texas.

## Henkell    CC    ★
142 Biebricher Allee, 6200 Wiesbaden, Rheingau

Henkell first started making Sekt in 1856. Today they produce an amazing 4m-plus cases a year. 1m cases is Henkell Trocken – a sparkler that has become so popular throughout the world that many think it is actually the name of a company rather than a brand name. Henkell's early-20th-century Henkellsfeld head-quarters, with majestic reception rooms above and cellars below, are as impressive as the sales figures. Adam Henkell started it all and in honour of their founder Henkell have introduced the smart black-bottled Adam Henkell Extra Brut. With such vast sales it is predictable that Henkell buy in their base wine from Germany, France and Italy. They are somewhat secretive about which wines are used for which blends but they are prepared to admit that the following grapes go into the base wines: Riesling, Silvaner, Chardonnay, Sauvignon, Chenin Blanc, Colombard, Folle Blanche, Pinot Noir and Trebbiano. All the wines are made by the tank method, with the new Adam Henkell the most expensive, followed by Henkell Trocken, the red Kardinal plus the white and red Csárdás range. Cheapest of all are the Carstens SC, Ruttgers Club, Caprice and Schloss Biebrich sparklers. Henkell Trocken's ripe, slightly rubbery fruit taste is aggressive but acceptable as is the sweet, dull, bland Henkell Brut.

### Landgräflich Hessisches Weingut            CC            ★
6225 Johannisberg, Rheingau

Now owned by the Landgrave (Marquis) of Hessen, this Riesling estate produces a Sekt called Kurhessen.

### Haus Hochheim            CC            ★
Postfach 1145, 6203 Hochheim am Main, Rheingau

Hummel & Co's Hochheim Sektkellerei was established in 1884 and today produces 83,000 cases of Sekt a year. These tank-method sparklers are mostly made from bought-in German, French and Italian base wine. The Dry and Extra Dry are the most popular sparklers and other brands include Goldlack, Rotlack, Grünlack and Sonder Cuvée.

### Gräflich von Kageneck'sche            TM/MC            ★→
35 Muggens-Turmstrasse, 7814 Breisach, Baden

Owned exclusively by the vast ZBW cooperative cellar at Baden. Both the transfer method and the *méthode champenoise* are used. Somewhat confusingly, the cooperative has given almost every varietal Sekt a separate brand name: Schloss Münzingen is made from Nobling and Weissburgunder, with a red Extra Trocken from Badische Rotgold. The Brut Badisch Rotgold sparkler is called Freiherr Heinrich and the *méthode champenoise* Müller-Thurgau Greiffenegg Schlössle. Riesling and Gutedel Sekts are also made. The cooperative considers its Riesling sparkler to be its best and the vineyards will eventually be replanted with this variety. The Extra Trocken Riesling Schloss Münzingen has a good mousse and warm, hefty green taste that many will enjoy.

### G. C. Kessler            TM/CC/MC            ★→
7300 Esslingen, Württemberg

Kessler are Germany's oldest Sekt producers, dating from 1826. The original Herr Kessler worked in Champagne for Veuve Clicquot. Kessler sparklers are made by the transfer method, those of subsidiary Gebrüder Weiss by the tank method.

### Kloss Foerster            CC/MC            ★→
Postfach 1207, 6220 Rudesheim, Rheingau

This family firm began to make sparkling wine in eastern

Germany in the 1850s. Four generations later they are in the Rheingau and produce 84,000 cases of Sekt a year. The vintage-dated Wappen Trocken, Halbtrocken and red Wappen-Rot wines form the biggest range. Apart from the blended Wappen wines, most Foerster Sekt is made from Rheingau Riesling. Brands include Riesling Extra Dry, Bereich Johannisberg Rheingauer Riesling and Traditions-Sekt Halbtrocken. Kloss Foerster use the *méthode champenoise* for their Imperator Brut, Rudesheimer Bischofsberg and red Assmannshäuser Steil sparklers. The firm makes Prinz von Preussen Brut from Schloss Reinhartshausen grapes, and the red Assmannshäuser Höllenberg from the Staatsweingut or state cellars' Spätburgunder. Base wines from the Loire and Soave regions are also used.

## Kupferberg                    CC/TM/MC                    ★→
19 Kupferberg-Terrasse, 6500 Mainz, Rheinhessen

Kupferberg, one of the best-known German sparkling wine names, are somewhat secretive about exactly what goes into their best-selling Kupferberg Gold. Not altogether surprising perhaps, as they sell almost 800,000 cases of the stuff and don't want to give too much away to the competition. Christian Adalbert Kupferberg founded this firm in Mainz in 1850 and two years later was selling Kupferberg Gold, making it the oldest Sekt brand in Germany. Herr Kupferberg obviously understood the importance of exports for until 1910 his Sekt sold more bottles in Britain than in Germany. Today Kupferberg produce 1m cases annually and besides the Gold a sweet red Blauer Spätburgunder is made. Fürst von Bismarck Brut and Sec are more expensive transfer-method Riesling-based sparklers. Kupferberg became part of the large Racke wine and spirit group in 1979 and are proud of the fact that they are the only German Sekt house to own a champagne firm – Bricout & Koch in Avize. Last year 30,000 visitors came to taste the wines and admire the Roman and medieval cellars, the carved wooden casks, the Art-Nouveau pavilion built for the 1900 Paris exhibition, and museum.

## Langenbach                    CC                    →★
31 Alzeyerstrasse, 6520 Worms, Rheinhessen

Julius Langenbach founded this firm in 1852 at Worms. Langenbach makes much of its part ownership of the original Liebfrauenkirche vineyards that surround the Church of our Lady at Worms. It was these vineyards that produced the first *liebfrauenmilch* or "milk of our lady", better known today as Liebfraumilch (and coming, it seems, from everywhere). Langenbach make a wide range of tank-method Sekt. The range includes vintage-dated Waldracher Riesling and Goldlack Riesling Brut plus the non-vintage Schloss Leutstetten, Sparkling Crown of Crowns, Silver Crown and Weisslack besides sweet Schloss Dalberg and red Purpur made from the Spätburgunder grape. The silver-labelled Silver Crown, originally launched in 1952 to celebrate the company's centenary, is, sadly, to be avoided. The gold label Crown of Crowns Sekt with its curious, sweet, tutti-frutti taste, is just acceptable, showing a family resemblance to Crown of Crowns Liebfraumilch.

## Fürst von Metternich                    TM/CC                    ★★
1–8 Söhnleinstrasse, 6200 Wiesbaden-Schierstein, Rheingau
*Star buy Fürst von Metternich Extra Trocken*

The Fürst von Metternich sparkling wine, produced by Söhnlein

Rheingold, is one of Germany's best. The Extra Trocken is made from Rheingau Riesling, part of which emanates from the Prince von Metternich's Schloss Johannisberg estate. This Sekt's intense, clean, classy, lime-juice-like Riesling character is worth seeking out, for it is one of the very few German sparklers with style.

## Matheus Müller    CC    ★
6228 Eltville, Rheingau

Seagram are obviously happy to keep on expanding their German interests for this 1836 firm was taken over by them in 1984. "MM Extra", their best known sparkler, gets its bubbles via the *cuve close* method.

## Rudolf Müller    CC    ★→★★
Postfach 20, 5586 Reil, Mosel
*Star buy 1984 Mosel Riesling Extra Dry*

Best known for its Bishop or Riesling still wine, this firm also produces a wide range of Sekts. The cheaper versions are sold under the Splendid label in Halbtrocken, Gold, Trocken and Mild versions. Two fancier, vintage-dated Riesling-based sparklers are also available, the Wwe Dr H. Thanisch Trocken from the Mosel-Saar-Ruwer region or the Mosel Riesling Extra Dry. For a firm that did not start making sparkling wine until 1956, Müller's current annual Sekt production of almost 300,000 cases is impressive. Dr Thanisch, Müller's most expensive sparkler, will soon be fermented in bottle rather than tank. Müller's splendid Halbtrocken is a popular, inoffensive fizz, sweet and fruity. But the real star here is the vintage-dated Mosel Riesling Extra Dry. The 84 vintage was a delicious, ripe, elegant, flowery-appley Riesling, made from fine fruit. As such it is probably Germany's finest Sekt.

## Söhnlein Rheingold    CC    ★→
1–8 Söhnleinstrasse, Wiesbaden-Schierstein, Rheingau

The firm that produces the Fürst von Metternich sparkling wine also makes sparklers of its own. Söhnlein Brillant is the best known, but Söhnlein Rheingold, launched in 1876 by Richard Wagner, a friend of the Söhnlein family, is still going strong.

## Rilling    CC    ★
2–18 Brückenstrasse, 7000 Stuttgart, Württemberg

Roman remains were found when the Rilling cellar was being built. But there appears to be little that is traditional about Rilling today. The tank method is used to make numerous different sparklers including Schloss Rosenstein, Rilling LR, Resed, Sabinchen, Rosé, Rubin, Moscato and Diadem. Better quality wines are the Bereich Kaiserstuhl Tuniberg from Baden plus the Württemberger Trollinger and Riesling. Finer still are the Brut de Brut and Jubilar plus the other vintage-dated, mostly Riesling-based, wines bearing the Hochgewächs stamp.

## Ritterhof    CC    ★→
51 Weinstrasse Nord, 6702 Bad Dürkheim, Rheinpfalz

The Fitz family have owned the Ritterhof Sektkellerei, the third-oldest Sekt cellar in Germany, since 1837. The associated Fitz-Ritter estate supplies half of Ritterhof's grapes: Riesling is the main variety. The remainder comes from elsewhere in the Rheinpfalz. 16,000 cases of Ritterhof Sekt are made, most of which is Ritterstolz, an ultra-dry sparkler that is suitable for diabetics. Ritterhof Riesling Trocken and Brut are also on offer, plus red Dürkheimer Feuerberg Halbtrocken Sekt.

## Schloss Affaltrach CC →★
15 Am Ordensschloss, 7104 Obersulm-Affaltrach, Württemberg

Over 52,000 cases of tank-method wine are made at the Schloss each year. Most of it however is made from imported French and Italian base wine. Baumann Riesling, in its Extra Dry and Brut styles, is however 100% Württemberg Riesling. The Franco-Italian Schloss Affaltrach wines comes in Brillant, Diamant, Smaragd, and a red or Rubin version. Schloss Affaltrach also produce the Burg Löwenstein sparkler.

## Schloss Rheingarten CC ★
6222 Geisenheim, Rheingau

The current Hallgarten Vater & Söhne, whose firm was founded in the Rheingau in 1898 and in London in 1933, must be as well-known today as their ancestors were. Schloss Rheingarten is their bland, sweet, acceptable *cuve close* sparkler.

## Schloss Saarfels MC ★→
Domanenstrasse, 5512 Serrig, Saar

Schloss Saarfels turn Riesling and Weissenburgunder into almost 11,000 cases of Sekt annually, using the *méthode champenoise*. The range includes Trocken, Brut Extra, Edelmarke (Halbtrocken) and a Trocken Sekt known as "*Aus dem Felsverlies*". Other Sekt brands include Scharzhofberger Trocken, plus the vintage-dated Staadter Maximiner Pralat Brut.

## Schnaufer CC ★
1 Im Mönchswasen, 7262 Althengstett, Württemberg

Most of the 208,000 cases of Sekt made here annually are sold under the Lichtenstein Halbtrocken, Trocken and Riesling Trocken labels. Other tank-method Sekts are Württemberg Riesling Trocken and Baden Riesling. Pricky Ananas and Pfirsich Royal are fruit-flavoured sparklers.

## Schorlemer CC ★→
14 Cusanusstrasse, Bernkastel-Kues, Mosel

This collection of Mosel estates once owned by the von Schorlemer family now belongs to Meyer-Horne. The production of Sekt is small, but various sparkling Rieslings from the estates are sold.

## Sichel Söhne CC ★
14–18 Werner von Siemenstrasse, 6508 Alzey, Rheinhessen

It had to happen, of course. Once the famous Blue Nun had visited 81 different countries, Sichel had to come up with something new. So this sparkler was relaunched. Today the slightly restyled Sparkling Blue Nun has been made fractionally sweeter to appear closer in style to Blue Nun Liebfraumilch. However its sweet, bland, fruity taste presents little to get worked up about.

## Sick MC ★
3 Bundesstrasse, 7830 Emmendingen-Mundingen, Württemberg

Better known as producers of cellar machinery, especially the paraphernalia of Sekt production, Weinbau Sick have just made

5,000 bottles of their own sparkling wine. Their 84 Mundinger Alte Burg is an Extra Trocken Riesling Sekt made by the *méthode champenoise*.

## Treis                    CC/MC                                    ★→
204 Provinzialstrasse, 5581 Zell-Merl, Mosel

Theodor Treis founded this firm in 1810 and today it is still a family-run business. The tank-method and bottle-fermented sparklers are 100% Riesling, which is alas something of a rarity in Germany today. As usual, numerous different sparkling wine brands are made. Apart from the Kongressmarke Schaumwein, the Sekts include Cabinet plus Möselchen and Moselgold, Tradition, Rotlack and a Saar-Riesling.

## Verband Deutscher Sektkellereien
46 Sonnenbergerstrasse, 6200 Wiesbaden, Rheingau

Members of this giant association of German sparkling wine producers account for about 98% of the country's total sparkling wine production.

## Verwaltung der Staatlichen Weinbaudomänen    CC  ★→
1 Deworastrasse, 5500 Trier, Mosel

The King of Prussia founded this estate in 1896. Today its vast vaulted cellars produce a Sekt made from Riesling from Serrig in the Saar Valley.

# Other German
## sparkling wine producers:

Peter Herres, Trier, Mosel; Schloss Böchingen, Böchingen, Rheingau; G.H. Mumm, Rheingau; Winzersekt GmbH, Sprendlingen, Rheinhessen; Schloss Wachenheim Sektkellerei, Rheinpfalz; Sektkellerei Spicka, Serrig/Saar.

# Austria

Even if one makes allowances for the Austrian wine industry's tragic problems during the last few years, it is hard to explain the disappointingly low standards in sparkling wine production.

Austria's chief obstacle to producing first-class sparkling wine is a lack of suitable grape varieties. Austria's climate should not be a drawback, for if Alsace on a similar latitude can produce good sparkling wines, then so can Austria. Yet the grape most widely used is the Welschriesling or Italian Riesling, which with its low acidity and dull flavours is not the ideal sparkling wine base. Nor is Austria's earthy, peppery Grüner Veltliner much better. Things are looking up however, for at least one Austrian Sekt house is using the Pinot Blanc, a relative of the Chardonnay.

As if to add to their problems, most Austrian Sekt houses buy in base wine rather than make their own, thereby losing control over quality at a vital stage. Few firms use any method other than *cuve close*; if the *méthode champenoise* is too time consuming and expensive, what about the transfer method?

Vienna is the sparkling wine capital of Austria, partly perhaps because there are plenty of festive occasions here at which to drink it. Falkenstein to the north of the city produces most of Austria's sparklers. The Viennese were sensible enough to allow vineyards within the city limits. Most *heurigen* – wine inns – deal in youthful, still wines, though several have their own sparklers too.

With such keen local customers and enthusiastic export markets, Austria's Sekt firms are expected to do well in the future.

---

### Austrian Sparkling Labels and the Law

The Austrian wine law of November 1985 introduced stringent new legislation, part of which relates to Sekt. (In Austria *Schaumwein* is interchangeable with Sekt.)

● Sparkling wine sold as Österreichischer Sekt must be made exclusively from Austrian wine.

● If any Austrian Sekt specifies a vintage or region it must come entirely from that vintage or region.

● Apart from the basic Österreichischer Sekt there is a superior category of Austrian sparkling wine known as Qualitätssekt or Qualitätsschaumwein. This must contain 10% alcohol and gain its sparkle via the tank method or *méthode champenoise* and not the carbonated method. Qualitätswein must be kept on yeast for an extended period. It must be cellared for nine months prior to sale.

● At the other end of the quality scale all carbonated Austrian wine such as Perlwein must bear the following words prominently on the label "*mit Kohlensäure versetzt*" ("carbon dioxide has been added").

● Most Austrian Sekt is made by the tank method but the words "*méthode classique champenoise*" or "*nach traditioneller Champagnermethode*" on a bottle denote a genuine *méthode champenoise* wine.

● Austria mostly uses the French terms for sweetness levels such as Brut. But also expect to see "*Trocken*" for Sec, "*Halbtrocken*" or "*Halbsüss*" for Demi-Sec.

## Karl Inführ                    CC                    ★ →
46 Kahlenbergerstrasse, 3042 Klosterneuburg

Königssekt or King's Sekt is the most famous sparkling wine of
this firm, which was founded in 1949 and today makes 167,000
cases a year. Königssekt is made by the cooperative at
Gumpoldskirchen using Spätrot Rotgipfler grapes. Similarly the
cooperative at Dürnstein in the Wachau supplies the Rhine
Riesling that goes into Ritter von Dürnstein, their oldest and most
expensive sparkler. "Darling Sekt" made from the Grüner
Veltliner and Welschriesling, complete with a Queen of Hearts
label, does well pre-Christmas and on Valentine's Day. Poste de
Vienne, made from the Samling 88 grape is another famous Inführ
wine, while Sekts such as Le Grand Rouge, Excellent, Pinot
Blanc and their fruit-based sparklers, including the strawberry
variety, are perhaps less well-known. Karl Inführ also make a
bone-dry sparkling wine that is suitable for consumption by
diabetics.

## Johann Kattus                  MC                        ★
Am Hof 8, 1011 Vienna

Since 1857 four generations of the Kattus family have been
involved in wine. Johann Kattus II founded the Kattus Sekt cellar
and established the Hochriegel brand name. Hochriegel means
"high hill" and before the Second World War the family owned
a vineyard by this name. Johann Kattus's heyday was probably
during the Austro-Hungarian empire when Hochriegel was
served at both the Imperial and Royal courts. Today it is unlikely
that even humble palates will greatly enjoy the curious, sherbety
Hochriegel Grosser Jahrgang Brut or the similarly sweetshop-
like bouquet of the Alte Reserve. However, Hochriegel's gold
foil Trocken Sekt, with its big, somewhat oily taste is worth
trying. Kattus is the largest Sekt producer in Austria.

## Kelleramt Chorherrenstift Klosterneuburg    CC    ★ → ★★
Am Renninger 2, 3400 Klosterneuburg

The Augustine monastery of Klosterneuburg was founded in
1108 by Duke Leopold. The majestic Baroque palace close by was
built in 1730 by the devout Emperor Karl VI. Its vast cellars date
from this period too. Like many monasteries Klosterneuburg
cultivated vines and made wine from the beginning. Today
Klosterneuburg own 100ha (247 acres) of vines in 4 different
regions but only 30% of their own grapes are used in the annual
production of 33,000 cases of Klostersekt. Grüner Veltliner
backed up by a little Riesling make up the Klostersekt Trocken
and Halbsüss Sekts (complete with gold and silver foils). The
Trocken or Brut version enjoys a good although slightly
simplistic Grüner Veltliner taste, clean, peppery and drinkable,
whereas the bronze-labelled Rosé made from the St-Laurent
grape has a worrying blue-pink colour and a pleasant, albeit
unexciting, sweet, fruity taste. The real Klosterneuburg treat,
however, is the 83 Grand Reserve Brut made from the Pinot
Blanc grape. Ignore its ridiculous label and concentrate instead on
the rich, full-bodied, pineappley Pinot Blanc flavour coupled
with that traditional spicy, peppery Austrian finish.

## Brüder Kleinoscheg                MC                    ★ →
66 Anton Kleinoschegstrasse, 8051 Graz

One of a handful of *méthode champenoise* producers in Austria.

They sell their *méthode champenoise* wines under three different labels: Herzogmantel, Goldmark and Derby.

## Krems Winzergenossenschaft   CC   ★
Sandgrube 13, 3500 Krems

Historic Krems with its onion-tower churches and pretty houses overlooking the Danube is one of the most attractive parts of the Wachau. The cooperative or Winzergenossenschaft, founded in 1938, is efficiently run and has since 1977 produced about 33,000 cases every year of Haus Österreich sparkling wine in Trocken, Halbtrocken and Rosé versions. All are made by the *cuve close* method.

## Rudolf Kutschera   CC   ★
250 Heiligenstädterstrasse, 1195 Vienna

Herr Kutschera obviously does a neat line in bottling sparkling wine for numerous other firms. Of the 50,000 cases produced here every year, few appear under the Kutschera label. What with the Marillenschaumwein, or apricot sparkling wine, for Lenz Moser and the Hotel de France, Vienna Hilton and Salzburg Sheraton sparklers it is a wonder that Kutschera finds time for his own Château de Belle Fontaine and Schloss Schönbrunn sparkling wines at all. The firm has links with Henkell, Germany, and Riccadonna, Italy.

## Lenz Moser   CC   ★
3495 Rohrendorf bei Krems

Lenz Moser's pretty, ornately-gabled Imperial Yellow winery has been the leading Austrian Weingut since the firm's foundation in 1849. The original cellars date back apparently to 970–980 AD and the Moser family appear to have been involved in wine almost as long. The 4,000 cases of Moser sparkling wine are made from Grüner Veltliner grapes grown mainly at the Schlossweingut Malteser Ritterorden, the estate of the Knights of Malta, and are sold under the Schloss Mailberg label. In addition Lenz Moser sell some curious, low-alcohol sparkling fruit wines called Mariandl (sparkling apricot), Romy (sparkling raspberry) and Strawby (sparkling strawberry). Most Moser sparkling wine is consumed in Austria but 20% is exported to America.

## P. M. Mounier   MC   ★→
20 Ungargasse, 1031 Vienna

Mounier are one of the very few Austrian Sekt firms to still use the old-fashioned *méthode champenoise*. Four different styles, Brut, Sec, Demi-Sec and Rouge, are made of the straight Mounier bubbly, mostly from the Welschriesling grape topped up with a little Grüner Veltliner. The new vintage-dated Cuvée 262, made from the nobler Rhine Riesling, is rather more stylish. With 18 months minimum on yeast and available in a wide range of sizes up to a Balthasar (16-bottle capacity), Mounier sparklers are worth seeking out.

## Schlumberger   MC   ★→★★
41–43 Heiligenstädterstrasse, 1190 Vienna

In 1842 Robert Schlumberger gave up his job in a leading Champagne house to live and work in his Austrian wife's country. He quickly acquired vineyards in Bad Vöslau south of Vienna and began to make *méthode champenoise* wines. Today Schlumberger's *méthode champenoise* sparklers spend about 18–30 months on yeast in Schlumberger's extensive Vienna cellars before being disgorged. Schlumberger do not actually own vineyards but buy in base wine from contract growers just as they have done for the last 60 years. Welschriesling is the basis of all Schlumberger sparklers but a little Grüner Veltliner is used too. Underberg bought out Schlumberger in 1973 and current cellar capacity of 250,000 cases, and annual sales of 125,000 cases could well double in the next five years as the cellars are enlarged and automatic *remuage* is introduced. While this sounds encouraging, many feel that Austria's oldest sparkling wine producer should concentrate more on quality rather than quantity. Recently Schlumberger's non-vintage Blanc de Blancs has had a big, earthy, biscuity character that is not really good enough for Austria's most important and prestigious Sekt house. The superior Goldeck Trocken with its fine, fruity taste is surprisingly sweeter (and spends one rather than two years on yeast) but again, worryingly, it has a slightly dank finish that should not be there. Schlumberger make a vintage-dated Ultra Brut – which they consider to be their finest wine – and there are also the Goldeck Halbsüss and red Don Giovanni sparklers.

| **Siegendorf** | CC | ★→ |
|---|---|---|

12 Rathausplatz, 7011 Siegendorf

Siegendorf, founded in 1860 and owned by the Patzenhofer family, enjoys a good reputation for both its still and its few sparkling wines. Siegendorf's Sekt is made by the *cuve close* method and sold under the Imperial label.

| **R. Zimmermann** | CC | ★ |
|---|---|---|

Agnesstrasse 46b, 3400 Klosterneuburg

Zimmermann make 3 sparkling wines: Zimmermann Extra Dry, made from Welschriesling, Charpentier Blaufränkisch Rosé and a vintage-dated Charpentier Brut made from Pinot Blanc. Zimmermann have *heurigen* at Grinzing and Klosterneuburg. They make just over 9,000 cases per annum of *cuve close* Österreichischer Sekt. Charpentier Brut is Zimmermann's finest sparkling wine.

# California

The USA is afloat on a sea of bubbles, consuming about 140m bottles of California sparkling wine every year, to say nothing of the annual tidal waves from Italy (38m bottles), France (18m bottles, of which more than two-thirds are champagne), and Spain (16m bottles). All over the country corks have been popping with increasing frequency at functions from modest brunches and poolside barbecues to grand banquets.

Americans, it seems, despite the anti-alcohol lobby and prohibitively high sparkling wine sales tax, need little excuse to crack open a bottle of bubbly, whether it be the rarefied heights of DPR – Dom Pérignon Rosé – or the distinctly ordinary yet phenomenally successful André from E. & J. Gallo.

The rate of growth may have slowed down slightly in the last few years but sales are still healthy, for production of California's own sparklers has doubled during the last decade and imports of champagne have trebled in the same period.

American sparklers (of which the vast majority are produced in California) can be divided into two camps: The original "American champagnes" are typified by the bland, sweet Korbel wines and the full-flavoured, hefty Hanns Kornells. The second camp comprises firms aiming to imitate French champagne. Many are succeeding. The arrival in California of six *grandes marques* Champagne houses confirms, and at the same time pays the highest compliment to, the starry goals of the second group. Other Champagne firms such as Lanson and Taittinger are on the way, it is rumoured, either joining forces with American firms, as did Piper-Heidsieck in founding Piper Sonoma, or else going it alone like Domaine Chandon and Roederer. The latest arrival has been Bollinger who have somewhat curiously linked with Whitbread (the UK brewers) and Chianti producers Antinori to set up a $30m winery in Napa's Foss Valley region. Spanish *cava* expertise has also arrived in California, with Freixenet and Codorníu both owning land there.

Some California *méthode champenoise* concerns have had time to build up experience: Schramsberg was founded in 1965 and Domaine Chandon in 1973. But most California winemakers are still puzzling over the intricacies of the *méthode champenoise* process. Selecting suitable grape varieties is still a problem: the big bouncy character of most California Chardonnay gives excessively strong fruit-salad flavours. Pinot Noir is much more successful, albeit rosy-tinted. But it is not always easy to find: California is thought to have three different grape varieties masquerading as the authentic Pinot Noir. Attempts to tone down excessive varietal flavour with bland, high-acid varieties such as Pinot Blanc (in California, alas, often confused with the humble Muscadet grape, the Melon de Bourgogne) have not always worked either.

The ideal places for growing sparkling wine grapes have not yet been entirely sorted out. Napa and Sonoma have had their successes, especially in their shared Carneros region. The cool Anderson, Redwood and Potter Valleys of Mendocino farther north, where latest newcomer Roederer is situated, could turn out to be the finest areas of all.

Comparative work on first- and second-fermentation yeast strains has only just begun, although at least half the industry uses an efficient Moët & Chandon yeast generously supplied by Domaine Chandon to its competitors. The time spent *en tirage* or

# CALIFORNIA

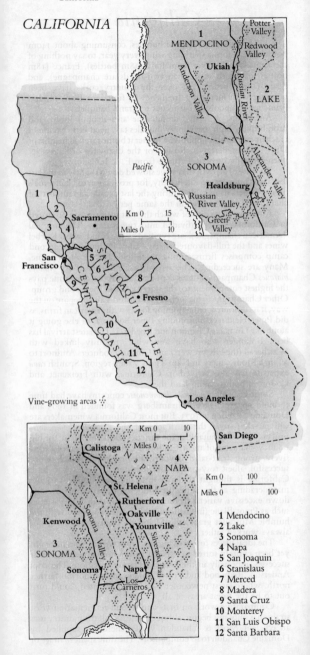

**1** MENDOCINO
Potter Valley
Redwood Valley
Ukiah
Anderson Valley
Russian River
**2** LAKE
Alexander Valley
Pacific
**3** SONOMA
Healdsburg
Russian River Valley
Green Valley

Km 0 — 15
Miles 0 — 10

Sacramento

San Francisco

CENTRAL COAST

SAN JOAQUIN VALLEY

Fresno

Los Angeles

San Diego

Km 0 — 100
Miles 0 — 100

Vine-growing areas

Calistoga
Napa Valley
**4** NAPA
St. Helena
Rutherford
Oakville
Yountville
Silverado Trail
Kenwood
Sonoma Valley
**3** SONOMA
Sonoma
Napa
Los Carneros

Km 0 — 10
Miles 0 — 5

1 Mendocino
2 Lake
3 Sonoma
4 Napa
5 San Joaquin
6 Stanislaus
7 Merced
8 Madera
9 Santa Cruz
10 Monterey
11 San Luis Obispo
12 Santa Barbara

on yeast varies, too, from about 12–18 months through to as long as 7 years for Reserve wines. *Dosage* trails are also still in the early stages with most firms using half the accepted French *dosage* levels. There is concern too about the use of brandy in the *dosage*. Important firms such as Schramsberg and Chateau St-Jean are in favour of brandy, whilst others such as Iron Horse are opposed to a *dosage* at all, although they occasionally allow a little polishing of the wine by blending back some of the same still wine.

The use of reserve wines in blending is contentious. Domaine Chandon is perhaps the chief protagonist, blending up to 15% of older reserves into its non-vintage wine. It is reputed that Roederer will follow suit. USA wine laws, unlike the French, can hardly be said to help the reserve wine devotees, for any sparkler with more than 5% of wine from another vintage in the blend cannot be sold as a vintage product. Gyropalettes for automatic *remuage* at least seem to be meeting with universal approval, with Domaine Chandon utilizing the aptly named VLMs or Very Large Machines and Piper-Sonoma conventional gyropalettes.

It has been difficult in this section to recommend specific vintages, for California has only released a handful of sparkling wine vintages and their supremacy or staying power is in many cases as yet unproved.

To have come so far so quickly does however mean that whatever happens California, and indeed America, look all set for a sparkling future.

---

### USA Sparkling Labels and the Law

● The words "champagne," "*méthode champenoise*" or "naturally fermented in *this* bottle" indicate a wine that has had its second fermentation in that bottle and has therefore been made by the genuine *méthode champenoise*.

● "Sparkling wine" *plus* the words "champagne", "champagne style" or "champagne type" can be made either by the bulk or transfer process and the method will be stated on the label.

● "Sparkling wine", including "sparkling red wine" and "sparkling white wine", by itself on a label indicates that the wine has been made by one of the lesser methods such as the bulk method.

● "Naturally fermented in *the* bottle" indicates a transfer-method wine.

● "Crackling wine", "perlant wine" and "frizzante wine" is sparkling wine with usually less effervescence than "champagne" or other sparkling wines.

● "Carbonated wine" is a sparkling wine that has gained its bubbles from artificial carbonation rather than a natural second fermentation.

● Sweetness levels of Brut, Sec and Demi-Sec tend to vary from brand to brand. Any wine designated "Natural", however, should have no *dosage*.

---

| Adler Fels | MC | ★ |
|---|---|---|
| 5325 Corrick Road, Santa Rosa | | |

This small family-run winery, on a steep Mayacamas mountain slope with a bird's eye view of the Sonoma valley, is obviously keen to stress its international connections: the tiny amounts of bone-dry Gewürztraminer/Rhine Riesling *méthode champenoise* wine produced are sold under the Melange à Deux label and the winery name is derived from the German for Eagle Rock – a nearby landmark.

## Almaden                TM                    ★
1530 Blossom Hill Road, San Jose

Founded in 1852, today Almaden produces more than half a million cases of basic transfer-method wine from thousands of acres in San Benito and Monterey. Pink-toned Eye of the Partridge, Le Domaine, Golden Champagne and other Almaden sparklers have their devotees in the home market. European palates, however, are more likely to appreciate the still California Chardonnay produced as a joint venture with Laurent-Perrier of France and sold as Caves Laurent-Perrier Chardonnay. This is, alas, about to be discontinued.

## S. Anderson           MC                    ★★
Winery and vineyard: 1473 Yountville Cross Road, Napa

California determination and grit enable Los Angeles dentist Stanley Anderson and his Davis-trained wife Carol to work weekends at their small Napa winery. Impressive new rock-hewn cellars are surrounded by 6ha (15 acres) of mostly Chardonnay plus some Pinot Noir and Pinot Blanc. Of their three released vintages the fresh, yeasty-smoky Blanc de Noirs is worthwhile, but eventually production will concentrate on a Pinot Noir/ Chardonnay vintage Brut blend.

## Beaulieu Vineyard      MC                    ★★
1960 St-Helena Highway, Rutherford

Grand old California wineman André Tchelistcheff supervised the first BV sparkling blend in 1952 and since then these wines have been served by every American President from Roosevelt to Reagan. European palates, however, are likely to find the light, fresh, flowery 81 BV Champagne de Chardonnay agreeable rather than exceptional. BV also sell a lesser quality Brut Champagne made from the Chenin Blanc grape.

## Jacques Bonet          CC                    →★
Italian Swiss Colony, 490 Second St., San Francisco

This ordinary, inexpensive bulk-method sparkler from Italian Swiss Colony is probably the closest competitor to Gallo's André. It's a mass-market wine with no finesse. The sweet and somewhat flabby Lejon Brut is similar. A range of flavoured "champagnes" is also sold under the Jacques Bonet label.

## California Cellar Masters   CC/TM              →★
212 West Pine Street, Lodi

Don't let the name confuse you. California Cellars does not grow its own grapes, nor in the case of its Coloma Cellars brand, ferment or bottle its own wine. All that is done for them by Weibel.

## Chateau St-Jean        MC           81    ★★→★★★
Winery and vineyards: 8555 Sonoma Highway, Kenwood
*Star buy 81 Chateau St-Jean Blanc de Blancs*

Since 1980 unglamorous Graton has been the headquarters of Chateau St-Jean's sparkling-wine empire. Apart from St-Jean's dry, stylish, vintage sparklers, made from bought-in Russian River grapes, accomplished winemaker Pete Downs also makes wine and bottles wine under contract for several firms; any California fizz with Graton on the label will have been made here. The superb silver-labelled 81 Ch St-Jean Blanc de Blancs (mostly Chardonnay) with its biscuity nose and rich, full, creamy taste is their finest wine but the elegant, similarly biscuity 82 Blanc de Blancs and the lively and flowery Pinot Noir-dominated 81 Brut are good alternatives. Watch out for St-Jean's new Reserve with five years on the yeast instead of the usual three. In 1984 Ch St-Jean was bought for $40m by Suntory International.

| The Christian Brothers | CC | ★ |
| --- | --- | --- |

Mont La Salle Vineyards, St-Helena

Big and bulky does not, alas, always mean beautiful too. This lay Catholic teaching order came to the USA from Reims in 1848 and by 1887 was making wine commercially. Their sparkling wine with its musk-melon taste is not recommended. Winemaker Brother Timothy's unobtainable birthday bubbly is their best effort yet.

| Cook's | CC/TM/IM | ★ |
| --- | --- | --- |

Guild Wineries and Distilleries, One Winemasters Way, Lodi

A fresh sweet sparkler, unexciting yet fruity, accounts for the bulk of the 1m case annual sales of Guild Wineries and Distilleries, the huge California growers' cooperative. The sweet Cribari, the even sweeter Roma and the Cresta Blanca range (including their dry citrussy/burnt toast Chardonnay) account for the rest. Predominantly non-classic varieties are used and all non-vintage Guild sparklers are made by the *cuve close* method, except Cresta Blanca (transfer method) and J. Pierrot (injection method). Latest innovations include orange-, almond-, and blackcurrant-flavoured fizz plus Cook's Sparkling White Zinfandel.

| Crystal Valley | CC | →★ |
| --- | --- | --- |

415 Hosmer, Modesto

Crystal Valley's Blanc de Noirs is not to my taste. The nose is curious and the colour unappealing. Crystal Valley also make the Spumante d' Franseca brand.

| John Culbertson Winery | MC | ★ |
| --- | --- | --- |

2608 Via Rancheros, Fallbrook

This medium-sized family-owned firm, founded in 1981, makes a wide range of reasonable, albeit unusually flavoured, sparkling wine from bought-in grapes, including a Cuvée de Frontignan. Half their production undergoes automatic *remuage*. The aniseed-nosed 83 Blanc de Noirs is their best wine.

| Domaine Chandon | MC | ★★→★★★ |
| --- | --- | --- |

California Drive, Yountville

*Star buys Chandon Reserve, Chandon Napa Valley Brut*

If Schramsberg are the Krug of Napa Valley, then Domaine Chandon are of course the Moët & Chandon. And at times Moët's California outpost, founded in 1973, has managed to outshine its Moët-Hennessy owners, consistently providing from the 1984 Vintage onwards both quantity and quality. 30% of the Domaine's Pinot Noir/Chardonnay/Pinot Blanc grapes (the latter advocated by consulting oenologist Edmond Maudière of Moët, Epernay) come from their own Napa vineyards. The remainder are supplied by numerous growers including nearby Trefethen. Annual production (utilizing their own Moët yeast strain plus 4,032 enormous Domaine-designed gyropalettes) is now almost half a million cases. This is mostly accounted for by the fine Pinot Noir-dominated Napa Valley Brut, fresh, fruity and smoky-nosed. Then follows the gulpable, pale salmon-pink Blanc de Noirs (100% Pinot Noir) and the elegant four-star Reserve (100% Pinot Noir and four years on yeast). The fragrant and flowery Reserve will be available again (in magnums only) in 1987. So far all Domaine Chandon bubbly has been non-vintage due to the high proportion (12–15%) of Reserve wines used in the blends. The Domaine also produce a ratafia-style Pinot Noir-based apéritif, Panache, and have their own excellent *haute cuisine* restaurant. Expect a new Blanc de Blancs-dominant deluxe *cuvée* (called Dom Chandon perhaps?) in 1988/89.

| Domaine Mumm | MC | ☆ |
| --- | --- | --- |

111 Dunaweal Lane, Calistoga

Secrecy is all, so it seems, at Seagram's West Coast outpost whose Franco-American winery is being built on Sterling's extravagant Napa property. Although a 1986 release is rumoured, Domaine Mumm are so far not allowing anyone to evaluate the wine.

| Domaine Montreaux | MC | ☆☆ |
| --- | --- | --- |

4242 Big Ranch Road, Napa

This new Monticello Cellars offshoot is part-owned by its European-influenced winemaker, the talented Alan Phillips. Since 1983 Domaine Montreaux have made minute quantities of a Pinot Noir-dominated Brut vintage wine, partly fermented and aged in barrel. Their first sparkling wine, 83 Domaine Montreaux, is due for release in late 1987.

| Estrella River | MC | ★ |
| --- | --- | --- |

Highway 46 East, Paso Robles

Situated in San Luis Obispo County. Tom Myers makes small amounts of a vintage-dated Blanc de Blancs Brut from the Chardonnay grape for the Giacobine family. Estrella River and Tonio Conti are currently sharing the same *méthode champenoise* equipment.

| Fetzer Vineyards | MC | ★→ |
| --- | --- | --- |

13500 South Highway 101, Hopland

Fetzer is definitely a family-run affair with ten brothers and sisters hard at work. They are only recently involved in sparkling wine: Fetzer's earliest attempts were experimental rather than commercial and fewer than 2,000 cases of a Pinot Noir-dominated Brut, rounded off with a little Chardonnay, were sold in California in 1985 and 1986. The nation-wide launch is due in 1987. So far Hopland grapes have gone into Fetzer sparklers, but future *cuvées* are likely to be made from fine Anderson and Redwood Valley fruit. Look out for a Fetzer Reserve with five years on yeast.

| Firestone | MC | ★ |
| --- | --- | --- |

Zaca Station Road, Los Olivos

1985 saw the trial launch of a new Santa Ynez Valley sparkler, Firestone's dawn-pink Princess Aurora, a 100% Pinot Noir *méthode champenoise* wine. From the winery's own vineyards, Princess Aurora is named after Brooks Firestone's wife, Kate, who once danced the role of Princess Aurora in The Royal

Ballet's The Sleeping Beauty. Previously available only for family celebrations, Princess Aurora will always be a limited line and will probably not be commercially available until 1987.

## Franzia                      CC                                    ★
17000 East Highway 120, Ripon

Vast amounts of tank-method flavoured Franzia fizz rejoicing in such non-vinous names as Bavarian Blackberry and Roman Raspberry are sold alongside the pink-hued White Zinfandel Champagne. The low-alcohol Franzia California Champagne Brut, sweet and beery, is their best wine.

## Freixenet Sonoma              MC                              ★★→
23555 Highway 121, Sonoma

Great things are expected from impressive Davis- and Domaine Chandon-trained winemaker Eileen Crane at this offshoot of the Spanish firm. The Freixenet President's wife gave her name to two early Gloria Ferrer Cuvée Emerald Brut non-vintage releases, fragrant and yeasty. These were made at Chateau St-Jean (Graton) and Piper Sonoma, but from late 1986 wine will be made at Freixenet Sonoma's handsome new winery, complete with underground cellars, near San Francisco. Freixenet's own fine, full-flavoured Carneros Pinot Noir and Chardonnay grapes will eventually supply half their needs. These grapes will be turned into two wines, a Pinot Noir-dominated Blanc de Noirs and a Brut.

## E. & J. Gallo                 CC                              →★
600 Yosemite Boulevard, Modesto

The gigantic Gallo winery, situated at the northern end of the Central Valley – the "fruitbowl" of America – produces more sparkling wine than any other North American winery: a cool 1m cases per annum minimum of the ubiquitous André and others. Clever advertising, hard-working salesmen and a low price have, since the early 1970s, made André (and to a lesser extent Ballatore) a staggering success story. Unfortunately, the taste is less impressive than the sales figures.

## Geyser Peak                   MC                                   ★
22281 Chianti Road, Geyserville

This winery dating back to 1880 is situated north of Geyserville on a hill overlooking the Alexander Valley. It was extensively modernized and expanded more than a decade ago. Production is large and mostly of the jug type, but Geyser Peak's vintage-dated Brut, which is made from Sonoma County grapes, is a notch up in quality.

## Gloria Ferrer
*See* Freixenet Sonoma.

## Handley Cellars               MC                                   ☆
2160 Guntley Road, Philo

This minute family firm has chosen a first-class location just down the road from Roederer at Philo in the cool Anderson valley. Until their own 4ha (10 acres) plot of Chardonnay and Pinot Noir vines yield, the Handleys are buying grapes locally to make just 375 cases per annum. Handley Cellars' first wine, a 1983 Pinot Noir-dominated Brut, is due to be released in late 1986, and a 1984 Rosé is on the way.

### Heitz Cellars                    MC                    ★
500 Taplin Road, St-Helena

350 cases of unexciting non-vintage Brut and Extra Dry are made for Heitz Cellars by another Napa winery.

### Hop Kiln Winery                  MC                    ★
6050 Westside Road, Healdsburg

Anyone who develops a taste for Hop Kiln's *méthode champenoise* Brut Verveux, made from Rhine Riesling grapes, will have no alternative but to keep going back to the winery housed in an old hop-drying barn, for it is only sold there.

### Robert Hunter                    MC                   ★→
3027 Silverado Trail, St Helena

This Sonoma Valley sparkler stems from a joint venture with Duckhorn Cellars in the Napa Valley. Grapes come mostly from Robert Hunter's vineyard to the west of Sonoma, and winemaking expertise from Duckhorn. The first release was 5,000 cases of a 1980 Pinot Noir-dominated Brut de Noirs topped up with Chardonnay, which was followed by a crisp, clean slatey 81 Brut de Noirs. Production is now approx. 8,000 cases per annum.

### Iron Horse                 MC              81 82   ★★→★★★
9786 Ross Station Road, Sebastopol
*Star buys 82 Brut, 81 Blanc de Noirs*

This remote hilltop winery grows Pinot Noir and Chardonnay in Green Valley and picks the grapes early. Since 1980 Forrest Tancer's winemaking expertise, and more recently that of Reims-trained Claude Thibaut, have made an impressive clutch of lean, elegant, low-*dosage* vintage wines. The Pinot Noir-dominated sparklers are the most stylish, especially the intense, rich, fruity 82 Brut and the fresh, racy 81 Blanc de Noirs. Reagan and Gorbachev are among those who have enjoyed the soft, smoky 82 Blanc de Blancs. Labels carry disgorge dates. Future plans include Brut Reserve and Rosé.

### JFJ Bronco                       CC                    →★
6342 Bystrum Road, Ceres

Cheap but not very enjoyable Modesto sweet sparklers, made by the bulk method, are sold under the JFJ Winery label. JFJ is best known for its ubiquitous (in California at any rate) jug and carafe wines. Extra Dry and Naturel are the two styles available. Sales are half a million cases annually.

### Korbel                           MC                  ★→★★
13250 River Road, Guerneville

Century-old Korbel's wide range of sweet, bland, inoffensive sparklers have recently notched up annual sales of over 1m cases, making it the biggest selling California *méthode champenoise* in the USA. The redwood forest backdrop plus gardens, museum and ultra-efficient automation merit a Korbel detour. Their best wine is the simple, fruity 100% Chardonnay Blanc de Blancs.

### Hanns Kornell                    MC                    ★
1091 Larkmead Lane, St-Helena

Four generations of Kornells have made sparkling wine, first in Germany and now in the USA. Kornell buy finished wine and add bubbles via the *méthode champenoise* including hand riddling. The wines sell well, but their strong flavours will not be appreciated by everyone. The Chenin Blanc-based 80 Blanc de Blancs, soft and peachy, is the best sparkling wine that Hanns Kornell produce.

## Thomas Kruse      MC      ★→
4390 Hecker Pass Road, Gilroy

Situated south of Saratoga in the Hecker Pass district of the Santa Cruz mountains, Thomas Kruse make small amounts of a Naturel-style *méthode champenoise* wine under the Insouciance label.

## Maison Deutz      MC      ☆→
454 Deutz Drive, Arroyo Grande

French tradition, from the Deutz champagne house, and California know-how join forces at Pressoir Deutz, situated down south in San Luis Obispo County at Arroyo Grande. Until their own Pinot Blanc/Pinot Noir/Chardonnay/Chenin Blanc grapes come on stream, fruit from nearby Santa Maria Valley is being used. Pinot Blanc looks set to be the backbone of the first late 1986 Maison Deutz release – a non-vintage blend backed up by some Pinot Noir and Chardonnay, as well as a proportion of reserve wines. Deutz are aiming for a full-flavoured old-style sparkling wine – principally non-vintage, but vintage too if quality merits it. Currently production of this sparkler is small but could rise to 30,000 cases per annum.

## Mark West Vineyards      MC      ★★→★★★
7000 Trenton-Healdsburg Road, Forestville
*Star buy 81 Blanc de Noirs*

First-time fluke it may have been, but Joan and Bob Ellis's only sparkling wine to date, the 81 Blanc de Noirs made exclusively from their own Russian River Pinot Noir grapes, is excellent: its slightly pink colour and fresh *fraise de bois* bouquet and taste augur well for future releases.

## Paul Masson      TM      ★→★★
13150 Saratoga Avenue, Saratoga

Now that Taylor California Cellars have been absorbed into Paul Masson this mighty Seagram name is even mightier than before. Paul Masson's fresh, green, vintage-dated Brut, from Chardonnay and Pinot Noir topped up with other less noble varieties, is one of the better transfer-method wines. Similarly the Extra Dry is attractive, but like the Brut could do with a shot more of invigorating acidity.

## Mirassou      MC      ★★→
3000 Aborn Road, San Jose

This fifth generation family firm was established in 1854 by French gold prospector Pierre Pellier (his daughter married a Mirassou). Today they use a blend of Pinot Noir, Chardonnay and Pinot Blanc grapes grown in cool Monterey County to make their fresh and lively *méthode champenoise* sparklers. Latest innovations from Mirassou include a mobile vineyard press and the curiously scented Brut Rosé bubbly sold alongside their Brut, Au Naturel, Blanc de Noirs and Late-disgorged. Try the well-made, clean, easy-to-drink 82 Monterey Brut with its smell of lime juice.

## Robert Mondavi    MC    ★★
7801 St Helena Highway, St Helena

Experimental sparkling wine has gone down well here with both
staff and visitors since 1978. After a thousand taste, technical and
harvest trials the rich, full 81 Mondavi Brut is likely to be the first
commercial release in 1987, made predominantly from Oak
Knoll Pinot Noir plus a little Carneros Chardonnay. Future
releases will continue to be Pinot Noir-orientated but a
Chardonnay-dominated Brut is also likely. All *cuvées* are to have
a lengthy four years on the yeast.

## The Monterey Vineyard    MC    ★→★★
800 South Alta Street, Gonzales

Part of the giant Seagram organisation. Grapes for The Monterey
Vineyard's only sparkling wine – the vintage-dated Brut – come
from the same 8ha (20 acres) Salinas Valley vineyard (planted to
60% Pinot Noir plus 20% each of the Pinot Blanc and
Chardonnay) every year. This must be Seagram's most upmarket
sparkling wine, as production (involving hand riddling) is tiny
(just 3,000 cases) and the wine is available virtually only at the
winery. The once mighty Taylor California Cellars were
previously associated with this winery. They have now been
absorbed by Paul Masson.

## Nevada City Winery    MC    ★→
321 Spring Street, Nevada

Situated east of the Central Valley and tucked away in the Sierra
foothills area (better known in earlier times as California's Gold
Rush country). This recently established winery was set up by
local people keen to revitalize the booming pre-prohibition wine
traditions of the region with, amongst other wines, a Brut
Naturel and a Cuvée des Enfants. Future production will be
limited to a Chardonnay/Pinot Noir blend, the Cuvée des
Montagnes.

## Nicasio Vineyards    MC    →★
483 Nicasio Way, Soquel

Situated in the Santa Cruz mountains just east of Santa Cruz, this
small enterprise owned by Dan Wheeler produces limited
amounts of Naturel *méthode champenoise* from Pinot Noir,
Chardonnay and White Riesling grapes.

## Novitiate Wines    CC    ★
300 College Avenue, Los Gatos

South of Saratoga and the Bay, Novitiate Wines have an
impressive history going back nearly one hundred years. The
wines are somewhat old-fashioned in style, including the sweet,
bulk-method Demi-Sec.

## Parsons Creek    MC    ★★→
3001 South State Street, Ukiah

Just down the road from Scharffenberger, Parsons Creek buys its
grapes from the cool Anderson and Potter Valleys. Winemaker
Jesse Tidwell makes just 4,000 cases annually and his first release is
the crisp, creamy and very drinkable Pinot Noir-dominated non-
vintage Brut, which also has some Chardonnay in the blend.
Future releases from Parsons Creek are likely to be in the same
mould as this wine.

| Piper Sonoma | MC | 81 | ★★ |

11447 Old Redwood Highway, Healdsburg

Piper Sonoma's stylish $8m showplace winery in Sonoma – a joint US/Piper Heidsieck venture – has since 1980 produced crisp, dry, vintage-dated wine from mostly bought-in Sonoma grapes. It is not a wine that will appeal to lovers of bigger, bouncier styles. Production via automatic remuage is now almost 75,000 cases a year. Most of this is accounted for by the austere, cinnamon-nosed Pinot Noir-dominated 82 Brut. This is followed by a small proportion of their fruity, somewhat earthy 82 Blanc de Noirs, and even tinier amounts of their 81 Tête de Cuvée – a fuller-flavoured and more complex 50/50 blend of Chardonnay and Pinot Noir.

| Martin Ray | MC | | ★→ |

1593 Willowmont Avenue, San Jose

North of Saratoga in the Santa Cruz mountains, this small winery run by yet another Stanford professor produces tiny amounts of wildly expensive *méthode champenoise* Naturel.

| Roederer USA | MC | | ☆→ |

Office: 2211 McKinley Avenue, Berkeley

Devotees eagerly await the first Roederer USA release planned for late 1988. 141ha (350 acres) of prime Anderson Valley land at Philo have been planted with equal plots of Pinot Noir and Chardonnay, yielding their first crop in 1986. The new winery's architecture is rumoured to be "French country/rustic California", with hillside caves hewn out of an old quarry. Production at the new winery is likely to be approx. 85,000 cases.

| Rosenblum Cellars | MC | | ★ |

1401 Stanford Avenue, Emeryville

The Rosenblum family and partners turn out just 300 cases a year of their idiosyncratic, spicy sparkling wines. These are made mostly from the Gewürztraminer grape topped up with White Riesling. The wine was originally sold as Napa Valley Sparkling Gewürztraminer and now as California Sparkling Brut.

| San Pasqual Vineyards | MC | | →★ |

13455 San Pasqual Road, Escondido

Just north of San Diego, San Pasqual must surely be California's most southerly sparkling wine producer. Some curious grape varieties (from their own vineyards) are turned into sparklers here: the Blanc de Noirs is predominantly Gamay, with a little Sauvignon Blanc and Chenin Blanc. The 81 vintage (only 750 cases) was the first release, with future production intended to be three times that amount.

| Scharffenberger | MC | 81 | ★★→ |

307 Talmage Road, Ukiah

Hotly tipped as one of the leading Mendocino County *méthode champenoise* winemakers, Dr Robert Porter has, since 1981, been making some stylish, sophisticated sparkling wine from the equally admired cool-climate Anderson and Redwood Valley grapes. *Remuage* is performed mechanically. Most of Scharffenberger's annual 20,000 cases are taken up by the Pinot Noir-dominated Brut. A little 100%-Chardonnay Blanc de Blancs is also made, however, together with smaller amounts of

Brut Rosé and a 50/50 Pinot Noir/Chardonnay Reserve. Cuvée No. 2 is a wine which spends longer on the yeast. Judging, from the positive, fresh, peppermint bouquet and elegant, flowery clean-cut palate of the 81 Cuvée No. 2 Brut, Scharffenberger is definitely a winery to watch. The fresh, green zippy 82 Blanc de Blancs is less impressive.

| Schramsberg | MC | ★★ → ★★★★ |
|---|---|---|
| Calistoga | | |

*Star buys 81 Blanc de Blancs, 75 Reserve*

Registered Historical Landmark No. 561 was founded as a winery by Jacob Schram in 1862, complete with an impressive mountain-top Victorian house and rock-hewn cellars. Schramsberg, which is clearly no ordinary California *méthode champenoise* producer, was bought by Jack and Jamie Davies in 1965. Schramsberg's big, rich, complex sparklers are, even competitors admit, California's answer to Krug. With part barrel-fermented base wine, long ageing on yeast (five years for Reserve wines), brandy in the *dosage* and noticeable use of old Reserve wines, Schramsberg are probably as Krugesque as any California producer can get. The wines are admired by wine buffs and American presidents (Nixon, Carter and Reagan) alike. 16ha (40 acres) of Schramsberg's own Pinot Noir/Chardonnay plus the neighbouring new 8ha (20 acres) plot, formerly McEckron's, provide more than 20% of their needs. Bought-in grapes supply the rest. Most of the annual 50,000 case production is hand riddled with 20% on gyropalettes. Of the five different Schramsberg wines, the glorious, elegant, full Chardonnay-dominated 81 Blanc de Blancs, smoky, racy and yeasty, accounts for more than half the total. This is followed by the 80 Pinot Noir-based Blanc de Noirs (rounded off with Chardonnay) with its pinky blush and big, fruity, exotic taste. Limited amounts of a pale, pinky-gold 81 Cuvée de Pinot, soft and fruity, are on sale as well as the Schramsberg curio, the sweet, aromatic 82 Crémant Demi-Sec pudding fizz, made from the spicy Flora grape. Schramsberg's most expensive bubblies however are their Reserve wines (avoid the excessively smoky-toasty 79) whose *cépage* varies slightly every year: the big, rich, fragrant 78 was 100% Chardonnay and the biscuity, almost overblown 80 mostly Pinot Noir. Schramsberg joined forces with Rémy Martin in 82 to launch RMS Alambic brandy.

| Sebastiani | MC | ★ → ★★ |
|---|---|---|
| 389 Fourth Street East, Sonoma | | |

After eight decades in California Italian traditions are as strong as ever at this third-generation family-run winery, right down to using Italian brandy in the *dosage* of its recently launched non-vintage *méthode champenoise* Sebastiani Brut. Sebastiani's base wine, made predominantly from Sonoma Valley Pinot Noir (plus a little Chardonnay), is trucked over twice to Chateau St-Jean at Graton, first for its *liqueur de tirage* and finally for riddling and bottling. Despite the journeys, Sebastiani's fresh, yeasty, doughy, pink-toned Brut is a palatable, clean blend.

| Shadow Creek | MC | 81 | ★★ |
|---|---|---|---|
| 2195 Corbett Canyon Road, San Luis Obispo | | | |

New owners (Glenmore Distilleries) mean that from 1986 Shadow Creek fizz will be made at its own Central Coast winery by an experienced ex-Korbel winemaker. Previous wines, including vintage and non-vintage Bruts, a Blanc de Blancs and a Blanc de Noirs all made by Chateau St-Jean at Graton, have had their ups and downs. But the seductive flowery 81 Cuvée No. 1 Blanc de Noirs (100% Pinot Noir) is a three-star plus wine.

| Sierra Wine Corporation | CC | →★ |

1925 North Mooney Boulevard, Tulare

This south Central Valley producer makes inexpensive, big-selling bulk-method sparkling wine sold under the Valley Mission label in both Brut and Extra Dry styles.

| Sonoma-Cutrer | MC | ☆→ |

4401 Slusser Road, Windsor

Based over the hill from Mark West and still in the Russian River Valley. Sonoma Cutrer's winemaker Bill Bonnetti is aiming for a high-quality 100%-Chardonnay wine from the winery's own grapes. Besides undergoing its first fermentation in cask, the wine will spend a very lengthy seven years on the yeast. The first *cuvée* is due out in 1987 and a limited production is planned.

| Stony Ridge | CC | ★→ |

818 Main Street, Pleasanton

Stony Ridge are a medium-sized winery situated east of the Bay in the Livermore Valley. They make an Extra Dry bulk-method bubbly.

| Tijsseling | MC | ★→ |

2150 McNab Ranch Road, Ukiah

Tijsseling, south of Ukiah, is not the easiest winery to find but its vintage-dated wine is becoming increasingly widely available. Unlike other Mendocino or indeed California fizz producers, fruit for Tijsseling's 10,000 or so cases come from one site – that of the Tijsseling farm just north of Hopland. So far the winery has produced a toasty 82 Pinot Noir-dominated Brut and a 100% Chardonnay non-*dosage* 82 Blanc de Blancs. A 100% Pinot Noir Blanc de Noirs is in the pipe-line. All wines are disgorge-dated.

| Tonio Conti | MC | ★→ |

Adelaida Star Route, Paso Robles

Named after its major Swiss shareholder and owned by Adelaida Cellars. Tonio Conti hope to plant vines where they now buy their grapes, in the Paso Robles area. For the moment the wines are made at Estrella River. Emphasis here is on the low-*dosage* vintage 100% Chardonnay Blanc de Blancs. Helpfully (for *dosage* devotees perhaps?) back labels give disgorge and *dosage* details.

| Van der Kamp | MC | ★→ |

PO Box 609, Kenwood

Martin and Dixie van der Kamp are the major shareholders in this tiny 3,000-case enterprise. The fruity 81 Pinot Noir-dominated Brut (plus a little Chardonnay) has gone down well with discerning palates, but quite why the van der Kamps have labelled it English Cuvée is anyone's guess. Likewise the 100% Pinot Noir 82 Brut Rosé which is called Midnight Cuvée.

| Ventana | MC | ★→★★ |

Los Coches Road, Soledad

Suppliers of grapes more than of wine, Ventana originally sold Chardonnay and Pinot Noir grapes to other wineries to turn into sparkling wine. They now produce very limited amounts of their own *méthode champenoise* sparklers. Some of Ventana's own Arroyo Seco grapes from cool Monterey were turned into Naturel Cuvée JDM in 1981 and 1982. The blend was two-thirds Pinot Noir and one-third Chardonnay.

| Weibel | CC/TM | ★ |
|---|---|---|

1250 Stanford Avenue, Mission San Jose

Swiss emigré Fred Weibel and his family now use their European winemaking experience to make vast quantities of distinctly Californian, mainly non-vintage *cuve close* sparkling wine from bought-in grapes. These wines appear under numerous labels including Sparkling White Zinfandel, Sparkling Green Hungarian and Crackling Rosé. From the 1985 vintage onwards Weibel's premium Mendocino fizz will be made via the *méthode champenoise* and the transfer-method sparklers will be phased out gradually.

| Wente | MC | ★ |
|---|---|---|

5050 Arroyo Road, Livermore

Established in 1833, this fourth-generation family-owned firm is based east of the Bay in the Livermore Valley. The handsome mission-style Cresta Blanca winery, along with its sandstone caves, was restored in 1981 and became the headquarters of Wente's own sparkling wine unit, complete with conference centre and restaurant. Night-picked and field-crushed Chardonnay, Pinot Noir and Pinot Blanc grapes from their own Arroyo Seco vineyards in Monterey are turned here into 25,000 cases of the Wente Bros' only sparkling wine – the fruity but dull Chardonnay-dominated Brut.

# — *The Rest of the USA*—

At the last count there were more than 120 American sparkling wine producers: it seems that almost every state has one or two sparklers of its own. California, of course, still accounts for about half of these producers (and the vast majority of all the sparkling wine made). However, New York State is in second place with roughly 20 producers, with Michigan and Missouri the next biggest sparkling wine producing states.

The chief drawback for American winemakers hoping to produce top quality sparkling wines is not the method they employ, for most firms are using the classic *méthode champenoise*, but the choice of grape variety. Severe winters and late springs mean that in many states outside California winemakers will always have a limited choice. At best, they can grow French hybrids such as the hardy Seyval Blanc, Aurora and Vidal, and at worst American hybrids, such as the Dutchess and Delaware with their mild, but still noticeable, foxy *labrusca* taste. The most foxy and *labrusca*-like of all the native American hybrids is Concord. The sparkling wines made from this all-American grape are unlikely ever to be admired internationally, despite their devoted local fans. Nor are the Scuppernong-based sparklers from the deep South with their sweet musky flavours.

Currently the producers who are making the most stylish American sparklers outside California are those using both the classic Champagne method and grapes: Chardonnay and Pinot Noir. A good alternative for those with impossible climates are the robust French hybrids, plantings of which are happily on the increase everywhere. This will mean that during the next five years or so, as the new plantings come on stream, there will be a definite improvement in the quality of American sparkling wine. In New York State a marked improvement in quality is already noticeable, for French hybrids and the milder American hybrids are beginning to replace the *labrusca*-dominant grapes, such as Niagara and Catawaba, in most firms' sparkling wine blends.

Michigan's sparkling wine figures in the 1960s and early 1970s had much to do with that curious sparkling pink party phenomenon Cold Duck. Made mostly from sparkling white and red wine, this sweet *labrusca*-like tipple is an Americanized version of the traditional German sparkling Kalte Ente or Cold Duck. Cold Duck is no longer as popular as it once was (although produced in numerous states). Those firms who still make it usually produce a similar "Sparkling Burgundy" as well.

The sparkling wine region to watch in America, outside California, is the Pacific Northwest. For it is here, especially in the cool, almost Champagne-like climate of Oregon, that the widely planted Pinot Noir and Chardonnay produce what could well prove to be the quintessential West Coast sparkling wine base: elegant, restrained wines with subtle fruit flavours, low alcohol and high acidity. This, together with the low price of vineyard land compared to California, has already started to attract winemakers from elsewhere.

## Arkansas

| Post Winery | MC | ★→ |
|---|---|---|
| Route 1, Box 1, Altus | | |

Emily Post herself would no doubt have approved of this tidy Alpine-style winery founded by Jacob Post from Bavaria in 1880.

The Post *méthode champenoise* Brut and Naturel are a cut above the other Franco–American hybrid wines here.

| Wiederkehr Wine Cellars | CC | →★ |
| --- | --- | --- |
| Wiederkehr Village, Altus | | |

Atop Champagne Drive lies the Wiederkehr family's mini Alpine village comprising winery, restaurant *et al*. Cousins to the Posts, whose winery lies at the bottom of St Mary's Mountain, the Swiss Wiederkehrs produce Extra Dry bulk-method wines under the Chateau du Monte and Hanns Wiederkehr labels.

## Connecticut

| Haight Vineyard | MC | ★→★★ |
| --- | --- | --- |
| Chestnut Hill, Litchfield | | |

Connecticut's first winery to open since the Repeal is now more than a decade old. It produces just 800 cases annually of Haight Blanc de Blancs made exclusively from its own Seyval Blanc grapes, with a dash of Chardonnay to lighten the hybrid load. The wine is made by the *méthode champenoise* (including hand riddling) and produced in either Dry or Naturel non-vintage versions.

## Hawaii

| Tedeschi Vineyard | MC | ★ |
| --- | --- | --- |
| PO Box 953, Ulupalakua, Maui | | |

Hawaii is not the first place anyone would connect with sparkling wine production, but the Carnelian *vinifera* grape thrives in the Tedeschi's sub-tropical dormant volcanic vineyard. The grape is turned via the *méthode champenoise* into the vintage-dated Erdman-Tedeschi Blanc de Noirs Brut. Pineapple wine, still and sparkling, is also on offer.

## Idaho

| Ste-Chapelle Winery | CC | ★★ |
| --- | --- | --- |
| Route 4, Caldwell | | |

Idaho is better known for potatoes than wine, but perhaps the well-distributed Ste-Chapelle, with its attractive octagonal chapel of a winery featured on the label, will change all that. This impressive decade-old concern deals only with the *vinifera* grape (mainly Chardonnay and Johannisberg Riesling). A bulk-method Blanc de Noirs Ste-Chapelle sparkling wine, made from the Pinot Noir, is currently sold.

## Illinois

| Thompson Winery | MC | ★ |
| --- | --- | --- |
| PO Box 127, Monee | | |

Small quantities of Père Marquette and Père Hennepin white and rosé *méthode champenoise* are made every year at this converted railway station. The grapes used are Franco–American hybrids.

## Maine

| Bartlett Maine Estate Winery | MC | →★ |
| --- | --- | --- |
| Box 598, Gouldsboro | | |

Maine's first and possibly to remain its only winery is run by Bob,

Mary and Kathe Bartlett. They make what they describe as "classic *méthode champenoise*" wine from pears and apples. Classic winemaking equipment is certainly much in evidence here including stainless steel tanks and French oak casks, but Bartlett Sparkling Pear/Apple Brut is unlikely to convert lovers of the grape.

## Massachusetts

| Chicama Vineyards | MC | →★ |
|---|---|---|
| Stoney Hill Road, West Tisbury | | |

Chicama's peach-coloured Sea Mist Sparkling Wine is predominantly Chenin Blanc topped up with a little Chardonnay and White Riesling. Only 125 cases are made annually at this Martha's Vineyard winery.

| Nashoba Valley Winery | MC | →★ |
|---|---|---|
| 100 Wattaquadoc Hill Road, Bolton | | |

Not to be outdone by Maine, this state also boasts a non-vintage *méthode champenoise* sparkling apple wine of which 200 cases are made every year.

## Michigan

| Fenn Valley | MC | ★→★★ |
|---|---|---|
| 6130–122nd Avenue, Fennville | | |

Fenn Valley make just 125 cases a year of their dry Blanc de Blancs Naturel (from their own Seyval grapes backed up by another French hybrid, the Vidal, plus a little Riesling). This is sold chiefly at the winery. Future plans include a 100% sparkling Riesling.

| Lakeside Vineyard | MC | →★ |
|---|---|---|
| 13581 Red Arrow Highway, Harbert | | |

Tourists love this easily accessible place, originally known as the Molly Pitcher winery. Wine-bibbers are likely to find that name, plus the sweet *méthode champenoise* wine called Touch of Bubbly, all rather too much.

| Leelanau | MC | ★→ |
|---|---|---|
| Box 68, Omena | | |

Just over a decade old, Leelanau make everything, it seems, from fruit wines through to hybrid wines and, more and more, wines from *vinifera*. Chardonnay and Pinot Noir are planted and small amounts of Extra Dry *méthode champenoise* are produced.

| St-Julian | CC/MC | ★→ |
|---|---|---|
| Kalamazoo Street, Paw Paw | | |

The wonderfully-addressed St-Julian winery is named after the Italian founder's home town patron saint. Most of the winery's vast production is made from hybrid grapes. Bulk-method sparkling wine is sold under the Chateau St-Julian label and tiny amounts of *méthode champenoise* San Giuliano are also made.

| Tabor Hill | CC | ★→★★ |
|---|---|---|
| Route Two, Buchanan | | |

Another Alpine-inspired place. The emphasis here is on French hybrids and *vinifera* varieties such as Chardonnay and Johannnisberg Riesling. A small amount of vintage-dated bulk-method wine goes out under the Tabor Hill and Brontë labels.

| **Warner Vineyards** | CC/MC | →★ |

706 Kalamazoo Street, Paw Paw

Next door to St-Julian, this is the largest Michigan producer, buying in grapes from all over the state. The vintage-dated Warner sparklers, sold under curious names, such as Very, Very Cranberry, Pol Pereaux and Warner, are the best of the uninspiring Warner range.

## Missouri

| **Hermannhof** | MC | ★→★★ |

330 East First Street, Hermann

An 8ha (20 acres) plot close to Hermannhof supplies Seyval Blanc, Vidal and Villard Blanc grapes for 2,500 cases of *méthode champenoise* Hermannhof's Hermann Brut Champagne. Brut, Extra Dry and Blanc de Blancs styles are all made.

| **Mount Pleasant Vineyards** | CC/TM/MC | ★→ |

101 Webster Street, Augusta

The century-old Mount Pleasant winery concentrates on French hybrids and *labrusca*. Since the winery was revitalized in 1968 small quantities of vintage-dated *méthode champenoise*, bulk-and transfer-method wine have been made in a variety of styles from Brut to Sweet.

| **Rosati Winery** | MC | →★ |

Route 1, St James

Hybrid grapes and Italian traditions sum up the Rosati style. The fruity, heavy Brut, Dry and Demi-Sec non-vintage Rosati Champagne is much liked locally.

| **St-James Winery** | MC | ★→ |

540 Sidney Street, St-James

The ten-year-old St-James Winery is owned by the Hofherrs whose Fresno State-trained son will no doubt want to move on from mead, fruit wines and Franco-American hybrids to *vinifera* wines. Pink champagne is popular here and Extra Dry and Naturel versions of St-James Winery's *méthode champenoise* sparklers are also produced.

| **Stone Hill** | MC | →★ |

Route One, Hermann

Prohibition has a lot to answer for: at the impressive hilltop winery of Stone Hill, founded by a German emigré, mushrooms grew where wine was once cellared. Now, more than a century after its foundation, the Helds and their Fresno State oenology department-educated children keep the local German traditions alive and make wine from the native American hybrid grapes via the *méthode champenoise*.

## North Carolina

| **Biltmore Estate** | MC | ★★ |

One Biltmore Plaza, Asheville

The celebrated Biltmore stately pile was built by George Vanderbilt. Chardonnay and other noble vines have been planted on the estate for some years now. The new vineyards, an imported French winemaker, and a new no-expense-spared winery promise well for the vintage-dated *méthode champenoise* Biltmore Estate and Chateau Biltmore wines.

| Duplin Wine Cellars | MC | →★ |
| --- | --- | --- |
| Highway 117, Rose Hill | | |

This group of North Carolina grape growers has joined forces to produce, amongst other wines, vintage-dated Brut and Sweet *méthode champenoise* sparklers. They are made from the curiously flavoured Scuppernong grape, unique to the southeastern states.

## New Jersey

| Gross Highland Winery | CC | ★→ |
| --- | --- | --- |
| 306 Jim Leeds Road, Absecon | | |

This establishment north of Atlantic City turns out tank-method sparklers under both the Gross Highland and Bernard D'Arcy labels. The move from *labrusca* to French hybrids and *vinifera*, together with the expertise of a Davis-trained winemaker augur well for future (possibly *méthode champenoise*?) releases.

| Renault Winery | MC | ★→ |
| --- | --- | --- |
| 72 Bremen Avenue, Egg Harbor City | | |

In 1864 champagne salesman Louis Renault travelled west, liked what he saw and planted vineyards. He was soon selling his own wine rather than that of the firm that had sent him. Today New Jersey's oldest winery receives thousands of visitors a day and hybrid/*vinifera* plantings are on the increase, which is good news for its Renault, Dumont and St-George's brands.

| Tomasello Winery | MC | ★ |
| --- | --- | --- |
| 225 White Horse Pike, Hammonton | | |

The first farming Tomasello founded this winery just after Prohibition and their first sparkling wine was made in the late 1940s. A few French hybrids introduced in the early 1970s are now blended in with the ubiquitous "foxy" grapes native to the East Coast. Today third-generation Tomasellos make no less than six different sparklers from the two grape varieties – two of which are sold under the Kainier label. Sparkling production however still only adds up to about 6,000 cases, of which the sweet Spumante and sweet (despite its label) Blanc de Blancs Brut are by far the most popular.

## New York

| Barrington | MC | ★→★★ |
| --- | --- | --- |
| Dundee | | |

Bought-in Chardonnay grapes (plus a little Pinot Noir) from the Finger Lakes are processed traditionally by hand here and turned into some 400 cases of Barrington Blanc de Blancs.

| Batavia Wine Cellars | TM | →★ |
| --- | --- | --- |
| School St. & Hewitt Place, Batavia | | |

This large wine firm sells non-vintage transfer-method sparkling wine under the Capri, Imperator and Royal Seal labels.

| Benmarl | MC | ★→ |
| --- | --- | --- |
| Highland Ave., Marlboro | | |

Chiefly a cooperative viti- and vinicultural research station for the Hudson River region, Benmarl sells its finest wines to its own members. However, diligent New Yorkers should be able to track down its vintage-dated Cuvée du Vigneron Mousseux Brut and Naturel.

---

**Bully Hill Vineyards**              MC              →★

Hammondsport

Bully by name and bizarre by nature, this quirky firm celebrates two decades of trading soon. Bully Hill's labels both back and front are extraordinary – the wine within, made mostly from the Seyval Blanc topped up with a little Vidal, is less so. Bully's latest idea is a 13% "champagne rouge" made from red hybrids and labelled "Mother Ship over Paris" to commemorate the owner's flight over the 1983 Paris airshow. Of course.

---

**Casa Larga Vineyards**             MC              ★★

2287 Turk Hill Road, Fairport

Some 500 cases of the 100% Chardonnay Casa Larga Naturel are produced annually from this estate's own grapes, grown in the Finger Lakes area.

---

**Clinton Vineyards**                MC              ★→★★

Schultzville Road, Clinton Corners

Clinton claim that they were the first to produce a *méthode champenoise* sparkler in the Hudson River Valley just north of New York City. Called Seyval Naturel, it is made exclusively from that hybrid and total production is just 250 cases.

---

**De May Wine Cellars**              MC              →★

Route 88, Hammondsport

This family-owned winery only sells wine at the door, so be prepared to make the trek to the Finger Lakes if you like the idea of purchasing a sweet red, rosé or white sparkler made by the *méthode champenoise*. The family follow the traditions built up at Vouvray in the Loire before the De Mays left France for the USA in 1974.

---

**Glenora Wine Cellars**             MC              ★★

Glenora-on-Seneca, Dundee

Nearly a decade old and with case sales to the order of 900 per annum, this tiny, quality-conscious winery uses the grapes from its own 3.6ha (9 acres) of Chardonnay and 0.4ha (1 acre) of Pinot Noir to create its vintage-dated Chardonnay-dominated Blanc de Blancs Naturel. The wine is hand riddled.

---

**Gold Seal Vineyards**              TM              ★→

Hammondsport

Founded in 1865 at Hammondsport in the heart of the Finger Lakes, this historic winery was making "Imperial champagne" as early as 1870. A series of Reims-trained winemakers turned *labrusca* grapes into bubbly until an ex-Veuve Clicquot wine-maker, Charles Fournier, started to work with the *vinifera* in the late 1950s. Today this Seagram-owned outfit uses the Charles Fournier signature to denote its finest sparkling wine – the disagreeable, burnt-toffee-like Blanc de Blancs made from Chardonnay, Vidal and Ravat grapes. (Henri Marchant is another label.) Other transfer-method sparklers here include Naturel, Brut, Extra Dry, Pink and Sparkling Burgundy, and all these are made principally from the native American hybrid grape – the Catawaba.

## Great Western Winery    TM/MC    ★→
Hammondsport

Great Western, founded in 1860, pips its Seagram sister Gold Seal at the post by being the oldest Finger Lakes winery by five years. Today the historic Bonded Winery Number One makes just one *méthode champenoise* wine (mostly from French hybrids): Great Western Naturel New York Champagne, sold in a Dom Pérignon look-alike bottle. Sparkling wine is also made here by the transfer method and sold under such labels as Blush, Cold Duck, Sparkling Burgundy and the more familiar styles of Brut, Pink and Extra Dry.

## Hudson Valley Wine Company    CC    →★
Blue Point Road, Highland

This firm, situated in the centre of the Hudson River region, was founded in 1907 and sells about 5,000 cases of sparkling wine per annum, made from a combination of American hybrids and the occasional superior French hybrid. Ultra-commercial labels include Sparkling Burgundy, Cold Duck, Brut, Extra Dry, Naturel and others.

## Knapp Farms    MC    ★→★★
2770 Country Road, Romulus

Knapp Vineyards Chardonnay Champagne Brut, made from the Chardonnay grape plus a little Pinot Noir, is the best sparkling wine here. Alternatively, for half the price try Knapp's "Champagne" made from hybrid grapes.

## McGregor Vineyard    MC    ★★
5503 Dutch Street, Dundee

Robert McGregor's 9.3ha (23 acres) *vinifera* vineyard, which amongst other noble vines is planted to Chardonnay and Pinot Noir, produces minute amounts of promising Chardonnay-dominated Naturel *méthode champenoise*.

## Monarch Wine Company    CC    →★
4500 Second Avenue, Brooklyn

Situated across the river from Manhattan, Monarch bring in *labrusca* juice from New York State to produce the Kosher Manischewitz sparkling wine and the Gallic-inspired Pol d'Argent, Chateau Laurent and Chateau Imperial in a variety of styles including Spumanti, Cold Duck and Sparkling Burgundy. Sales are impressive but the wines are less majestic than they sound.

## J. Roget    CC    →★
Canandaigua Wine Company, 116 Buffalo Street, Canandaigua

J. Roget is a brand name of the Canandaigua Wine Company, situated at the head of the odd-sounding Canandaigua Finger Lake (Canandaigua means "Chosen Place" in Seneca Indian). Total sales of flavoured sparkling wines, a style pioneered by the company, are now in excess of 1m cases. Their most popular line is L'Orangerie, an odd-sounding blend of coloured, low-alcohol fizz, orange juice, triple sec and "other natural flavours".

## Royal Wine Corporation    CC    →★
Dock Road, Milton

As this corporation's brand names of Kedem and Star of

Abraham suggest, the Herzogs produce sizeable amounts of kosher wine in the heart of the Hudson River area. Styles made here include Cold Duck, Sparkling Burgundy, Naturel and Demi-Sec among others.

---

### Schapiro's    CC    →★
126 Rivington Street, New York

Manhattan's last-remaining winery, founded in 1899 by Samuel Shapiro, produces kosher-approved sparkling wine under the ubiquitous Cold Duck, Sparkling Burgundy and Spumante labels besides pink and dry fizz.

---

### Taylor    TM    →★
Country Route 88, Hammondsport

Seagram's third historic Hammondsport winery was founded in 1880. It bought out its next door neighbour, Great Western, in 1961, only to be bought out in turn by Coca-Cola in 1977 and, eventually, by Seagram in 1983. Until 1968 Taylor's sparklers were made by the *méthode champenoise* but phenomenal sales (with 12m bottles ageing at any one time) soon necessitated a switch to the transfer method. Cold Duck and Sparkling Burgundy are made principally from the foxy *labrusca* Concord, while Brut, Extra Dry, Pink and Blush rely heavily on native American hybrids such as Catawaba and Delaware.

---

### Wagner Vineyards    CC    →★
Route 414, Lodi

Celebration Cuvée is a cheap tank-method sparkler made here from hybrid grapes.

---

### Widmer's Wine Cellars    CC/MC    →★
West Avenue & Tobey Street, Naples

The Swiss Widmers arrived at Naples in the west Finger Lakes in the 1880s. Today there are over 35 Widmer wines, including some 20,000 cases of bulk-method bubbly sold under the Lake Niagara name plus a little *méthode champenoise*.

---

### Hermann J. Wiemer Vineyard    MC    ★→
Route 14, Dundee

Teutonic traditions continue here, for Wiemer's *méthode champenoise* sparkler, the Naturel Vintage Brut, is made entirely from the Riesling grape. Future plans include a Chardonnay/Pinot Noir blend.

---

### Windsor Vineyards    MC    ★
Marlboro Champagne Cellars, 104 Western Avenue, Marlboro

This winery situated in the centre of Marlboro sells sparkling wine under the Great River Winery and Windsor labels. It has recently been bought out by Windsor Vineyards, a subsidiary of Sonoma Vineyards, which used to be connected with Piper Sonoma. All rather confusing. Small amounts of non-vintage *méthode champenoise* Brut are made.

---

### Woodbury Vineyards    MC    ★→
South Roberts Road, Dunkirk

The Woodburys have tended their vines here on the shores of Lake Erie since 1910. It took another 60 years, however, for the family to become interested in the *vinifera* vine. Small amounts of a Chardonnay Champagne Brut are made.

# Ohio

| Cedar Hill Wine Company | MC | ★ |
|---|---|---|

2195 Lee Road, Cleveland Heights

A doctor-cum-restaurateur-cum-winemaker, who is nothing if not enterprising, makes a *méthode champenoise* sparkler called Chateau Lagniappe in the restaurant's cellar. The wine is only sold upstairs.

| Mantey Vineyards | CC | →★ |
|---|---|---|

917 Bardshar Road, Sandusky

Sandusky on the shores of Lake Erie is the centre of Ohio's wine industry and this revamped 100-year-old winery now produces bulk-method bubbly from French-American hybrids.

| Meier's Wine Cellars | CC | →★ |
|---|---|---|

6955 Plainfield Pike, Silverton

At the other end of Ohio from Sandusky and close to Cincinnati, these cellars are under the same ownership as Mantey and Mon Ami. Production of Reim and Meier's *cuve close*-method Blanc de Blancs (made in part from French hybrid grapes grown on a small Lake Erie island) is considerably larger here than at the other two firms.

| Mon Ami | MC | →★ |
|---|---|---|

325 West Catawaba Road, Port Clinton

As the address suggests, the foxy *labrusca*-redolent Catawaba grape has much to do with the Mon Ami's *méthode champenoise* sparkler. This wine is produced in century-old cellars above which the Mon Ami restaurant is now housed.

| Moyer Vineyards | MC | ★→ |
|---|---|---|

3859 US Route 52, Manchester

Wineries-cum-restaurants seem to be the thing in Ohio, for the Moyers run both at No. 3859. *Méthode champenoise* wine is made here from French hybrids.

| Steuk Wine Company | MC | →★ |
|---|---|---|

1001 Fremont Avenue, Sandusky

*Labrusca* reigns supreme at this small winery, whose Extra Dry, Brut and Naturel *méthode champenoise* wines take some getting used to by palates not attuned to the *labrusca* style.

| Stillwater Wineries | MC | ★→ |
|---|---|---|

2311 State Route, 55 West Troy

Hardly the most appropriate name for a sparkling wine house! Stillwater Wineries' non-vintage *méthode champenoise* Brut comes from French hybrid grapes which are grown close to the Stillwater River.

# Oregon

| Arterberry | MC | ★★ |
|---|---|---|

905 East 10th Street, McMinnville

Situated in the heart of the Willamette River Valley. Oregon's first *méthode champenoise* wine was made here in a spare corner of the Eyrie Vineyards winery by a Davis-trained winemaker. Both a vintage-dated Brut and Naturel are produced here at Arterberry.

| Chateau Benoit | MC | ★→ |
| --- | --- | --- |

Route One, Charlton

The Benoits make limited amounts of a vintage-dated *méthode champenoise* Chateau Benoit Brut, among other wines, from nearly 16ha (10 acres) of Willamette River Valley grapes, including Chardonnay and Pinot Noir.

| Hillcrest Vineyard | MC | ★ |
| --- | --- | --- |

240 Vineyard Lane, Roseburg

Hillcrest was one of the first wineries to plant noble vines in Oregon and now grows Chardonnay and Pinot Noir. The Vineyard Lane address is reassuring, even if the Extra Dry *méthode champenoise* wine is sold under the less elegant name of Oregon Mist.

| Knudsen-Erath Winery | MC | ★★ |
| --- | --- | --- |

Worden Hill Road, Dundee

This leading Oregon winery with 28ha (70 acres) in the Willamette Valley is owned by Richard Erath and C. Calvert Knudsen. Every year they make 2,000 cases of a Chardonnay-dominated non-vintage Brut, mechanically riddled and topped up with Pinot Noir. The prospects look promising.

## Pennsylvania

| Bucks Country Vineyards | MC | ★ |
| --- | --- | --- |

Route 202, New Hope

This winery, complete with its own wine museum, is housed in an old barn. It produces, among other wines, a non-vintage *méthode champenoise* Brut which is made from mostly bought-in grapes.

| Penn Shore Vineyards | MC | ★→ |
| --- | --- | --- |

10225 East Lake Road, North East PA

Davis expertise turns mostly *labrusca* grapes into wine here, but French hybrids and some *vinifera* have been planted too. About 5,000 cases of non-vintage fizz are sold in total, including a *méthode champenoise* Seyval Blanc sparkler.

## Texas

| La Buena Vida Vineyards | MC | ★→ |
| --- | --- | --- |

Springtown

The Smith family's hybrid-dominated vineyards are situated west of Fort Worth and south of Springtown. The *méthode champenoise* non-vintage La Buena Vida Brut and Naturel are recent introductions.

## Virginia

| Ingleside Plantation Vyds. | MC | ★→ |
| --- | --- | --- |

PO Box 1038, Oak Grove

Virginia's first *méthode champenoise* sparkler was made here from hybrid grapes by the Flemer family, aided by retired Belgian oenology professor Jacques Recht. The infinitely more classy Chardonnay grape, plus some Pinot Noir and Pinot Meunier, are now being used to create a non-vintage Dry and Rosé. The new Chesapeake Sparkler is also available.

## Oasis Vineyard  TM/MC  ★→
Route One, Highway 635, Hume

An oasis indeed, for this 12ha (30 acres) vineyard turns part of its production into both transfer and *méthode champenoise* wines, made mostly from Chardonnay and Pinot Noir and sold under the Domaine de la Venne label in Brut and Extra Dry versions.

## Rapidan River Vineyards  MC  ★→
Route Four, Culpeper

The German owner and the German Geisenheim-trained winemaker obviously make a good team here, for both Riesling and Chardonnay have been planted and their Extra Dry *méthode champenoise* sparkler is going down well with locals.

# Washington

## Chateau Ste-Michelle  MC  ★★
One Stimson Lane, Woodinville

This "French chateau" in the Yakima Valley produced its first wines in the mid-1960s. Its sizeable vineyards are now planted with both Pinot Noir and Chardonnay. Sparkling wine production is currently limited to a vintage-dated Blanc de Noirs Brut made by the *méthode champenoise* that spends four years on yeast. Future releases will include a Chardonnay Blanc de Blancs and a Pinot Noir/Chardonnay Brut blend.

## Hinzerling Vineyards  MC  ★→
1520 Sheridan Avenue, Prosser

The Wallace family, complete with their own Davis-trained winemaker, run this winery on the north side of the Yakima Valley. They grow a wide range of noble grape varieties and make vintage-dated Brut and Extra Dry Hinzerling wines.

## Mont Elise Vineyards  MC  ★→
315 West Steuben, Bingen

Local German traditions have not stopped the Henderson family from planting Pinot Noir and Chardonnay, in addition to noble German grape varieties, in their hilltop vineyard overlooking the Columbia River gorge – the border with Oregon. So far only a vintage-dated *méthode champenoise* Brut has been released.

## Preston Wine Cellars  MC  ★→
Star Route One, Pasco

Powerful Preston is the third-largest winery in the Pacific Northwest. 79ha (180 acres) of noble *vinifera* vines (including Chardonnay and Pinot Noir) are planted close to the Columbia and Snake Rivers, and they also buy in grapes. Among the wines produced here by Preston's Davis-trained winemaker is a non-vintage *méthode champenoise* Extra Dry.

# Other USA firms
## producing sparkling wines:

Georgia Wines, Georgia; Wines of St Augustine, Florida; Bloomington Winery, Indiana; Moore Dupont, Missouri; Winery of the Abbey, Missouri; Conestoga Vineyards (Landey), Pennsylvania; Highland Manor, Tennessee; Moyer, Texas.

# Australia

Australia is close behind California in the making and drinking of sparkling wine. Indeed, sparkling wine is (along with "coolers") the big growth area in the Australian drinks business: in 1985 Australians drank an impressive 40m bottles of sparkling wine. Or, to put it another way, more than one bottle of wine in three consumed was sparkling.

Given such a bullish market it is not surprising that the more internationally-minded French champagne houses should set up joint sparkling wine ventures with Australian firms, just as they have done in California. So far California appears to be winning the joint venture race with six *grandes marques* firms to its credit. But Australia has signed up three so far. The ventures involve Roederer and Heemskeerk, and Bollinger and Petaluma. Moët & Chandon is currently setting up shop in Victoria and more, it is thought, are on the way. Drink business insiders point out that several of these firms share the same Australian distributor. And one need not be clairvoyant either to see where the next sparkling wine marriages might be made.

The chief difference between Australia and California when making sparkling wine is the excessive heat that Australian winemakers have to deal with. This is especially a problem at vintage time, when grapes have been known to reach the winery at temperatures of 35°C or more. True, the quest for, and planting of, cool-climate vineyards has helped. But it looks as if many Australian winemakers will be forced for some years to attempt the impossible: to turn low-acid, high-alcohol, coarse, intensely-flavoured base wines into top-quality sparklers.

The Australian sparkling wine industry is thus forced to attempt to make silk-purse wines out of sow's ear grapes. But many firms compound their difficulties by choosing indifferent grapes even when better ones are available. Sultana (California's Thomson's Seedless), from the irrigated Riverland vineyards and elsewhere, is the lowest of the low. But neither Ugni Blanc/Trebbiano, Semillon from the Hunter Valley nor Victoria's bizarre Ondenc provide the ideal sparkling wine base. Despite this the younger generation of winemakers are convinced that the classic Champagne mix of Chardonnay and Pinot Noir, and even Pinot Meunier, is the way to go. And this trend, together with the French joint-venture influence, should shortly result in some dramatic improvements in the quality of Australia's sparklers.

One problem that will continue to beset the industry as a whole is that just five brands owned by three firms dominate Australia's sparkling wine sales. One of the big three, the giant Penfolds, has recently swallowed up the large Seaview/Wynns group. This in turn has already persuaded another important wine firm, Lindemans, that it should wind down its sparkling wine operation. Many envisage that the cheap Australian sparklers will become the monopoly of Penfolds, Orlando and Seppelts, while the expensive, high-quality, hand-riddled *méthode champenoise* wines made from top quality grapes will become the prerogative of smaller, specialist wineries. It is clear that the medium-sized firms inbetween are the ones who are likely to suffer.

With so many changes in the air it is hard to predict the eventual style of the still embryonic Australian sparklers. The late 1960s to 1970s was the era of transfer-method and *cuve close* wines.

The 1980s to 1990s should be the era of high-quality, small producer *méthode champenoise* wines, closer to the understated style of French champagne than ever before. In the past, Australia's sparkling wines tended to be sweet, coarse and earthy. It looks likely that the first division Australian sparkling wines of the future will reflect the quality of fine Australian Chardonnay, Pinot Noir and Pinot Meunier fruit. It will be an exciting evolution to witness.

---

### Australian Sparkling Labels and the Law

Australian sparkling wine laws are a mess. The words "*méthode champenoise*" on a bottle in Australia do not guarantee that the wine within has been made by the authentic *méthode champenoise*. The word "champagne" can indicate either a genuine *méthode champenoise* or a transfer-method wine: the law merely stipulates that Australian "champagne" has to be fermented in a bottle and aged on its lees for not less than six months.

- The words "fermented in *this* bottle" indicate a traditional *méthode champenoise* sparkler and "fermented in *the* bottle" denotes a transfer-method wine.
- Any sparkling wine without these words on the label is likely to have been made by the *cuve close* or Charmat method.
- Australia has thankfully taken a responsible attitude towards carbonated sparklers, for any sparkling wine that has acquired its bubbles by this method will carry the words "Carbonated wine" on the label or else "Carbonated . . . ." followed by the brand name.
- Terms such as Brut de Brut, Ultra Brut and Natur indicate a non-*dosage* wine.

---

| All Saints Winery | MC | →★ |
|---|---|---|
| Wahgunyah, Vic. | | |

This imposing red-brick castle of a winery sells a sweet sparkling wine, which receives its bubbles elsewhere, called All Saints' Lyre Bird Champagne.

| Baskerville Wines | MC | →★ |
|---|---|---|
| Haddrill Road, Baskerville, W.A. | | |

Swan Valley winery Baskerville sends some of its Ugni Blanc grapes away to be turned into *méthode champenoise* sparkling wines.

| Berri-Renmano | IM | →★ |
|---|---|---|
| Renmark, Riverland, S.A. | | |

Passion Wine, based on passion fruit juice, is among the products of this giant concern. Vast quantities of cheap, carbonated sparkling wines are also made.

| Best's Wines | MC | ★★ |
|---|---|---|
| Western Highway, Great Western, Vic. | | |

Best's, like nearby Seppelt's Great Western Winery, was one of the wine pioneers in Victoria's gold country. Early sparkling wines were mostly cheap and carbonated. Now, having toyed with a wine from Ondenc grapes, Best's limited amounts of *méthode champenoise* wines are made from Chardonnay. The restrained, low-crop 83 Chardonnay has been much admired.

## Wolf Blass                    TM                          ★
PO Box 396, Nuriootpa, S.A.

Kellermeister, bow-tie fiend and wine promoter extraordinary, Wolfgang Blass is not easy to ignore. Neither are his best-selling wines. Yet behind the kitsch labels and marketing hype lie some skilfully-made and blended wines. The transfer-method 83 Chardonnay Cuvée Champagne is no exception.

## Bleasdale Vineyards           CC                        →★
Wellington Road, Langhorne Creek, S.A.

Bleasdale was the first vineyard to be planted in this area in 1860. Today the sparkling wines are made by the *cuve close* process from a blend of grape varieties and are sold in Brut, Demi-Sec and sweet Muscat-based Spumante styles.

## Bonnonee Wines               IM                         →★
Campbell Avenue, Irymple, Vic.

Bonnonee are producers of inexpensive flavoured sparkling wines such as Sparkling Passion (made from passion fruit) and Strawberry Sparkling as well as the more familiar Spumante.

## Cambrai Vineyards            MC                        ★→
PO Box 206, McLaren Vale, S.A.

Cambrai Vineyards were founded a decade ago. They offer the contract-bottled Mount Wilson Brut.

## Chateau Remy                 MC                       ★→★★
Vinoca Road, Avoca, Vic.
*Star buy Cuvée Speciale Brut*

Chateau Remy was originally set up in 1961 to make brandy as a joint venture between Rémy Martin and a local firm. Chateau Remy suddenly switched to producing sparkling wine a decade later, starting with vineyards still planted with grape varieties intended for brandy. Chateau Remy's Cuvée Speciale Brut is still mostly Ugni Blanc-based with a touch, if any, of Chardonnay. However the wine has a crisp, positive flavour, fragrant bouquet and a creamy mousse: an excellent achievement for the Bordeaux bred and trained winemaker. If the Cuvée Speciale has a fault it is the slightly too high alcohol level. Great things are expected, once their Chardonnay and Pinot Noir come on stream.

## Chateau Yaldara              CC/IM                      →★
Gomersal Road, Lyndoch, S.A.

German traditions live on at this ornate Barossa Valley "Chateau", founded by Hermann Thumm. Yaldara's vast range of sparkling wines do not, alas, always match up to the splendid surroundings. Take your pick from dry, sweet and pink Sekt, Yaldara's Pearl wines, plus Sparkling Burgundy and Moselle, Fiesta Spumante and the more promising "Champagne" range, of which the best are Great Barossa Brut and vintage Reserve.

## Cinzano                      IM                         →★
PO Box 488, Griffith, N.S.W.

This Turin firm, now as famous for its *spumante* sparkling wines as it is for its vermouth, arrived in Griffith half a century ago. However, Cinzano's inexpensive carbonated Australian-made brands are not up to the standards set by its Asti Spumante produced in Italy.

## The College Winery     MC     ★→
Barooma Street, Wagga Wagga, N.S.W.

The wine course at Riverina College, set up more than ten years ago, soon acquired its own commercial winery, which enabled the students to practise what their teachers had preached. Early releases from this well-equipped winery, using their own as well as bought-in grapes, were impressive. However their *méthode champenoise* wine made from Chardonnay and Pinot Noir grapes does not thrill.

## De Bortoli     CC/IM/MC     →★
De Bortoli Road, Bilbul, N.S.W.

The De Bortoli family have achieved miracles with their glorious, sweet Sauternes-like botrytis wines. But as yet their sparkling wines, the sweet Muscat-based *cuve close* Vittorio Spumante as well as carbonated wines, merit less enthusiasm. However, experiments with a Chardonnay-based *méthode champenoise* wine sound more promising.

## Ellendale Estate Wines     IM     →★
18 Ivanhoe Street, Bassendean, W.A.

Retired army man and trained winemaker Robert Hudson makes just 1,000 cases annually of carbonated Sparkling Moselle from Muscadelle and Muscat of Alexandria grapes. This is sold direct from the winery alongside 30 other wines including "Chateau du Plonque"

## Thomas Hardy & Sons     CC/TM/MC     →★
Reynell Road, Reynella, S.A.

The Hardys still own and work in their family firm which, given the large number of take-overs and mergers in the Australian wine industry, is something of an achievement. Their cheap *cuve close* Ugni Blanc-based Courier Brut and Demi-Sec account for almost 70,000 of the 90,000 cases of sparkling wine that they make annually. The transfer-method Demi-Sec Victory, another Ugni Blanc-based sparkler, adds another 10,000 cases. Smaller quantities of transfer-method Brut and Demi-Sec Grande Reserve, with some Chardonnay and Pinot Noir in the blend, are made. Hardy's finest sparkling wine, the *méthode champenoise* Grande Cuvée based on Pinot Noir topped up with Chardonnay, is made in small quantities. It spends about three years on yeast.

## Heemskerk     MC     ☆→
Pipers Brook, Tasmania

Champagne house Louis Roederer, it is rumoured, had their eye on several mainland wineries before they plumped for Heemskerk as a joint-venture partner. It is too early to tell whether Roederer have made the right choice in opting for cool-climate Tasmania. The island's Pinot Noir and Chardonnay are promising, but as yet unproven. The wine, when it appears, will be *méthode champenoise*. So far Heemskerk, the largest Tasmanian winery, have planted 8.9ha (22 acres) of Pinot Noir and Chardonnay and currently they are busy working on experimental blends.

### Hoffmans            CC                          ★
Para Road, North Para, Tanunda, S.A.

This large Barossa Valley winery sells two types of sparkling wine, the Muscat-based Spumante and the superior Hoffmans Brut.

### Houghton          MC                          ★→
PO Box 79, Guildford, W.A.

Houghton was the first and is still the most famous winery in Western Australia. However sparkling wine has only been made here since 1984. The first Houghton sparkler, of which just 750 cases were produced, is a predominantly Pinot Noir and Chardonnay blend topped up with Pinot Meunier. Houghton's obvious winemaking expertise combined with the cool Frankland River fruit should mean that their *méthode champenoise* wine will be worthwhile.

### Hungerford Hill          MC                  ★→
Broke Road, Pokolbin, N.S.W.

One of the Hunter Valley's biggest visitor attractions, with its inn, cellar visits and restaurant. The HH Collection Champagne 82 is partly made from Coonawarra grapes and from equal proportions of Chardonnay and Pinot Noir. It is a zippy, flavoury wine and shows high acidity.

### Katnook          MC                           ☆
PO Box 6, Coonawarra, S.A.

Katnook are best known for their stylish, classic Sauvignon Blanc still wine, which is one of Australia's best examples of this grape variety. Only a tiny proportion of their sizeable Coonawarra crop appears under the Katnook label, most of the wine being sold off to other wine firms. None too surprisingly Katnook, advised by wine consultants Oenotec, keep back *la crème de la crème* for themselves. This augurs well for future releases of their Chardonnay/Pinot Noir *méthode champenoise* wine, which is only experimental at present.

### Krondorf          MC                          ★→
Krondorf Road, Tanunda, S.A.

Barossa Valley winery Krondorf was founded in 1978, although parts of the winery and vineyard are much older. They have swiftly made a name for themselves in Australia for their well-made varietal wines. Their Chardonnay-based *méthode champenoise* wine is also good.

### Peter Lehmann          MC                     ★
PO Box 315, Tanunda, S.A.

Ex-Saltram winemaker Peter Lehmann buys in grapes from all over the Barossa valley to turn into a wide range of wines. His Brut Absolu is made from equal parts of Muscadelle and Rouschette and spends three years on yeast. Future releases may well have some Pinot Noir and Chardonnay in the blend.

### Lindemans          MC/CC                       ★
31 Nyrang Street, Lidcombe, N.S.W.

Lindemans made a *méthode champenoise* wine called Sparkling Empire back in 1944, so it is sad to learn that competition is forcing the group (including its Leo Buring and Rouge Homme subsidiaries) to lease its sparkling wine facilities. This could mean that in several years' time there will be no Lindemans sparkling wines apart from small lots of expensive Coonawarra Pinot Noir *méthode champenoise* wine. However, if you are quick there is still time to enjoy a bottle or two of Lindemans' *méthode champenoise* vintage and non-vintage Imperator, Rouge Homme's Coonawarra Brut and Leo Buring's Brut "Champagne". Alternatively you could slake your thirst with Lindeman's *cuve close* cheaper wines such as Sparkling Moselle, Leo Buring's Sparkling Ringolde and Ringolde Spumante.

| McWilliam's Wines | IM/CC/MC | →★ |
| --- | --- | --- |
| PO Box 1, Pyrmont, N.S.W. | | |

Occasionally, McWilliam's make magnificent wines, such as the 78 Mt-Pleasant Maria Riesling. But the general run are dull, and occasionally faulty. The sparkling wines are sound if undistinguished. Among them are the sweet tank-method Bodega Sparkling, the slightly less sweet *méthode champenoise* McWilliam's Champagne, Pink Champagne and Brut Champagne plus the less-distinguished *cuve close* sparklers, Sparkling Moselle, Burgundy and Rosé. The most stylish sparkler is the light, frothy, barley sugar-like Markview Champagne Brut. This is made mostly from Semillon, with 20% of Chardonnay to lighten the load.

| Maglieri | IM | →★ |
| --- | --- | --- |
| 13 Douglas Gully Road, McLaren Flat, S.A. | | |

Italian Steve Maglieri sells the style of fizz that his countrymen enjoy including Lambrusco, a sweet Muscat-redolent Gran Spumante and Demi-Sec Spumante.

| Middlebrook | CC | →★ |
| --- | --- | --- |
| PO Box 320, McLaren Vale, S.A. | | |

Middlebrook has had its fair share of upheavals over the years, but this traditional winery is gradually moving into the 21st century with the help of Oenotec, the high-tech wine consultancy. No doubt improvements will soon be made to the *cuve close* sparkling wine.

| Miranda Wines | CC/IM | →★ |
| --- | --- | --- |
| Griffith, N.S.W. | | |

The Miranda Golden Gate Brut and Golden Gate Spumante are popular, inexpensive and sweet.

| Mitchelton | MC | ☆→ |
| --- | --- | --- |
| PO Box 2, Nagambie, Vic. | | |

This vast winery, overshadowed by its faintly ridiculous witch's hat of a look-out tower (an apt observation by James Halliday, Australia's leading winewriter), is barely a decade old. Yet, with the help of wine consultancy Oenotec, its wines, especially the whites, are as crisp, lively and palate-pleasing as anyone could ask for. Prospects look good for what is at present an experimental *méthode champenoise* wine.

| Montrose Winery | MC | ★→ |
| --- | --- | --- |
| Henry Lawson Drive, Mudgee, N.S.W. | | |

This Italian-owned winery is just over ten years old, but has only recently started making sparkling wine. Consultants Oenotec are thought to be helping with the first Pinot Noir *méthode champenoise* releases. Montrose have recently bought out Craig-moor, the historic Mudgee winery, and its production, once again on the advice of Oenotec, is likely to be transferred to the Montrose premises at Henry Lawson Drive. This could mean the rapid phasing out of Craigmoor's sweet, muscat-based sparklers for something altogether more stylish.

| Mountadam | MC | ☆→ |

High Eden Ridge, Eden Valley, S.A.

Bordeaux oenology graduate Adam Wynn is the third genera-tion of winemaking Wynns at Mountadam. Together with his father he is the driving force behind this winery. As the name suggests the winery sits atop High Eden Ridge, east of the Barossa Valley. *Méthode champenoise* experiments here have used blends of both Pinot Noir and Chardonnay and the first commercial releases are eagerly awaited.

| Norman's | MC | ★ |

183–187 Holbrooks Road, Underdale, S.A.

Jesse Norman planted the first vines here in 1853. The Norman family no longer own the winery, which has expanded consider-ably since the early days. For those who do not wince at the name, their non-vintage *méthode champenoise* Norman's Conquest Brut is a well-made wine.

| Olive Farm | MC | →★ |

77 Great Eastern Highway, South Guildford, W.A.

This was one of the earliest estates in the Swan Valley, indeed in Western Australia. Vines as well as olive trees were grown from the beginning. Olive Farm Champagne is made here in addition to a wide range of table and fortified wines.

| Orlando Wines | TM/CC | ★→ |

Rowland Flat, Via Tanunda, S.A.

This large, well-known Barossa Valley firm was founded in 1847 and is now owned by Reckitt & Colman. Orlando pioneered the *cuve close* sparkling wine method in Australia in 1956 with the launch of their Barossa Pearl. Today Orlando make a wide range of sparkling wines, mostly from bought-in Chardonnay, Semillon and Palomino grapes. The Carrington range of transfer-method wines, launched in 1980 in vintage and non-vintage styles, along with the new, multi-variety Brut de Brut, are among Australia's best-selling sparkling wines. The vintage-dated Carrington Brut Chardonnay is Orlando's finest, but *cuve close* pink, white and Gran Spumante versions of Starwine are also made.

| Penfolds Michinbury | MC/TM/CC | ★ |

634–726 Princes Highway, Tempe, N.S.W.

Penfolds make not only Australia's biggest-selling sparkling wines but, according to some statistics, the country's biggest-selling wines of any sort. Sales of the transfer-method Michinbury Brut and White Seal and the *méthode champenoise* Chardonnay/Pinot Noir Special Brut were 540,000 cases in 1985. Unfortunately the quality of this vast production is not up to the standards set by Penfolds' best still wines. Other sparkling wines in Penfolds' range, such as the transfer-method Kaiser Stuhl Brut or sweet Demi-Sec Special Reserve, also disappoint. The sweet-toothed, however, may find Kaiser Stuhl's popular Muscat-based *cuve close* Summer Wine acceptable along with sparkling April Gold, White Duck, Cold Duck or even the Stock Spumante range of white, rosé and Gala Gold.

| Petaluma | MC | ★★→ |
| --- | --- | --- |

Spring Gully Road, Piccadilly, S.A.

Wine wizard Brian Croser was paid what is probably his greatest winemaking compliment to date when in 1985 Bollinger, the Champagne house, bought a 20% share in Petaluma. In other New World sparkling wine joint ventures Gallic expertise has usually formed an equal partnership with the local firm. Here it seems that Bollinger has merely invested in Petaluma. It would appear that all decisions concerning Petaluma's *méthode champenoise* wines are to be left entirely to Croser and his eminently capable young team, backed by European-style expertise from Petaluma's Chairman Len Evans. So far 40ha (100 acres) of immaculate, new, closely-spaced Chardonnay and Pinot Noir vineyards have been planted in the cool Adelaide Hills region, overlooked by Mount Bonython. These vineyards are close to the original 4ha (11 acres) Chardonnay/Pinot Noir home plot, which surrounds the well-equipped Petaluma winery. As yet only a limited-edition rich, pineappley, lemon clove-like 84 Chardonnay has been released, but the first commercial *cuvée* of the 85 sparkling wine, mostly Chardonnay backed up by Pinot Noir, will be on sale in 1987. Eventually, when the new vineyards start yielding, it is intended that the grapes will be processed at a press house in the vineyards, then fermented at Petaluma and transported to nearby Bridgewater Mill for the ageing, riddling and disgorgement process. This handsome three-storey mill, built in 1860, with its giant "Old Rumbler" wheel, is to be restored and turned into a restaurant/wine cellar and shop/wine museum/concert hall. As if all this were not enough, the dynamic Croser hopes to set up a sparkling wine venture in America's cool Pacific Northwest state of Oregon. This man never stops.

| Rosemount Estate | MC | ★→★★ |
| --- | --- | --- |

Rosemount Road, Denman, N.S.W.

In just ten years Rosemount has leapt from nowhere to become an impressive winemaking and marketing force. With such dramatic growth slight variation from bottle to bottle is perhaps inevitable. However, Rosemount's fine, buttery-oaky Chardonnays, which are quick to mature, are amongst Australia's best and this augurs well for their first sparkling wine release, the 83 Chardonnay Brut. This wine, made at Rosemount's new winemaking facility at the delightful-sounding Tumbarumba, enjoys a pale gold colour and youthful, fresh, yeasty-smoky taste, although it is let down by a slightly metallic finish. Future releases may well contain some Pinot Noir and Pinot Meunier in the mix.

| The Rothbury Estate | MC | ★ |
| --- | --- | --- |

Broke Road, Pokolbin, N.S.W.

Mature Rothbury Semillon from the Hunter Valley is one of the great white wines of Australia. However, the Semillon is not a grape that marries well with bubbles, as the contract-bottled *méthode champenoise* wine from this estate demonstrates.

| Saltram Winery | MC | ★ |
| --- | --- | --- |

Angaston Road, Angaston, S.A.

Saltram has had changing fortunes over the years, but since the firm was sold to Seagram in 1979 life has been calmer. Saltram's Dry Brut Champagne is a good example of a traditional Barossa Valley sparkling wine. Despite its name, Saltram's Dry Champagne is sweeter.

| San Bernardino | CC | →★ |
|---|---|---|

PO Box 938, Griffith, N.S.W.

San Bernardino is owned by the Pilloni and Aliprandi families. Its *cuve close* Spumante, made principally from a blend of Muscat/ Semillon grapes grown in the hot Murrumbidgee irrigation area, is an inexpensive, sweet sparkling wine.

| Seaview | MC/CC/TM | ★→★★ |
|---|---|---|

Reynell Road, Reynella, S.A.

Leading Australian sparkling winemaker Norman Walker and his capable winemaking team are the force behind Seaview's *méthode champenoise* wines. Now that Seaview and its associate company Wynns have been bought out by Penfolds, their giant new sparkling wine cellars are being built in the Barossa. The reasonably-priced range of Seaview non-vintage sparklers, based on several grape varieties, includes a full, fruity Seaview Brut and a sweet Demi-Sec Grand Cuvée, both of which spend more than a year on yeast. Other Seaview/Wynns sparkling wines include the 82 Tulloch Brut Champagne made from 100% Hunter Semillon, the 82 Killawarra Vintage Brut and the Muscat-redolent *cuve close* Wynns Black Label Spumante. Seaview's *pièce de resistance*, however, is the stylish 81 Edmond Mazure, a *méthode champenoise* wine, made mostly from Pinot Noir with a little Chardonnay, that spends four years on yeast. Even competitive winemakers rate this sparkling wine as one of the best currently available on the Australian market.

| Seppelt Great Western | TM/MC | ★→★★★ |
|---|---|---|

Seppelt, 181 Flinders Street, Adelaide, S.A.

*Star buy 1972 Great Western Show Champagne*

This firm dates from 1851 and today produces vast quantities of several sparkling wines. Great Western's ripe, pleasant, fruity Imperial and Brut Reserve are the most popular in the range. They account for sales of about 480,000 cases per annum (although Seppelt will not confirm this figure). This means that in terms of sales they take second place on the market after Penfolds' Michinbury. The Great Western Imperial and Brut Reserve are made by the transfer method from several grape varieties including the curious Ondenc. Most of Seppelt's other sparkling wines are made by the *méthode champenoise*. These include the strange, aromatic 100% Ondenc Great Western 79 Brut and the non-vintage Brut, which smells very strongly of lychees. Fleur de Lys is another major Seppelt brand: it is a relief to know that the aggressive proportion of Ondenc in the blend is gradually being replaced by Pinot Noir and Chenin Blanc, as in the much-heralded 82 vintage. Seppelt also produce limited quantities of numerous varietal and show sparkling wines from Chardonnay, Pinot Meunier and Ondenc, as well as the more classic and well-received 83 Chardonnay/Pinot Noir. The most fascinating wine of all to Europeans is sadly being phased out. It is Seppelt's answer to Bollinger's RD: the Great Western Show Champagnes which spend ten years or more on yeast. The 1970, made from the Ondenc grape, had real class with a delicious, smoky bottle-age character. Not everyone appreciates the qualities of Great

Western's Shiraz-based red sparkling burgundy, but the excellent 44 vintage was still going strong last year.

| Taltarni | MC | ★ |

Moonambel, Vic.

This well-kept and well-run winery is just down the road from Chateau Remy. It is managed by the well-travelled Dominique Portet whose father was formerly *régisseur* at Chateau Lafite. Dominique's brother Bernard runs the Clos du Val winery in California. Dominique Portet trained at Montpellier and then spent some time at Clos du Val before he came to Taltarni, and his cosmopolitan experience is evident. So far Taltarni, has been producing about 8,000 cases per annum of four different sparkling wines, none of which however are quite as good as Taltarni's still wines. The best sparkling wine is the 100% Chardonnay Blanc de Blancs, followed in quality by the fruity, bonbon-like 82 Cuvée de Brut and the pale pink, fruity, almost banana-flavoured 83 Brut Taché. The latter two have a noticeable proportion of Ugni Blanc in the blend. Taltarni's latest, Royale, is a sparkling kind of kir with a little blackcurrant juice blended in with the Ugni Blanc.

| Tollana | MC/IM | ★ |

Sturt Highway, Nuriootpa, S.A.

This Barossa Valley winery started life as a brandy distillery and gradually became involved in producing table wine. Despite the somewhat humble grape varieties used in their sparkling wine production, Tollana's *méthode champenoise* Brut Champagne has a good reputation in Australia as does their basic Sparkling Brut.

| Tolley's | CC/MC | ★ |

30 Barracks Road, Hope Valley, S.A.

Three brothers run this large family winery. Apart from their cheap, sweet Hope Valley sparkling white, pink and Spumante, the brothers make two *méthode champenoise* wines, which are much more upmarket: the Crouchen-based Pedare Champagne Brut and the more classy Pedare Champagne Dry Premium based on the Riesling grape.

| Tyrell's | MC | ★ → ★★★ |

Broke Road, Pokolbin, N.S.W.

*Star buy 1982 Pinot Noir*

This grand old Hunter Valley winery is run by Murray Tyrell and his son Bruce. They currently produce only the base wines for their sparklers, sending them elsewhere to receive their bubbles. Gold medals at the 1985 Sydney Show prove the success of the system. The medal-winning wines include a gutsy 82 Chardonnay made by Yellowglen and an excellent 82 Pinot Noir, made by Wynn's, with a fresh, biscuity nose and lively, crisp palate let down by a slightly coarse finish. Ashman's non-vintage Brut is a lower quality 100% Semillon sparkling wine.

| Vasse Felix | MC | ☆ |

Cowaramup, Margaret River, W.A.

Margaret River's pioneer winery founded in 1967 by the Gregg family. The first commercial release of their non-vintage Brut, which is Pinot Noir-dominated with some Chardonnay and Pinot Meunier in the blend, will be available in 1987. This *méthode champenoise* wine includes vintages going back as far as 1981 and is made from grapes grown in the Margaret River region, about 32km (20 miles) from Vasse Felix.

## Woodley Wines                    TM                    →★
### Blyth Street, Glen Osmond, S.A.

Woodley's have had a somewhat chequered albeit colourful past, but the recent construction of a new winery may herald an improvement in their wines. Woodley's Queen Adelaide Champagne, also available in a Brut style, is a vintage-dated transfer-method sparkler made from a blend of mostly bought-in grapes. Woodley Wines are now owned by Seppelt.

## Wyndham Estate                   MC                    ★
### Dalwood, Branxton, N.S.W.

This Hunter River estate, founded by George Wyndham in 1828, claims to be Australia's oldest operating winery. The strong, sweet, yeasty 83 Semillon Brut Cuvée, with its greeny-gold colour and citrussy Semillon character is a good although not great wine.

## Yalumba                          TM/MC                ★→★★
### Eden Valley Road, Angaston, S.A.

Yalumba in the Barossa Valley was founded by Samuel Smith, using the proceeds of a successful 19th century gold strike. Today the Hill-Smith family still own the winery and produce a wide range of still wines as well as 70,000 cases per annum of sparkling wine. Most of this is accounted for by the Semillon-based Yalumba Angus Brut, a non-vintage wine made by the transfer method. There is also a vintage-dated well thought of Brut de Brut with increasing proportions of Pinot Noir/Chardonnay blended in with the Semillon. Yalumba's most exciting news however is the production (which Deutz the Champagne house were involved in early on) of a Chardonnay/Pinot Noir *méthode champenoise* wine, due to be released in 1986. The results are eagerly awaited.

## Yellowglen                       MC                    ★→
### White's Road, Smythesdale, nr. Ballarat, Vic.

If anyone in Australia can make the perfect *méthode champenoise* wine it is Dominique Landragin. His family come from Champagne and he himself worked at Lanson and Deutz before coming to Australia and working for Seppelt. Yellowglen, which he set up in 1982, has recently been bought by Mildara. Yellowglen produces 84,000 cases of six different *méthode champenoise* wines, including Mildara's Windsor brand. They show future promise rather than current pleasure, despite their popularity. Monsieur Landragin certainly knows his stuff, even if he is hampered by Victoria fruit. Yellowglen's best sparkling wine, the 100% Pinot Noir Cuvée Tradition from their own vineyards, is worth trying. The new Cuvée Victoria, made from equal parts of Victoria Chardonnay, Pinot Noir and Pinot Meunier grapes, is also worthwhile, as is the overt, strong 100% Chardonnay. Until the *cuvées* improve however Yellowglen's curious elderflower-redolent multi-variety non-vintage wine will find little favour in either Brut, Crémant or sweet Rosé forms. The fresh, invigorating Windsor Brut Chardonnay is better and a sparkling Kir-Royale-in-a-bottle is also made under this label. Yellowglen also bottle wine under contract for numerous firms.

# Other Australian sparkling wine producers and brands:

Capogreco, N.S.W.; Casella's Wines, N.S.W.; Franco's Wines, N.S.W.; St. Peter's, N.S.W.; Verona, N.S.W.; West End Wines, N.S.W.; Taranga Estate, S.A.; Tarawein, S.A.; Ward's Gateway Cellars, S.A.; Robinvale Wines, Vic.; Wantirna Estate, Vic.; Jane Brook Estate, W.A.

# New Zealand

Australian sparkling winemakers must look enviously across the sea to New Zealand. Their neighbours have a temperate, maritime-influenced climate and a plethora of naturally acid, crisp, low-alcohol white wines. The Australians, with their much warmer climate and consequent struggle against over-ripeness, must wonder why they bother. New Zealand's cool climate plus her already impressive Chardonnay and Pinot Noir wines ensure that it will not be long before some world-class *méthode champenoise* sparklers are made here.

What does seem curious to outsiders is how reluctant the New Zealanders have been to develop their natural sparkling wine potential. Cheap carbonated and Charmat method fizz is much more common here than classic *méthode champenoise* wines. Few firms seem prepared to spend time and money on *méthode champenoise* equipment and the inevitable riddling experiments, yeast trials *et al* that go with it.

Still, Montana have set a fine example with their stylish *méthode champenoise* Lindauer Brut. Vidal and Morton Estate are following this lead. Hopefully others will soon do so too.

---

### New Zealand Sparkling Labels and the Law

- "Fermented in this bottle", "bottle fermented" and "*méthode champenoise*" denote a genuine New Zealand *méthode champenoise* sparkler. So do the words "New Zealand Champagne".
- Without such words on the label other New Zealand sparkling wine, no matter how French the names sound, is made by the tank or Charmat method. "Naturally fermented" also indicates a Charmat process wine.
- A great number of carbonated New Zealand sparkling wines are also available. The only clue on the label as to their method of production is that in addition to the brand name there will simply be the words "Sparkling wine" without the usual "Reserve" and "Première" to confuse.
- Sparkling New Zealand Spumante will usually have been made from Muscat grapes.

---

Daniel le Brun      MC      ★→

28 Gee Street, Renwick, Blenheim

South Island soil and French expertise have recently come together to make Daniel le Brun *méthode champenoise* sparkling wine. Monsieur le Brun, from the Champagne family of the same name in France, acquired vineyard land planted to Chardonnay and Pinot Noir close to Blenheim along with a brand new Coq champagne press. So far the still Chardonnay and sparkling Brut and Blanc de Blancs show future promise rather than current pleasure. Le Brun, is however a determined man and his future releases should be better.

---

Cooks      CC      ★

Paddy's Road, Te Kauwhata

Founded in 1969 by a group of Auckland businessmen, Cooks is one of New Zealand's most important wine companies. The firm has had its fair share of financial problems, but rarely has this been reflected in the wine, for Cooks have always insisted on quality. Fernhill Sparkling Chenin Blanc is their leading brand. Sparkling Chasseur is also made as well as a new product, Casavino, made from Dr. Hogg Muscat grapes. This firm has recently merged with McWilliams, New Zealand.

| Corbans Wines | CC | →★ |
|---|---|---|
| Great North Road, Henderson | | |

This large winery was founded by a Lebanese in 1902 and now has a German winemaker. Grapes from three different production units at Auckland, Gisborne and, more recently, Marlborough are turned into the *cuve close* Premiere Cuvee and the less toothsome teutonic-inspired Sparkling Liebestraum.

| Glenvale Vineyards | IM | →★ |
|---|---|---|
| Main Road, Bay View, Napier, Hawkes Bay | | |

Situated in Hawkes Bay, Glenvale is now run by Don and Rob Bird and produces mostly sweet, ordinary sparkling wine under the Bianco, Spumante and Reserve Cuvee labels.

| Korepo Wines | MC | ★ |
|---|---|---|
| Korepo Road, Ruby Bay | | |

No one could be that keen on the name Korepo's Olly's Folly, but this recently launched *méthode champenoise* Pinot Meunier/Chardonnay blend from a husband and wife team is popular here.

| Lombardi Scintilla | IM | →★ |
|---|---|---|
| Lombardi Wines, Te Mata Road, Havelock North | | |

However scintillating Lombardi Scintilla may be in the eyes of its creators, its sweet, carbonated taste is unlikely to charm international tastebuds. The Bianco style is a Müller-Thurgau/Muscatel blend, and Rosato a cloying, pink Pinotage/Pinot Noir.

| McWilliams Wines | CC | →★ |
|---|---|---|
| Church Road, Taradale, Hawkes Bay | | |

This traditionally-minded firm founded in 1929 produces wines with flavours that non-New Zealanders can find hard to take. McWilliams' popular Charmat-method Marque Vue, made from a blend of down-to-earth grape varieties including Chasselas, is sold under both Brut and Medium labels. Marque Vue Gold is the superior version made from Müller-Thurgau grapes. McWilliams has recently merged with Cooks.

| Montana Lindauer | MC/CC | ★★→ |
|---|---|---|
| Ormond Winery, Main Road, Rd 1, Ormond | | |
| Riverlands Winery, Rd 4, 82–099 Blenheim | | |
| *Star buy Montana Lindauer Brut* | | |

Pinot Noir and some Chardonnay grown at both the Ormond and Riverlands Wineries make up the Montana Lindauer Brut Champagne. This sparkling wine, with its stylish biscuity bouquet, elegant taste and fine mousse, is New Zealand's finest, ageing well in bottle for three years or more. It was the first commercial *méthode champenoise* wine available in New Zealand and there is also a Sec version. Fans of the sweeter Muscat grape could try Montana's sweet Bernardino Spumante and Sparkling Muscato Bianco. Montana also produce Mont Royale sparkling wine as well as the new pink Pascale, whose blush comes from the addition of a small amount of red wine made from Pinotage, the South African grape.

## Morton Estate MC ☆☆
State Highway 2, Aongatete via Kati Kati

Locals mistook the bizarre, fake Cape Dutch façade of this winery for a mosque or crematorium during its construction. Don't be put off by appearances, though; the winemaker here, John Hancock, is probably the best in New Zealand. Morton Estate's non-vintage *méthode champenoise* Brut, which is mostly Chardonnay with some Pinot Noir, will be released in 1987.

## Penfolds Wines IM/MC ★
190 Lincoln Road, Henderson

Penfolds produce more than 2m bottles of sparkling wine annually, mostly from bought-in grapes. As the population of New Zealand is a mere 3.2m, this firm could well have reached its saturation point on the domestic market. Their most popular sparkler is the carbonated Demi-Sec Chardon, sweet and low in alcohol, and made in either white, pink or Gran Spumante versions principally from the Müller-Thurgau grape. A recent introduction, the carbonated Le Papillon, a Chenin Blanc/Müller-Thurgau mix, is thankfully both drier and higher in alcohol. The Verdenay Champagne, a Chardonnay/Pinot Noir *méthode champenoise*, is in a more classic style.

## Selaks MC ★
Selaks Wines, Old North Road, Kumea

Selaks' wines have greatly improved over the past year or two and this non-vintage Brut *méthode champenoise* sparkler, made from mostly Pinot Noir grapes plus some Chardonnay, is a notch or two up from the old Champelle they once made.

## Soljans Wines IM →★
263 Lincoln Road, Henderson

This winery, better known for its fortified wines than its Sparkling Spumante, is now run by Frank Soljan's two sons.

## Vidal Wine Producers MC ★★
913 St Aubyn Street East, Hastings
*Star buy Vidal Brut*

Warwick Orchiston is Vidal's capable winemaker. One of his latest creations is the *méthode champenoise* Vidal Brut, a two-thirds Pinot Noir, one-third Chardonnay sparkler, made from bought-in Hawkes Bay grapes. It is, alas, scarce.

## Villa Maria IM →★
5 Kirkbride Road, Mangere, Auckland

Yugoslav descendant George Fistonich owns both Villa Maria and Vidal but the wineries are run separately. Sparkling production here is limited to about 20,000 cases of the sweet, carbonated Villa Maria Gold Label, a Müller-Thurgau/Muscat mix, plus the finer, drier Müller-Thurgau-based Black Label.

## Weingut Seifried IM →★
Sunrise Valley Road, Upper Moutere

Hermann and Agnes Seifried make a soft, low-alcohol, carbonated Sparkling Sekt from Rhine Riesling grapes with a dash of Pinot Noir. Just 2,500 cases are made annually.

# — South Africa —

South Africa's sparkling wines have recently taken a giant leap forward in quality with the arrival of several new *méthode champenoise* sparklers. Simonsig's Kaapse Vonkel, launched in 1971, was the Cape's first *méthode champenoise* wine, followed in 1978 by Boschendal's Brut and joined during the last few years by at least four new brands. Achim von Arnim's Pierre Jourdan looks the most promising of all the newcomers, due to its uncompromisingly classic Chardonnay/Pinot Noir blend. The other producers, too, are gradually working towards this classic *cuvée*, reducing the quota of the Cape's workhorse sparkling wine grapes, such as South African Riesling, Chenin Blanc and Steen, year by year.

Apart from the intense heat which creates low-acid, high-alcohol wines, South Africa's sparkling wine producers are hampered chiefly by poor clones and strains of both Chardonnay and Pinot Noir. Resorting to low quality grapes, such as South African Riesling, Steen, Colombard and Clairette Blanche, as an alternative does not, alas, produce first-division sparkling wine. Nor do the high yields (about three times those of most European vines) that most Cape growers expect help either.

Still, although there are as yet few Cape sparklers to enthuse about, South African winemakers have done extraordinarily well given their viticultural problems. And, provided the country's sparkling wine momentum is not sidetracked by recent arrivals such as Cold Duck, flavoured fizz and curious Sauvignon-based sparklers, the expanding sparkling wine market (over 6m bottles per annum) could continue to develop, both in terms of the quantity of wines produced and in the quality of the wines available on the market.

---

### South African Sparkling Labels and the Law

Most South African sparkling wines are made by the *cuve close* or Charmat method. The carbonated method is also used, most commonly for the cheaper wines, but apart from price there will usually be no indication on the label or elsewhere to tell you which is which. However, any sparkler with the words "*perlé*", "*perlant*", or "*pétillant*" on the label will have been made by the carbonated method. These semi-sparkling wines, with less than two atmospheres of pressure, carry a lower rate of tax than fully sparkling wines. *Méthode champenoise* wines, of which there are scarcely a handful in South Africa, are usually designated by words such as "fermented in this bottle", "*fermenté en bouteille*" and "*méthode champenoise*". Thankfully, South Africa has agreed with France not to use the word "champagne" to describe these or any other styles of sparkling wines it produces.

---

| Ashton Cooperative | CC | →★ |
| --- | --- | --- |
| PO Box 40, Ashton | | |

In spite of its location in the hot, arid Robertson region, this cooperative still manages to produce a dryish Dry Mousseux and a sweet Medium Mousseux from the Clairette Blanche grape, in addition to a sweet, pink, Pinotage-based sparkling wine which has recently changed its name to Cold Duck.

| Bellingham | IM/CC | →★ |
| --- | --- | --- |

Franschhoek Road, 7690 Franschhoek

Bellingham's Paarl estate, founded in 1693, dates back to the early Cape pioneering days. Since 1970 Bellingham has belonged to the Union Wine group and its distinctively labelled wines have been selling well. Just 4,000 cases each of Bellingham Extra Dry Brut (50/50 Sauvignon Blanc and South African Riesling) plus a vintage-dated Blanc de Noirs (100% Pinotage) are made each year via a combination of the carbonated and tank methods. Union also market a sweet sparkling wine.

| Boschendal | MC | ★★→ |
| --- | --- | --- |

7680 Groot Drakenstein

*Star buy 82 Boschendal Brut*

This 300-year-old estate boasts one of the finest examples of H-plan Cape Dutch farmhouses. And since 1979 it has offered the *méthode champenoise* Boschendal Brut. Made currently from a blend of Pinot Noir and Riesling, this will from the 1984 vintage onwards contain increasing proportions of Chardonnay/Pinot Blanc at the expense of the Riesling. Even so the complex, mature, flowery 1982 vintage with its creamy mousse and steady stream of small bubbles is the country's finest sparkling wine.

| Cinzano Spumante | IM/CC | →★ |
| --- | --- | --- |

Gilbey House, Stellentia Road, 7600 Stellenbosch

Europeans could be forgiven for imagining Italy to be the source of this best-selling sweet sparkling wine. But it is made and bottled by Gilbey's, South Africa. Last year Gilbey's produced 108,000 cases of non-vintage carbonated/tank method sparkling wine. Labels include the Chamblanc range (Cuvée Brut, Demi-Sec, Doux and Blanc de Noirs), as well as the sweet, pink pair St-Louis Cold Duck and Sparkling Symphony. Montagne Cuvée Brut is their best sparkler: it may well be renamed Hartenberg soon.

| Delheim | CC | ★ |
| --- | --- | --- |

Knorhoek, 7605 Koelenhof

Ebullient "Spatz" Sperling has made two styles of sparkler so far at his hilltop Stellenbosch Delheim estate: a dry Chenin Blanc-based wine and a finer Riesling-based Brut.

| Douglas Green | CC | →★ |
| --- | --- | --- |

10 Bolt Avenue, Montagu Gardens, 8000 Cape Town

Closely connected with the KWV operation in Paarl, Douglas Green buy in wines from elsewhere and simply blend and bottle them. Currently their list of sparkling wines includes a Cuvée Brut, Demi-Sec and Blanc de Noirs, as well as Chantel Pétillant, a sweet *perlé* wine.

| Fleur du Cap | CC | →★ |
| --- | --- | --- |

Papegaaiberg, Stellenbosch

This firm, part of the large Oude Meester group, offers two sparkling wines: a South African Riesling-based *cuve close*, which is somewhat curiously named Premier Grand Cru, and the sweet, soft Cuvée Doux.

## Franschhoek Cooperative      CC      →★
PO Box 52, Franschhoek

Nestling beneath the dramatic Franschhoek mountains, this cooperative produces a sweet sparkling wine under the Fleur de Lis label made from Chenin Blanc and Clairette Blanche grapes.

## Grand Mousseux      TM/CC      →★
SFW, Stellentia Road, 7600 Stellenbosch

Grand Mousseux is the biggest-selling brand of sparkler in South Africa. It is made by Stellenbosch Farmers' Winery, who are also responsible for the Nederburg sparkling wines. Grand Mousseux, which is made from Chenin Blanc and Clairette Blanche grapes, comes in Extra Brut, Vin Sec and Vin Doux versions. SFW also make the popular, sweet, salmon-pink Fifth Avenue Cold Duck and Bentley's Buck's Fizz, a sparkling wine/orange juice mix.

## Here XVII      CC/MC      ★→
Oude Meester, Papegaaiberg, Stellenbosch

Oude Meester, one of the largest and most powerful South African wine groups, own this brand, of which they sell about 25,000 cases a year. Here XVII is a sweet, sherbety *cuve close* blend of several varieties, dominated by the South African Riesling. In addition Oude Meester also sell small amounts of a 1984 *cuve close*, the positive, grassy J.C. Le Roux Sauvignon Blanc, made exclusively from that grape. Best of the bunch is the vintage-dated J.C. Le Roux Pinot Noir *méthode champenoise*, recently released and as yet available only in small quantities. With its earthy, hefty flavour it is not the finest *méthode champenoise* wine that the Cape produces.

## KWV (Ko-operatiewe Wijnbouwers Vereniging)      CC/MC      ★
Laborie Estate, Taillefer Street, Paarl

This powerful semi-official cooperative was set up in 1918 to help farmers dispose of bulk wine and obtain a fair price for their crop. The cooperative now has 6,000 members. Few KWV wines are sold in South Africa; most are reserved for export. KWV's mediocre *cuve close* Mousseux range, made principally from Chenin Blanc and available in a pear-drop-like Brut, Demi-Sec and jammy, redcurranty Rouge Doux, accounts for most of the sparkling wine sales. Small amounts of KWV's Laborie estate *méthode champenoise* Blanc de Noirs are on sale in the Cape.

## Nederburg      CC      ★→★★
Meaker Street, 7646 Huguenot

Nederburg is part of the large Stellenbosch Farmers' Winery Group. Two styles of sparkling wine are made here by German winemaker Gunter Brözel, one of the Cape's most impressive winemakers. The South African Riesling-dominated silver-labelled Première Cuvée Brut is raw and assertive (there is also a Cuvée Doux version for export). The superior German-inspired gold label Kap Sekt has some Rhine Riesling in the blend: this shows in its attractive lime-juice-like taste.

## Pierre Jourdan (Clos Cabrière)      MC      ★→★★
Cabrière Street, 7690 Franschhoek

*Star buy Pierre Jourdan Brut*

Winemaker and *méthode champenoise* enthusiast Achim von

Arnim runs the Clos Cabrière business in addition to his cellarmaster duties at nearby Boschendal. The Clos Cabrière estate, founded in 1694, has so far released one sparkling wine: the non-vintage Pierre Jourdan Brut, a *méthode champenoise* wine made from bought-in Chardonnay and Pinot Noir grapes. It is the first of such *cuvées* to be available commercially in the Cape. Eventually Clos Cabrière's own vineyards will provide these grapes. Its rich, mature nose and flowery, flavoursome palate is an excellent first effort and amongst the best *méthode champenoise* wines the Cape produces.

| Simonsig Kaapse Vonkel | MC | ★→ |
|---|---|---|

Simonsig Estate, Kromme Rhee Road, 7605 Koelenhof

Frans Malans, joined now by his three sons, launched Kaapse Vonkel, the Cape's first *méthode champenoise* wine, in 1971. The wine has improved considerably since some Chardonnay and Pinot Noir were added to its Chenin Blanc base. Eventually this vintage-dated bone-dry sparkler will be made entirely from the Pinot Noir and Chardonnay varieties.

| Tradition Charles de Fère | CC | ★→ |
|---|---|---|

Villiera Estate, Old Paarl Road, 7646 Paarl

The Villiera estate in Paarl is owned by the Grier brothers, one of whom worked for a short time in Champagne. Exactly which *champenois* traditions rubbed off on this pleasant, ripe, fruity, biscuity sparkler, made mostly from Pinotage and Pinot Noir plus a little Chenin Blanc, is difficult to judge. However this inexpensive wine has gone down well with locals.

# — The Rest of the World —

## Bulgaria

Bulgaria produces some of the finest white and red wines in eastern Europe. Whether this applies to their sparkling wines, known as *Iskra* (or *spark*), is difficult to say for few are exported. West Germany however imports one of the better Bulgarian sparklers, Schwarze Meer, which is made by the efficiently run modern plant at Tchirpan. Tchirpan's Balkan Crown sparkling Riesling and sparkling Chardonnay will soon be exported, to the UK at least. Both of these should be worth seeking out. Another Bulgarian winery, Targovishte, sells the basic Biliana and Albena sparklers. The best Bulgarian fizz however is Magura, which comes from the town of the same name. About 2m cases of Bulgarian sparkling wine are produced annually.

## Canada

Canada's sparkling wine producers appear to concentrate on Cold Duck and the like made from *labrusca*-redolent hybrids rather than anything more serious. Andrés' Baby Duck is probably the country's most successful sparkler in this category, but numerous other firms including Jordan and Barnes make similar styles. In addition Bright's, an old Ontario firm, use French and American hybrids as well as the *labrusca* grapes to make their range of du Barry sparklers. They now also have a "champagne" made from the Chardonnay grape. Château des Charmes, who are launching two "champagnes" shortly, are also based in Ontario as are Château Gai who use hybrid vines as the base for their Charmat-method sparkling wines. Inniskillin, another Ontario house founded in 1974, have a *méthode champenoise* vintage-dated Blanc de Blancs Chardonnay plus the non-vintage L'Allemand. The latter is apparently a German Sekt-style sparkler, still made by the *méthode champenoise* but from the Grey Riesling and Gamay Beaujolais grapes. Karl Podamer, another Ontario house, make *méthode champenoise* wines from a range of grape varieties including the Chardonnay.

## Central and South America

Surprisingly Mexico is responsible for the foundation of much of South America's wine industry. Spanish missionaries first planted the vine in Mexico around 1524 and gradually it was transported south to Chile, Peru and Argentina. In general the South American taste for both its own sparkling wines and imported champagne is for the sweeter or Doux styles. Many champagne houses now produce only a Doux champagne for this market. Most of Mexico's wine regions are situated north of Mexico City and although there are numerous growers there are very few producers. Several international names are to be found here but most of Mexico's sparkling wines are made by Mexicans. Cavas de San Juan with their Carte Blanche *méthode champenoise* wine is a well-known producer as is Bodegas de Santo Tomas. Vinicola de Aguascalientes with their Champ d'Or brand plus Hacienda Alamo and Marqués del Aguayo are other sparkling wine producers. The base wines for the majority of these sparklers come from a wide range of grapes including Chenin Blanc, Chardonnay, Ugni Blanc, Colombard, Semillon and Pinot Noir amongst others.

Working south Colombia and Venezuela both make sparkling wines but on a small scale. Venezuela is one of the few South American countries to restrict the use of the word "champagne" to genuine imported French champagne. Brazil on the other hand makes sizeable quantities of sparklers, about 417,000 cases annually – the same as Argentina and Chile. Brazilian bubbly is mostly produced in the Rio Grande do Sul region where the majority of still wines are also made. The first Brazilian bubbly was produced by Armando Peterlongo in 1913 and the firm still makes sparkling wine today. The grapes that are used for this and other Brazilian sparklers are gradually switching from *labrusca*-redolent hybrids to more noble varieties including Riesling, Trebbiano, Pinot Noir and Semillon. Other Brazilian sparkling wine brands include George Aubert, Bernard Taillan, Heublein do Brasil's Bratage plus Companhia Vinicola Riograndense's Moscato Espumante. International sparkling wine firms are also firmly established in Brazil. Moët & Chandon along with their partners, Cinzano and Monteiro Aranha, are the force behind Provifin's successful M. Chandon label. Martini & Rossi are responsible for the Brazilian Champagne de Greville plus a locally made Spumante.

There are fewer Chilean sparkling wine producers but they make roughly the same amount of bubbly as Brazil. The biggest producer is Alberto Valdivieso who uses the *méthode champenoise* to make his range of sparkling wines. Concha y Toro have a range of *cuve close* wines made for them by their subsidiary Subercaseaux. The other major *cuve close* producers are Santa Ana and Santa Carolina with their Champagne Chileno Santa Carolina. Undurraga, the important table wine producers, also sell fizz and cheap carbonated sparklers made by Viña Manquehue. Perhaps the most exciting Chilean sparkling wine news is that Torres, the leading Spanish wine firm, are now about to make *méthode champenoise* sparkling wine at their Chilean outpost.

Argentina's biggest sparkling wine producer is probably the Casa de Saint Remy with their Duc de Saint Remy and Marie Boucau *méthode champenoise* wines. Finca Flichman is another big Argentine sparkling wine name. International companies have a foothold here too, the most notable of which is Proviar (run jointly by Cinzano and Moët & Chandon). Proviar sparklers include Baron B, M. Chandon and H. Mercier.

## England

The world's winemakers are amazed that England grows grapes at all in its distinctly cool climate, let alone makes wine from them. But England has had vineyards since Roman times. The earliest English *méthode champenoise* wine was made by Nigel Godden at Pilton Manor near Shepton Mallet in Somerset. This *méthode champenoise* wine made from the Müller-Thurgau and Seyval Blanc scores points for trying but not for finesse. In 1985 David Carr Taylor introduced Carr Taylor Dry Sparkling Wine, again a *méthode champenoise* wine, from his vineyards close to Hastings, Sussex. So far only limited amounts of the young, green, acidic 83 vintage, made from the Kerner and Reichensteiner grapes, have been released.

# Hungary

Hungarian sparkling wine is divided into two categories: *pezsgö*, sparkling wine made by the *méthode champenoise*, and the lesser-quality *habzobor* foaming wine made by the transfer or Charmat method that is about half the price. The Hungarians, like their eastern European neighbours, enjoy sweet or medium-sweet fizz with distinctive regional flavours. The most famous and traditional *pezsgö* sparkling wine house is Törley in Budafok, close to Budapest. Törley was founded in 1880 and today produces some 83,000 cases of *méthode champenoise* wine annually. Hungarovin, who own Törley, also own two other big Budafok sparkling wine plants whose brands, Hungaria and Francois, made by the Charmat and transfer methods, account for some 242,000 cases annually between them. Hungarian sparkling wines are produced in a wide range of styles from Brut to Delicatesse, the sweetest. Apart from the Hungarovin sparklers leading Hungarian sparkling wine producers include Hosszuhegyi, Kiskunhalas, Villaany-Mecsekaljai, Balatonboglaar, Koezeep-Magyarorszaagi and Szikra.

Hungarian sparkling wine is mostly sweet and mediocre in quality. Kiskunhalas do however produce a Sparkling Chardonnay, which is highly thought of, and Balatonboglaar make a good sparkler from the Muscat grape. Henkell, the German Sekt house, are thought to be involved with Balatonboglaar. Charmant and Pompadour are two other Hungarian sparkling wine brand names. Visitors to Hungary will see vast quantities of cheap Russian sparklers on sale there as well as Hungarian *habzobor*. Hungary exports a great deal of its sparkling wine to the USSR, East Germany, Poland and elsewhere in Eastern Europe.

# India

India is probably the last place in the world anyone would look to as the origin of a *méthode champenoise* wine, but since 1983 it has indeed produced one: Royal Mousseux. This sparkling wine is made by the Indage group under advice from Piper-Heidsieck's Champagne Technologie. Ugni Blanc, Pinot Blanc and Chardonnay grapes grown at Narayangaon near Bombay in the Maharashtra region are turned into sparkling wine at a £4m winery that is exclusively French-equipped. What is remarkable, given India's hot climate and lack of winemaking expertise, is just how good Royal Mousseux is. Its pale gold colour is backed up by a flowery bouquet and a soft, flowery, perfumed palate. Royal Mousseux was previously sold under the Marquise de Pompadour label but is now sold as Omar Khayham. A Royal Mousseux made by the *cuve close* method is produced by the same firm and is available in India.

# Israel

Baron Edmond de Rothschild established the modern Israeli wine industry by founding two wineries to the north and south of Tel Aviv. Today these process more than two-thirds of the country's grapes. The vintage-dated President's Sparkling Wine under the Carmel label is made at the southern winery. This *méthode champenoise* sparkler is made in two versions, the classier Brut Sambatyon and a Demi-Sec style.

## Luxembourg

Luxembourg, sandwiched between Belgium and Germany, is overlooked by most wine drinkers. A pity because its cool, northern vineyards are beginning to produce some good wines from noble grapes and Luxembourg is especially keen to make fine upmarket sparkling wines. So far there are only four companies of note involved in the sparkling wine industry: Caves Bernard-Massard at Grevenmacher, run by the Clasen family, is the largest producing some 167,000 cases of *méthode champenoise* wine annually. Most of this, made from Elbling, Pinot Blanc and Riesling, is sold as Brut but the range also includes a classier Pinot Blanc-, Riesling- and Chardonnay-based Cuvée de l'Ecusson sparkling wine. Gales & Cie at Bech-Kleinmacher produce some 67,000 cases of fizz every year. Once again most of this is sold as the Riesling-based Brut Private Cuvée, but there is a cheaper St-Martin range whose Carte Blanche is the only *cuve close* wine – the rest are made by the *méthode champenoise*. Two-thirds of Luxembourg's wines are made in cooperatives and the Vins-moselle Coopérative at Stadtbredimus makes about 17,000 cases of Duc Henry *cuve close* sparkling wine every year. Most of this is made from the lesser-quality Elbling and Rivaner grapes. Caves St-Remy-Desom at Remich also make *cuve close* sparkling wine, sold under a variety of labels including St-Remy, Desom, Dicks, Albert-Georges, Calvador and Duc de Monclair. The best place to taste Luxembourg sparkling wine is in Luxembourg but it is also exported, mainly to Belguim and the Netherlands.

## Romania

Like those of its eastern European neighbours Romania's *spumos*, or sparkling wines, are sweetish and not very exciting. Still, Romania has plantings of Chardonnay and Pinot Noir and hopefully it will not be too long before commercial quantities of sparkling wine from these grape varieties are available. Premiat, made by the *méthode champenoise*, is Romania's most famous sparkling wine. Romania makes about 1.5m cases of sparkling wine annually.

## Switzerland

Swiss sparkling wine is confusing. Most of it is not Swiss at all, just a blend of local grapes mixed in with a hefty proportion of, usually, Chenin Blanc from the Loire to create the Blanc de Blancs styles and Muscat from northern Italy to make the *spumante* sparklers. Detecting the genuine Swiss sparkling wine from the imported, often blended product is not difficult. The majority of Swiss sparkling wines made from imported wine usually carry the words "*elaboré en Suisse*" or "*imbottigliato in Svizzera*" followed by "*produit de France*", "*spumante d'Italia*" etc. There are, however, true Swiss sparkling wines sold under labels such as Grand Vin Mousseux du Valais, an important Swiss wine-producing region to the east of Lake Geneva, and also Grand Vin Mousseux du Vaud, a region just to the north of the Lake.

The fruity but slightly dull Chasselas is the white grape used for these and other Swiss sparkling wines. Swiss sparkling wine is made either by the *méthode champenoise* (which will mostly be marked on the label) or else by the *cuve close*. Mauler & Cie at Môtiers, founded in 1829, with their range of *méthode champenoise* wines are thought by many to produce the finest Swiss sparklers. About 20% of their needs comes from their own Pinot Noir and Chardonnay vines; the rest, generally Pinot Noir, is imported from France.

# The USSR

Russians are devoted sparkling wine or *shampanskoye* drinkers. Before the Revolution, vast quantities of the finest French champagne enlivened the tedium of long, frozen Russian winters – for those who could afford it. The *dosage* levels were high – about three times those of the current Doux or Rich champagnes. Today modern Russians appear to have the same sweet tooths. Most Russian sparklers, whether white or red, are very sweet. There are however some dry sparkling wines available. Most Russian fizz is produced by the transfer method or the continuous method – a system which the Russians perfected. This Russian continuous flow system (see page 6) is both speedy and cheap. The USSR produces about 21m cases of *shampanskoye* annually – a dramatic 45% increase during the last five years (no doubt as a result of the continuous system). The USSR hopes to double this figure before too long. West Germany, the Communist bloc and the USSR itself are the chief consumers of *shampanskoye*. The three main export brands are Krim, Nazdorovya or Rossiya. Quality is mostly sweet, flabby and mediocre, with white Krim a strange, perfumed fizz and the red not unlike an unpleasant, sulphury version of Italian Lambrusco. Only the USSR Abrau-Durso from the Crimea, made by the *méthode champenoise*, is said to be the finest Russian *shampanskoye* and therefore worth seeking out. The red Tzimlianskoe and white Zolotoye are also available. Sovietskoye, in a variety of styles, is the most widely distributed *shampanskoye*.

# Yugoslavia

Yugoslavia is much better known for Laski Riesling than it is for sparkling wine. Yet the Yugoslavians do make fizz. Sparkling wine in Yugoslavia is known as *biser* or *pearl*. One of their best-known sparklers is called Fruskogorski Biser, made by Navip who also produce a finer fizz called Milion. Another Yugoslav sparkling wine, Bakarska Vodica, is made by Istravino. Slovenia is the only area that produces *méthode champenoise* wines and Radgona make a *méthode champenoise* sparkler called Zlata Radgonska Penina.

# Glossary

**AC Appellation Contrôlée** Superior French quality wine designation which guarantees the source and production method.

**Blanc de Blancs** See page 8.

**Blanc de Noirs** See page 9.

**Bodega** A Spanish firm that makes wine. *Bodega* also means wine cellar.

**Buyer's Own Brand, or BOB** See page 9.

**Cantina** Italian wine cellar or winery.

**Cava** Spanish sparkling wines made by the *méthode champenoise*. Also used to describe a sparkling wine establishment or producer.

**Charmat method** Another name for *cuve close*. See page 5.

**Chef de cave** The cellar manager and winemaker.

**Continuous, or Russian Continuous Flow method** A continuous sparkling wine method where the second bubble-inducing fermentation takes place in a series of tanks.

**Coteaux Champenois** Still red or white wines of the Champagne region.

**Crémant** Softly sparkling or "creaming" sparkling wines. See page 8.

**Cuve close** An inexpensive wine method where a second bubble-inducing fermentation takes place in a tank.

**Dégorgement, or disgorging** See page 8.

**Dégorgement à la glace** See page 8.

**Dégorgement à la volée** Disgorging performed by hand without ice.

**Deutscher Sekt bA** The finest German Sekt, on a par with still QbA wines.

**Deuxième taille** Juice from the final pressing of the *méthode champenoise*.

**Dosage** A blend of wine and sugar added to champagne and other sparkling wines before the final cork is put in.

**Girasol** Literally "sunflower" in Spanish. A metal riddling frame containing about 500 bottles. Used in Spain.

**Grande marque** Term applied to a leading champagne house.

**Gyropalettes** See page 7.

**Injection or carbonated method** The meanest and least lovely method of producing sparkling wine. $CO_2$ is pumped into a closed tank containing still wine and the wine is then bottled under pressure.

**Liqueur de tirage** See page 7.

**Malolactic fermentation** A secondary fermentation in which harsh malic acids are converted into gentler lactic acids.

**Méthode champenoise** Traditional, costly, time-consuming champagne and sparkling wine method where bubbles are produced by a second fermentation in bottle.

**Méthode dioise** A refined version of the *méthode rurale* involving a 3–4 month fermentation before bottling and used exclusively for making Clairette de Die.

**Méthode gaillaçoise** A variation on the *méthode rurale*.

**Micro-billes** Porous yeast capsules for *remuage*. See page 7.

**Mousseux** Fully sparkling wines. See Crémant on page 8.

**Non-vintage** See page 8.

**Perlant** Wines with the least sparkle of all. See page 9.

**Pétillant** Slightly sparkling wines. See page 9.

**Première taille** The second pressing from the *méthode champenoise*.

**Pupitres** Wooden riddling or *remuage* racks. See page 7.

**QbA Qualitätswein eines bestimmten Anbaugebietes.** German quality wines of defined geographical origin.

**Remuage** See page 7.

**Remueur** Person who performs the *remuage*.

**Rosé** Pink champagne or sparkling wine made from a blend of red and white wine.

**Schaumwein** German for sparkling wine at the cheapest level.

**Sekt** German for sparkling wine; a step up from *Schaumwein*.

**Spumante** Italian sparkling wine.

**Transfer method** Compromise method where a second bubble-inducing fermentation takes place in bottle and is transferred to a tank.

**Vigneron** French grape grower.

**Vin de cuvée** Finest quality juice from the first pressing of the *méthode champenoise* process.

**Vintage** See page 8.

**VMQ Vins mousseux de qualité** French quality sparkling wines.